PRE-CAPITALIST IRAN
A Theoretical History

Pre-capitalist Iran
A Theoretical History

Abbas Vali

WITHDRAWN

NEW YORK UNIVERSITY PRESS
Washington Square, New York

First published in the U.S.A. in 1993 by
NEW YORK UNIVERSITY PRESS
Washington Square
New York, N.Y. 10003

Library of Congress Cataloging-in-Publication Data

Vali, Abbas.
    Pre-capitalist Iran : a theoretical history / Abbas Vali.
      p.   cm.
    Includes bibliographical references and index.
    ISBN 0–8147–8773–8
    1. Iran–Economic conditions–Historiography.
    2. Feudalism–Iran—Historiography.
    3. Asiatic mode of production–Iran—Historiography.
    4. Land tenure—Iran–Historiography.
HC474.V34 1993   93–23837
330.955–dc20   CIP

Manufactured in Great Britain

In memory of A. R. Ghassemlou
whose tragic murder set back the cause of
peace and democracy in Iran.

CONTENTS

ACKNOWLEDGEMENTS

This study was originally planned as a doctoral thesis on the problems of the transition to capitalism and the emergence of the modern nation-state in Iran. It has undergone many transformations since; and my first thanks must go to Paul Hirst, who supervised it through all its changes with unflagging patience and interest. The work, as will be apparent, owes much to him. I also wish to thank Athar Hussein, with whom the original idea was discussed, although a very long time ago. Friends and colleagues in the Middle Eastern Study Group have also offered support and encouragement; my thanks are due particularly to Roger Owen and Sami Zubaida. I wish also to remember with gratitude conversations with David Rosenberg, who took an active interest both in pre-capitalist societies and in the completion of this work; sadly he did not live to see it finished. I am more than grateful to Anna Enayat, who has been an editor of exemplary tolerance in the face of seemingly endless delay, as well as an informed and intelligent commentator on the text. Thanks also to Phyllis Roberts for the initial typing out, and to my friend Rose Gann, who retyped and reorganised the final draft. In the last stages, Katharine Hodgkin read through and revised the text; without her it would have been far more difficult to read.

PREFACE

This essay is neither an exercise in historiography, nor a case for the necessity of theory in historical writing; rather, it is an argument for the theoretical character of historical discourse. A consideration of this issue involves a brief preliminary discussion of the object and the nature of historical knowledge.

Iran is a key case in the social scientific literature on pre-capitalist societies. Conceptual definitions of pre-capitalist Iran and characterizations of its economic structure, social relations and political institutions are as old as the discipline of social theory. In the Iranian context, it is the use of theory in historical argument which distinguishes modern from traditional historiography, marking the point of departure from the scholastic antiquarianism and chronologism which dominated the field before the early decades of the present century. This move towards the use of theory and conceptual knowledge in Iranian historiography was neither an arbitrary choice nor a purely scholastic undertaking; theory proved indispensable to historical writing when a new generation of historians and social scientists began to emphasize the contemporary value of historical knowledge. The historical studies which subsequently appeared during the 1960s, especially those concerned with the pre-capitalist era, assumed a specific form. They were genealogies of the present rather than studies of the past, entailing conceptions of causality grounded in specific philosophies of history, whether positivist, Marxist or Weberian.

This emphasis on the contemporary value of historical knowledge, which precipitated the use of theory in historical argument, arose out of the prevailing political and ideological conditions. The introductory chapter of this study shows that politics (rather than the subjective interests of the historians and social scientists) determined the choice of the object of investigation. The idea that definitions of the pre-capitalist past and characterizations of its social relations and political institutions are essential to the analysis and understanding of the capitalist present, its structural dynamics and developmental tenden-cies, was shared by different groups among the Iranian intelligentsia. The prevailing historicism, despite its diverse philosophical bases, thus affirmed the necessity of theory, and the revolution of 1979 gave a powerful impetus to this popular but still nascent trend in historical writing. The spate of work which has followed this historic event has further consolidated the tenuous link between theory and history: philosophies of history have proved indispensable to analyses which are primarily concerned with causal explanations of the demise of the Pahlavi autocracy and the rise of the Shii theocracy.

The practitioners of modern Iranian historiography, in Iran and in the West, for the most part use conceptual frames and definitions rather liberally, and often with no methodological restraint or regard for their theoretical validity, either as ideal type models for compar-ison or as means for the analysis of concrete conditions. The conceptual definitions of pre-capitalist Iran deployed in modern historical writing signify a real social totality which existed in the past in a continuous manner, evolving in the course of time into different forms expressive of the modality of its uniform essence. This real social totality, be it feudal, Asiatic, patrimonial or traditional, is held to be present in the facts of Iranian history. The conceptual definitions of pre-capitalist Iran, whatever their theoretical found-ations, constitute these facts as the object and the means of validation of historical knowledge. The evidence, selected by the historian, is both the point of departure and the ultimate court of appeal in historical enquiry. The theoretical forms from which the conceptual definitions of pre-capitalist Iran are derived remain external to the process of the selection and investigation of the evidence; they are means to knowledge, which enter and leave the process of its production without influencing the result, in much the same way as a catalyst in natural scientific experiments.

This particular relationship between fact and theory which under-pins the conceptual definitions of pre-capitalist Iran is not arbitrary, but rooted in the epistemological assumptions of the modern his-torical discourse on Iran; and these assumptions are empiricist. To characterize them as such is neither an unfounded assertion nor an unwarranted generalization. The concept of empiricism deployed in this essay refers to the common consequence of diverse theoretical and philosophical traditions which identify knowledge with the essence of the real as present in the fact, given and self-explanatory. It is a methodological procedure for the production of knowledge: the knowledge of the real is abstracted from within given facts by theoretical and conceptual means which facilitate the process without affecting its outcome. This doctrine of method is the hallmark of the modern historical discourse on Iran, and diversity in the philosophical bases of the discourse does not invalidate its characterization as empiricist. The empiricist character of the modern historical discourse on Iran will persist so long as it continues to insist on the unassailable status of the fact as both the object and the means of evaluation of historical knowledge.

The empiricist tradition characteristically identifies history with the past as signified in the body of the evidence available for investigation; historical knowledge is thus the knowledge of the past present in the evidence. The validity of the empiricist conception of history and historical knowledge is dependent on certain key assumptions: that the fact is identical with the real signified in it; that the evidence of the historical past is identical with it; and that the past, the object of historical knowledge, exists as presence in discourse. Central to these assumptions is the concept of the fact as pre-given and self-explanatory.

This essay rejects the central tenet of the empiricist tradition in historical writing. The contention is that facts are not given, but constructed in discourse; thus they are discursive constructs rather than autonomous objectivities. The constitution of the facts as objects of knowledge is a conceptual process premised on determinate theoretical forms and conditions. The investigation of the evidence, the process of production of knowledge, presupposes conceptual means and procedures which are informed by specific theoretical forms. These forms determine the conceptual structure and the order of the historical discourse in which the knowledge of the real signified in the evidence is represented. Facts, therefore, are representations of the real in discourse by specific conceptual means and determinate theoretical forms; they are not identical with the real signified in them. Contrary to the empiricist assumption, history is not identical with the past, nor is historical knowledge the essence of the past present in given facts. History is the representation of the past in discourse, and the theoretical forms and conceptual means which inform and facilitate the process of production of historical knowledge have determinate effects on the order and the structure of historical discourse which is the order and the structure of historical knowledge.

The constructive concept of the fact suggested by a critique of the empiricist procedure of modern historical writing on pre-capitalist Iran has wider implications for the project of this study. It implies above all that the ontological distinction between fact and concept, historical and theoretical knowledge, central to the empiricist tradition in history, can no longer be sustained. For this distinction rests on the pre-given and auto-significatory attributes of the fact, attributes which underpin the empiricist identification of the evidence with the real signified in it; hence the characterization of the evidence as the raw material of historical knowledge, factual and objective, distinct from conceptual knowledge which belongs to the field of the subjective. Empiricism absolutizes the distinction between facts and concepts in order to establish an exclusion zone around historiography, treating it as a field of objective knowledge governed by its own rules of investigation, modes of proof and means of validation, which defy the theoretical forms of evaluation of discourse appropriate to other disciplines in human and social sciences.

The rejection of the empiricist conception of the fact proposed by this study undermines the privileged status assigned to historiography in human and social sciences. Historical facts are no more given and self-explanatory than theoretical concepts. Both are discursive constructs, although of different kinds; the difference between them is conceptual rather than ontological. History is essentially a theoretical discipline; historical knowledge is no less conceptual than philosophy or social theory. It requires theoretical forms of reasoning, proof, and evaluation of discourse, radically different from that prescribed by the empiricist tradition. There is no valid justification for its exemption from the theoretical forms of evaluation of discourse. The validity of an argument depends on its discursive coherence and logical consistency. History is no exception to this rule.

This, then, is the argument behind the idea of a theoretical history, which forms the project of the present study. The project has two aims: first, to examine the conceptual structure of the modern historical discourse on pre-capitalist Iran; and second, to develop an alternative theoretical frame for the conceptualization of its social relations, economic structures and political institutions. Reference to the evidence of Iranian history is frequently made in the course of the enquiry; this invocation of the historical evidence serves a particular purpose, namely, to illustrate and substantiate the theoretical arguments developed in the course of the enquiry. It is not the means for the evaluation of historical knowledge. Chronology is not the organizing principle of the enquiry, determining the order and the sequence of analysis; the order of discourse in this enquiry is imposed by the concepts deployed in the analysis.

This essay is divided into three parts. The opening chapter explores the state of historiography in modern Iran, and discusses the political and ideological conditions which precipitated the surge of interest in studies of pre-capitalist Iran, both within and outside the country. It further surveys the contours of the controversy over the periodizations of Iranian history, and the characterizations of the Iranian social formation before the advent of the constitutional state in the early twentieth century. This survey focuses on the political and ideological undercurrents of the controversy, which largely specify the theoretical stance of the main contributors to the debate.

The remaining chapters of Part I deal with the definitions of pre-capitalist Iran as a feudal and an Asiatic society respectively. They examine the theoretical status and validity of the most influential of such definitions, tracing their inconsistencies to the Marxist concepts of the Asiatic and feudal modes of production, and in particular to the anthropological concept of economic property and ownership on which the political definitions of the relations of production associated with them are grounded. Chapter 2 finds the concept of the Asiatic mode of production theoretically inconsistent and discursively incoherent. Taxation as a political measure, it is argued, cannot by itself constitute the relations of production; and the tax-rent couple, emphasizing the state ownership of the land, can provide the basis for these relations only if the forces of production entailed in the concept of the Asiatic mode of production are radically modified to include state power. Thus the theoretical inconsistency of the concept of the Asiatic mode of production could be rectified by a redefinition of the forces of production in which the state would be reconceptualized as an economic force; but the conditions necessary for such a reconceptualization—namely, large-scale, state-controlled, labour-intensive public projects—did not exist in pre-capitalist Iran.

Chapter 3 argues that the concepts of Iranian feudalism deployed by the Marxist historians are also theoretically inconsistent. These historians attempt unsuccessfully to conceptualize Iranian feudalism as a variant of the Marxist concept of the feudal mode of production; a failure, it is further argued, which results not so much from the alleged structural differences between Iranian and European conditions, as from the inconsistencies of thĕ classical Marxist concept of the feudal mode of production serving as the frame of reference. This concept, which conflates the relations of production with their juridico-political conditions of existence, regards the political as the constitutive of the feudal mode of production, thus preventing the conceptualization of its variants in terms of the specificity of the forces and relations of production on a local or regional level. The chapter concludes with an argument for the reconceptualization of feudal rent as a necessary condition for the conceptualization of the economic structure of feudalism in Iran.

Part II, consisting of a single chapter (Chapter 4), thus begins with a critical evaluation of the political concept of feudal rent in Marxist discourse and of some authoritative accounts of it in contemporary Marxist theory, identifying the causes of its incoherence and the theoretical consequences thereof. Throughout the course of investigation, the mode of the conceptualization of capitalist relations of production in *Capital* serves as a point of reference as well as the basis for the construction of an economic concept of feudal rent. Feudal rent as an economic category is structured by exchange relations emanating from the possession of and separation from the means of production between the economic agents involved in the process of production. The crucial factor in this respect is a conception of economic property which results from the subsumption of the producer in the process of production, and which as such invariably involves his separation from the means and the conditions of production. The final section of this part uses the economic concept of feudal rent to outline the specificity of feudal economic structure. This then serves as the frame of reference for the conceptualization of the economic structure of Iranian feudalism, the constituent elements of which are outlined in Part III.

Part III consists of three chapters, dealing with the conceptualization of the processes of the formation and appropriation of economic property in land, and their juridico-political conditions of existence in medieval Iran. This involves a critique of the political conception of the *iqta*, by which it is maintained that the *iqta*, though a form of land grant, did not constitute private property in land. The prevailing

Islamic conception of power, and the resultant structure of command
and obedience, prevented the formation of private property in land
and the corresponding emergence of an autonomous land-owning
class along West European lines. The political conception of the *iqta*,
it is argued in Chapter 5, presupposes specific juridico-political
conditions of existence which were not present in medieval Iran. The
medieval state in Iran, exemplified by the Saljuq state, was a
particular articulation of the political and the economic, which
thwarted the development of conditions for territorial centralism,
instituting instead a decentralized political and military structure
sustained by the exchange of military service for land revenue. This
chapter further shows that the conditions of production of land
revenue do not bear any relevance to the political definitions of the
iqta, which insist on the ownership of land by the Sultan or the State.
These conditions are treated as external to the processes of the
formation and appropriation of landed property in medieval Iran.

Chapter 6 focuses on the concept of absolute ownership of the land
entailed in medieval political discourse, and also in recent statements
in the standard and authoritative social and economic histories of pre-
capitalist Iran. It is argued that the concept of absolute ownership
does not have an autonomous discursive status, but is an adjunct of
the ancient Persian (Sassanian) theory of government, which argues
for autocratic rule as prerequisite to order and stability. An
examination of the conditions which precipitated the revival of the
theory in medieval political discourse confirms this argument. In this
case too, autocratic rule is considered as the condition of social stability
and economic prosperity. The invocation of the concept of absolute
ownership in contemporary historical writing, however, is rooted in
the popular but erroneous identification of autocratic rule with
sovereign power. The autocratic state in pre-capitalist Iran lacked the
capacity to institute territorial centralism, and effective rule depended
in practice on a decentralized military power structure based on landholding. In other words, the institutional conditions of existence of
absolute ownership are given to the discourse, without being
theorized with reference to the specificity of the polity in medieval
Iran. In the final section of this chapter, the analysis argues for the
importance of control over the land in the conceptualization of the
process of the formation and appropriation of private property in land,
and emphasizes the significance of the conditions of subsumption of
the direct producer which underpins this process. This issue is taken

up and explored in Chapter 6, which involves a detailed analysis of
the organization of production, the forms and conditions of tenancy,
and the modes of extraction and realization of surplus in pre-capitalist
Iran.

The last and concluding part of the essay is an attempt to construct
a concept of Iranian feudalism, drawing on the analyses in the
preceding parts. The concept of Iranian feudalism signifies a
structure of social relations specific to the Iranian social formation
from the Saljuq to the constitutional period. It is intended as a means
for historical enquiry, to enable students of Iranian history to outline
the general structural characteristics of the Iranian social formation at
various points during this long period. Feudal social relations are
conceptualized in terms of their economic, juridico-political and
ideological conditions of existence. But the concrete forms in which
these conditions existed historically—i.e. the specific form of the
state, the political and ideological processes and practices, and
cultural relations—in pre-capitalist Iran are not given in the concept
of Iranian feudalism. It follows that no definite form of state and
politics can be deduced from this concept. Such forms are included in
the concept of the Iranian social formation, and should be theorized
in terms of the concrete conditions of Iranian history in various
phases of its development in the feudal era. This is the task of
historical writing dealing with specific episodes of the feudal period. It
is hoped that this essay can assist such studies to avoid some obvious
pitfalls of the empiricist tradition in their quest to extract the truth
from the evidence.

PART I

1. MARXISM AND THE HISTORIOGRAPHY OF PRE-CAPITALIST IRAN

The land reform of 1962 and the ensuing social and economic transformation in the Iranian countryside fundamentally altered the political and intellectual scene in Iran. It revealed the striking persistence and relative strength of pre-capitalist relations in agriculture, and the historical and political writings that followed this crucial event assigned to them an unparalleled significance in the history of modern Iran.[1] Social scientists, economic historians and political activists began to reassess the conventional interpretations of contemporary Iran in the light of new developments in the countryside. The result was a revival of interest in the question of the transition to capitalism, with a view to explaining the persistence of pre-capitalist features and the underdeveloped state of capitalist relations in Iranian agriculture.[2] Conceptual definitions of pre-capitalist relations, therefore, became an indispensable part of the study of the dynamics and direction of capitalist development in modern Iran.

Studies of the transition to capitalism in Iran focused, almost invariably, on the Constitutionalist period, 1891–1912. Historians and social scientists of different political and ideological persuasions viewed this as a turning point in Iranian history, a historical landmark separating the capitalist present from the pre-capitalist past.[3] While there was a general consensus on the predominantly transitional and increasingly capitalist character of the post-Constitutionalist era, opinions on the precise nature of pre-capitalist relations in the preceding period were sharply divided. The opposing views on this issue offered two distinct periodizations of Iranian history, both associated, in different ways, with Marxist theory, which for reasons of convenience will be termed the Soviet and the Asiatic periodizations of Iranian history; that is, the periodizations and interpretations

3

of Iranian history advocated by Soviet scholars, and those promul-
gated by their Iranian adversaries.

The Soviet and Asiatic interpretations of Iranian history both
presuppose a unilinear and teleological schema of history and
historical development. The schema, which is commonly attributed to
Marx, is a generalization of European history, entailing a notion of
periodization which is based on the concept of the mode of
production: the evolutionary succession of the modes of production
constitutes the structure of history. The Soviet historians assigned a
universal and deterministic character to the schema, and emphasized
the essential conformity of Iranian history with it.[4] The proponents of
the notion of an Asiatic Iran, on the other hand, admit to the general
theoretical validity of the schema in the European context, but are
opposed to its universalization and application to non-European
societies, arguing that such a universalization ignores the fundamental
dissimilarities between European and Iranian histories. In both cases,
however, European history serves as a model for reference and a
criterion for judging the consistency of historical argument about
Iran. Ahmad Ashraf and Homayoun Katouzian are the chief
proponents of this mode of analysis. They both consider the Marxist
concepts as 'ideal type' models and attempt to prove or disprove their
applicability to Iranian history with reference simply to the latter's
similarities and dissimilarities with European feudalism. This is then
considered as an example of 'scientific' methodology (Ashraf 1975,
Katouzian 1980, esp. Chapter I).

The Soviet and Asiatic historiographies of Iran share the same
empiricist method of analysis. The consistency of the historical
argument is thus judged by the supposed correspondence between
the concept and the real, in this case between the concepts of the
various modes of production and Iranian history. This is held as a
proof of the 'scientificity' of the analysis. In the case of Iranian
history, however, the correspondence is established within a comparative framework and through a process of parallel and contrast with
European history, which dominates the analysis. Similarities and
dissimilarities with European history are thus presented as proof
of correspondence between a given concept and Iranian history.
While, for example, the Soviet historians view 'similarities' with
feudal Europe as a proof of the correspondence of the concept of the
feudal mode of production with a particular period of Iranian history,
their opponents consider 'dissimilarities' as a justification for the

application of the concept of the Asiatic mode of production to the history of the same period. Accordingly, both feudal and Asiatic analyses of Iran usually include lengthy expositions of European feudalism. The work of the Iranian economic historian Farhad Nomani, who adheres to the Soviet concept of an Iranian feudalism, is a clear example of this mode of analysis: almost a third of his work *The Development of Feudalism in Iran* (Tehran 1980) is devoted to an exposition of the specificity of the feudal socio-economic system in Europe. In these studies the Marxist concept of the feudal mode of production and the history of feudal Europe are treated as identical, on the basis of another and equally empiricist assumption: that the correspondence between the Marxist concept and European feudalism has already been proved by the experience of European history, and the two can, therefore, be treated as interchangeable. In fact, what is often called the 'reality' of Iranian history by these writers is only an effect of its similarity/dissimilarity with European history. In the Soviet and Asiatic historiographies of Iran, Iranian history, as a discursive entity, has no independent existence.

Although Marxism was introduced to Iran in the early decades of the present century, systematic debates on the periodization of Iranian history began only in the late 1960s.[5] The intervening period is marked by the ideological dominance of the Tudeh (Communist) party in the Iranian intellectual scene as a whole. The Tudeh party was formed in 1941 and soon became the standard-bearer of scientific socialism and the single most important intellectual force in the history of modern Iran. Ideologically, the Tudeh party was distinguished by its strict allegiance to the Soviet Communist Party and Soviet Marxism. It was instrumental in introducing the official Soviet conception of history and historical development to the Iranian intellectual scene. This conception, identified with classical Marxism by the Tudeh intelligentsia, subsequently became the theoretical foundation of the standard Marxist periodization and interpretation of Iranian history.

The Soviet theory had its origin in the debates that surrounded the question of the transition to socialism in the predominantly agrarian and economically backward Russian social formation, before and after the October Revolution.[6] But the official version was conceptually based on a materialist interpretation of history associated with Stalin's *Dialectical and Historical Materialism*.[7] It outlined a universal theory of history according to which every human society must pass through the same process of development, divided into five distinct stages, each marked by the dominance of a particular mode of production. This universal process begins with primitive communism and, after passing through the three successive stages of slavery, feudalism and capitalism, ends with advanced (socialist) communism. The theory, as such, entails a mode of determination which stems from the development of productive forces and underlies the process of a succession of modes of production in a teleological order. The forward march of the productive forces, it is believed, constitutes the internal dynamics and inner essence of this universal teleology. The teleological and essentialist character of this theory of history is too obvious to need further explanation; instead I shall briefly dwell on the conditions which led to its rapid dissemination and subsequent dominance among the Iranian intelligentsia before considering the Soviet periodization of Iranian history.

As noted above, the Tudeh party was instrumental in introducing the Soviet view of history and historical development to the Iranian intellectual scene. But the party and the Marxist intelligentsia grouped around it did little in the way of substantiating the Soviet theory with the evidence of Iranian history. The conformity of the universal theory with the development of Iranian history was merely asserted, in the most general terms, in the party and related publications. Nevertheless, the political and ideological supremacy of the Tudeh party during 1941–53, coupled with the chronic poverty of non-Marxist historiography, both Iranian and non-Iranian, led to the rapid growth in popularity of the Soviet view among the Iranian intelligentsia.

Historiography in the modern sense of the term was little known in Iran prior to the Second World War. The traditionalist historians dominated the scene and their works were, on the whole, alien to any methodological rule, let alone theoretical and conceptual disciplines. They focused basically on political history: annotated chronologies of events expressed in terms of the voluntarist action of the kings and their retinues. This traditional historiography was, for the most part, anchored in an underlying nationalism which was stock in trade of the official ideology under the Pahlavis. This largely reduced its appeal to the Iranian intelligentsia which was ideologically distinguished, above all, by its opposition to the Pahlavi regime.[8] In Western Europe, meanwhile, historical writing on Iran was scarce, for historical and political reasons. Iran, unlike the Indian sub-continent and the countries of South-East Asia, never officially became part of the European colonial empire, nor did it enjoy the Ottoman privilege of proximity to Europe and Christian culture. Iran's political and cultural isolation during the eighteenth and nineteenth centuries meant that it did not receive its fair share of 'Orientalist scholarship', certainly much less than its later political and economic weight on the European scale deserved. European scholarship on Iran before the Second World War focused, by and large, on the spheres of literature and archaeology, accompanied at times by manuscript illumination and travel accounts, and memoirs written mostly by statesmen and members of official delegations to the royal court. Archaeological research often formed the basis of historical narrative, which characteristically paid little attention to the sphere of social and economic relations.[9]

After the Second World War, European historiography showed more interest in Iran, but still remained insensitive to theoretical and conceptual analysis. Although concepts such as slavery, feudalism and capitalism are frequently used to designate particular social and economic institutions in particular periods, their contents are always left unspecified. These concepts, when used, function as general terms illustrating similarities and differences between Iranian and European histories. The comparative historical narrative informs the bulk of European scholarship on Iranian society and history. It is a legacy of the 'Orientalist tradition' which has dominated the European vision of non-European society and history ever since the early sixteenth century.[10]

Although the political supremacy of the Tudeh party was short-lived, its forced expulsion from the political field did not end its ideological influence.[11] The Marxism of the Tudeh party, its interpretation of historical and dialectical materialism, remained the single most important influence on the Iranian intelligentsia in the decades to come. The socialist break away from the Tudeh party, the so-called Third Force, the only significant intellectual grouping during the decade 1953–63, did little to undermine this ideological dominance. It challenged the Tudeh's Stalinism and overt subservience to the Soviet Communist Party, but seldom questioned the theoretical status and validity of its interpretation of Marxism. The socialists failed to draw a theoretical demarcation line between the Stalinism of the Tudeh party and what they termed the genuine Marxism of the founders of scientific socialism.[12] In fact, in their writings on history and society, for the most part, they retained the very same conception of historical and dialectical materialism. The contention that the development of human society and nature were governed by the same universal dialectical laws was often cited by the socialists as a living proof for the scientificity of Marxism.[13]

Similarly, the Tudeh party's intellectual dominance outlived the rapid rise and increasing popularity of the Chinese and Cuban Marxisms during the decade 1965–75. The new trends in Iranian Marxism established their claim to orthodoxy by denouncing Soviet and Tudeh Marxism for revisionism and deviation from the revolutionary path. The works of Pouyan, Ahmadzadeh and Jazani exemplified this nascent but increasingly influential trend in Iranian Marxism. The first two were among the founding members of the Sazeman-e Cherikha-ye Fada'i-ye Khalq (the Organization of the People's Fedayeen). Their works were heavily influenced by Latin American Marxism, the Dependency School and its leading figures, especially Debray and Frank. The works of Debray, Guevara and Marighela were duly translated and circulated underground, and soon became the text-books of revolutionary Marxism in Iran. Jazani's work, on the other hand, was informed by Mao and Chinese Marxism. He adhered to Mao's classification of contradictions and, unlike the two others, believed in a two-stage transition to socialism in Iran. However, the new trends in Iranian Marxism and their principal rival, the Tudeh Party, shared a common theoretical ground: the dependency theory, and the characterization of Iran as a dependent capitalist society. This conception continued to dominate Iranian Marxism up until the early 1980s, when it suffered a fatal blow at the hands of the Islamic government.[14]

The political opposition to Soviet Marxism and the Tudeh party, though widespread, was not accompanied by a radical theoretical break, least of all in the field of history and historical writing. The proponents of the Dependency School in Iran, in particular those associated with the radical left, produced no work of any significance. In the field of historiography the new generation of Iranian Marxists continued to translate Soviet writing on Iranian history, and this despite their avowed political opposition to Soviet Marxism and the Tudeh Party.[15] In fact the new generation of the Marxist intelligentsia, who had been strongly influenced by the new and emergent trends in international Marxism, enthusiastically read and heavily drew upon the educational texts of the Tudeh party: selected texts of classical and Soviet Marxism, mostly translated and introduced by members and sympathisers of the Tudeh party during the formative period of 1941–53. These texts, selected and introduced under particular political and ideological conditions, circulated in a clandestine manner, and constituted the bulk of Marxist theoretical writing available to the Iranian intelligentsia prior to the 1979 revolution.[16] The prevailing 'party line' was the main criterion for the selection and publication of works of classical Marxism in Iran; for example an incomplete version of Engels's *Anti-Duhring* and Stalin's *Dialectical and Historical Materialism*, translated and introduced by the Tudeh Party, were for a long time the only sources on Marx's philosophy available to the Iranian intelligentsia. After the 1979 revolution, the Tudeh Party suppressed the publication of Marx's *Eighteenth Brumaire of Louis Bonaparte* on the grounds that it contained a conception of the petty bourgeoisie and petty-bourgeois politics which ran counter to the party line.

If, despite a crushing and largely self-inflicted political defeat, the Tudeh Party's ideological dominance in the intellectual field remained unchallenged, the key to this paradox was its close association and identification with Soviet Marxism, which was able to retain its influence on the Iranian intellectual scene during the period of the Tudeh Party's political demise, 1953-79.[17] Historiography was the main channel through which Soviet Marxism exercised and maintained its influence on the Iranian intelligentsia during this period. The last two decades preceding the 1979 revolution witnessed a slow but steady introduction of works of Soviet historiography to Iranian society. These works, which covered different periods of Iranian history, were theoretically grounded in the official scheme and, combined together, contained an almost complete version of the Soviet periodization of Iranian history.[18]

A brief outline of the Soviet periodization and interpretation of Iranian history, constructed on the basis of works available in Persian, is as follows. The Median (713–550 B.C.), Achaemenian (559–330 B.C.) and Parthian (250 B.C.–224 A.D.) periods signified the slave epoch in Iranian history during which the Iranian economy was dominated by a slave mode of production.[19] The Sassanian period (224–651 A.D.), on the other hand, signified the onset of the feudal epoch in Iranian history.[20] The development of the feudal mode of production, however, was retarded by the Arab conquest of Iran (651 A.D.), which led to a concentration of the land in the hands of the state and the consequent disruption of feudal property relations.[21] This trend was modified by the gradual disintegration of the Eastern Caliphate, under the increasing decentralizing pressures exerted upon it by the emergence and consolidation of Iranian dynasties with local power bases, and the formation of a centralized state by the Saljuqs in the early eleventh century put an end to the disruption. The Saljuq period (1038–1157), marked by the universalization of *iqta*, witnessed the revival of the feudal mode of production proper.

Iranian feudalism continued to flourish under the succeeding dynasty until its temporary disruption by the Mongol invasion in the thirteenth century.[22] The invasion considerably weakened the foundation of Iranian feudalism, but the organization of agricultural production and the prevailing property relations remained largely intact. The main feature of Iranian feudalism during this period (1220–1349) was peasants' bondage to the land, introduced by the Mongol rulers to ensure feudal exploitation in the face of a declining peasant population in the Iranian countryside.[23] The Mongol rule was followed by a period of political decentralization and economic chaos, during which dynasties with local and provincial power bases ruled in various parts of the country.[24] The constitution of the Safavid state (1501–1722) restored centralized government and gave a fresh and powerful impetus to the declining feudal economy. The outcome was a highly centralized feudal order, characterized by the systematic introduction of land assignments, known as *tuyul*, and a reorganization of the system of land-ownership.[25]

The Safavid achievements, however, were undermined by the economic chaos and political disorder that followed the Afghan invasion of Iran (1722–1736). The Afghans were defeated and replaced by the Afsharids who, with the notable exception of Nadir, did little to restore the centralized feudal order. Nadir's reign (1736–1747) signified the establishment of an 'absolutist feudal monarchy' in Iran; feudal exploitation was intensified to finance his numerous and often inconsequential military expeditions, which eventually brought the economy to decline.[26] The foundation of the Qajar dynasty (1794–1925) by Agha Mohammed Khan slowed down the process of political decentralization and economic stagnation that followed Nadir's death, but only temporarily, and the disintegration of the feudal economic system continued down to the second half of the nineteenth century.[27]

This period marked the beginning of the end of the feudal epoch in

Iranian history. Feudal relations began to dissolve, owing primarily to the development of commodity relations stimulated by the integration of the Iranian economy into the capitalist world market. The major political consequence of the new socio-economic development in Iran was the Constitutionalist revolution (1905–6), which signified an effort on the part of the nascent bourgeoisie to assume political power.[28] The post-Constitutionalist period is interpreted by the Soviet historians in terms of the development of a 'dependent capitalist economy', increasingly geared to the requirements of capitalist accumulation in the imperialist countries of the West. The Pahlavi state (1925–79) was thus a product of dependent capitalism, serving the economic and political interests of the dependent Iranian bourgeoisie and big landowners and their imperialist allies.[29]

The main feature of the Soviet periodization of Iranian history is thus a prolonged period of feudalism, lasting no less than sixteen centuries, 224–1906. The development of Iranian feudalism, as presented by the Soviet historians, is an expression of the institutional form and functioning of the Iranian state. The successive periods of economic prosperity and decline in the history of Iranian feudalism follow successive periods of political centralization and decentralization. The institutional form of the Iranian state, therefore, determines the rhythm and direction of the development of the feudal mode of production in Iran. The political essentialism entailed in Soviet historiography of Iranian feudalism is an index of the domination of the Soviet theory of history by a particular definition of the concept of mode of production.

The Soviet theory defines history as a universal and teleological process structured by the succession of modes of production. The concepts of these modes are defined in terms of the dominance of forces over relations of production in their structures. This definition of the concept of the mode of production has serious implications for the conceptualization of national and regional 'variants' of the universal theory. The dominance assigned to the forces of production in the structure of the concept, and the mode of determination that it entails, effectively exclude the possibility of conceptualizing national and regional variants in terms of variations within the structure of the mode of production. Thus, although the Soviet theory in principle allows for national and regional variants (e.g. the concept of an Iranian feudalism), these are, on the whole, conceived as empirical 'deviations' from the purity of the universal model of development;

that is, as effects of non-structural elements—geographic conditions and superstructural forms—on the pace and direction of the development of the productive forces. Soviet historiography of pre-constitutionalist Iran, in particular its conceptualization of the specificity of Iranian feudalism, is a clear illustration of this mode of analysis.

It was only in the late 1960s and early 1970s that the Soviet periodization and interpretation of Iranian history was directly and seriously challenged. The challenge came mainly from the academic sphere: a number of Iranian writers criticized Soviet historiography for its unwarranted generalizations, and for overlooking the 'reality' of Iranian history in favour of the official Soviet ideology. These critics were thus concerned mainly with the universalization of the European schema of development, rejecting its application to Iranian history. The focus of criticism was the supposed existence of slave and feudal periods in Iranian history. The contention was that the existence of these periods in Iranian history had been merely asserted by the Soviet historians, and the assertion could not be verified by the evidence of Iranian history; Iran, it was maintained, never experienced either slavery or feudalism.[30] Instead, it underwent a prolonged period of development marked by specifically Asiatic forms of social, economic and political relations and institutions which could not be deduced from any general theory of history.[31]

The Asiatic definitions of Iran postulate a prolonged period of development which can be said to correspond roughly to the slave and feudal periods in the Soviet historiography of Iran. Although the actual duration of Iranian Asiatism has never been specified, it seems to be seen as beginning with the formation of the first centralized sovereign state in Iranian history, and continuing down to the Constitutionalist period: 550 B.C.–1906 A.D. Most definitions, however, also include post-Constitutionalist Iran in the Asiatic period, seeing it basically as a restructured/redeployed Asiatic state: an amalgam of Asiatic despotism with an imported capitalism. Particular concepts are thus produced to define this amalgam and explain its relevance to the analysis of contemporary Iranian society and history.[32] These concepts, although they often derive their authority from Marx, on the whole strive to deny the relevance of Marxist categories and concepts to the analysis of contemporary Iranian society and history. Their main function is to displace the 'specificity' of Iranian history in favour of its 'uniqueness'.[33] The notion of the uniqueness of Iranian history implicit in Asiatic definitions of Iran indicates a unitary and self-generating field of history and historical discourse conditioned and perpetuated by constantly contrasting Iranian history with the history of Western societies.

Asiatic definitions of Iran vary, theoretically and conceptually. Broadly speaking, they identify two distinct components: a centralized despotic state characterized by the arbitrary nature of political power; and a stagnant economic structure defined by the absence of the institution of private property in land and by the prevalence of isolated self-sufficient peasant communities. The despotic state, superimposed upon the society at large, usually by the act of conquest, exercises near-total control over economic institutions and processes; the economic role of the state is the essential condition of its despotic domination over society. The state determines the stagnant character of economic institutions and processes and specifies the field of economic activity in the countryside and in the towns. The political and economic functioning of the state, which is ultimately reduced to effects of geographic-climatic conditions, is held to account for the Asiatic character of Iranian society and history.

Asiatic definitions of Iran thus explain the development of Iranian history in terms of the functioning of the state structure. This is defined by the term despotism, which refers to the arbitrary nature of political power, sustained and reproduced by the intrinsic relationship between political and economic centralism characteristic of all Asiatic societies. This element of political essentialism is central to all variants of Iranian Asiatism. It defines Iranian history as a teleology of state structure perpetuated by social and economic stagnation. Social classes and strata, i.e. landlords, peasants, artisans and merchants, have no historical existence; they are economic agents, so defined by the state, and are subsumed in general and indeterminate categories such as 'the Iranian people/nation', appearing in history only through their real or alleged relations with the state and political authority.

The term despotism, however, is not an attribute of political power alone. Rather, it denotes the real essence of Asiatic Iran as an undifferentiated community of unfree subjects lacking individuality and will. The community is ruled by 'fear', which is said to be the principal regulator of political relations as state-subject relations. The notion of despotism as such generates a field of discourse characterized by the absence or minimal development of civil society; the assumed relationship between subjectivity, private possession and individual rights is the main underlying theme. The absence of civil society in Asiatic Iran, on the other hand, meant that political opposition was internalized within the existing power structure. Dissensions and mutinies were frequent, but were usually led by tribal chieftains who simultaneously held high rank in the command structure of the armed forces. The army was organized on tribal lines and the intermingling of military hierarchy with tribal lineage formed a powerful decentralizing nexus within the centralized power structure. The loyalty of the tribal soldiery depended on the loyalty of the chief to the reigning despot, and this was a function of the military and economic strength of the central government. The weakness of central government usually precipitated tribal rebellions against the state, often leading to the constitution of a new but essentially similar despotic state. The state-tribe conflict and the similarities in the pattern of its recurrence and development has resulted in interpretations of Iranian history in terms of a constant conflict between centralizing and decentralizing forces in Iranian society.[34]

External forces—neighbouring states and tribes—were also important decentralizing factors. Foreign invasions, motivated by desire for territorial conquest, access to new pastures or just plunder and booty, succeeded when the military strength and financial resources of Iranian despotism had been exhausted. But the decentralizing effects of internal and external factors upon the centralized state structure were temporary and short-lived. They gave way to centralizing tendencies inherent in the need to consolidate power after the military conquest. The victors established their own centralized states and exercised power over the subjects in much the same manner as the vanquished. The 'storm clouds of the political sky' seldom affected the essentially static social structure of Asiatic Iran. The repeated cycles of political change led to little more than the succession of one dynastic rule by another.

Asiatic Iran is thus characterized by its static social structure, which essentially lacks the capacity to change. This characterization indicates the domination of Asiatic definitions of Iran by the 'Orientalist tradition' in European historiography. Orientalism constitutes a heterogeneous body of discourse on non-European society and history which is internally unified by the notion of the uniqueness of the West. The term 'Orient', therefore, does not designate a specific geographical location, but rather refers to all societies which allegedly fail to fit into the European model of history and development.

Oriental history is a discursive construct constituted by a series of absences: the alleged absence in Oriental society of the elements which define the characteristic uniqueness of the West and of Western history. The function of the Orientalist discourse is, therefore, to define Oriental history as a negative determination of European history.[35]

In the sphere of historiography, the Orientalist tradition focuses on the absence of those institutions and processes which constitute the dynamics of Western societies under the feudal and capitalist economic systems: the institution of private property in land, and rational economic activity in the sphere of trade and commerce. The absence of these elements in Oriental society is commonly related to the specific form and functioning of the Oriental state, characterized in contrast by the arbitrary nature of political power and the state's domination and control over major economic resources, institutions and processes within the society. These conditions are thus held to account for the essentially stagnant nature of Oriental society and the Oriental mind. The Orient lacks a dynamic social history. Its history is essentially political: it is the history of despotic states whose form and functioning determine the modality of the development of Oriental society.

Orientalist historiography entails a typology of Oriental society constituted in terms of variation in the institutional form and functioning of state structure, which becomes the main index for differentiating between Oriental societies: what distinguishes Qajar Iran from Chinese or Ottoman society during the same period is the specific form and functioning of the Qajar state. The Orientalist typology thus serves to assert both the common history and the diverse development of Oriental societies. This political essentialism is central to the Orientalist conception of history. It reduces non-European societies to a general category, i.e. the Orient, identified by a despotic state and a static social structure.

The Orientalist conception of history and the associated form of political essentialism dominate the Asiatic definition of Iranian history. The notion of the uniqueness of Iranian history entailed in such a definition is the assertion in reverse of the Orientalist problematic: the uniqueness of the West. The Orientalist problematic has influenced the Asiatic definitions of Iran in three different ways, each informed by a different theoretical and conceptual discipline: Marx's concept of the Asiatic mode of production, Weber's notion of patrimonial domination, and Wittfogel's idea of Oriental despotism. Although Asiatic definitions of pre-Constitutional Iran often claim scientificity by referring to Marx and his concept of the Asiatic mode of production, in particular its political component, Asiatic despotism, Marx's theoretical influence on the Asiatic definitions of Iran remains secondary. Repeated references to Marx mostly serve a 'tactical' rather than 'scientific' purpose, in that his authority is often invoked to countervail and challenge the equally unfounded claim to scientificity by the Soviet historians and their Iranian followers. Conceptually, however, the Asiatic definitions of Iran are influenced largely by Weber and Wittfogel. While some, like Ashraf, clearly acknowledge their debt to Weber, others—like Katouzian, who rather presumptuously claims originality—remain reluctant to acknowledge their debt to Marx or Wittfogel in an explicit manner. Marx and Weber share a common mode of approach to the conceptualization of Eastern societies, that is, in terms of their differences with the West and Western development; the common model is Western feudalism, against which the diversity of Iranian development is conceptualized. It should, however, be noted that the significance of feudalism in their discourse is due to the role that it plays in the development of capitalism as a uniquely Western phenomenon.

Marx's concept of the Asiatic mode of production[36] and Weber's notion of patrimonial domination[37] both presuppose a genealogy of capitalism and capitalist development conceived in terms of the structural dynamics of feudalism. They seek to explain, though in quite different ways, why Eastern forms of social and economic organization did not develop into a capitalist system. The answer is found in the absence of characteristically Western feudal relations and institutions in the East; thus the significance of feudalism as a model for reference is due primarily to the role that it plays in the development of capitalism in the West. This point is important in that it reveals the evolutionary and teleological character of the Marxist and Weberian concepts and of studies which are, in one way or another, informed by them. They all presuppose a teleological conception of capitalism and capitalist development.[38]

Further, Marx's concept of the Asiatic mode of production and Weber's notion of patrimonial domination refer to forms of economic and social relations and organizations which are constituted by political relations. They are functions of the mode of distribution of political power in Eastern societies. In these societies, unlike those of feudal Europe, the distribution of political power, and hence the institutional organization of the state, does not require a territorial basis and the associated forms of reciprocal obligation between the king and his subordinates. In the East, political relations are concentrated in the state, which is the personal domain of the despotic ruler. The result is the absence of feudal landed property and of an autonomous landed aristocracy in the East.

Clearly the concept of the Asiatic mode of production and the notion of patrimonial domination both presuppose a concept of feudalism which is defined by political rather than economic relations. To be more precise, it is the decentralized character of the feudal state and the associated parcellization of sovereignty which determine the specifically feudal character of social and economic institutions and relations in feudal Europe. The host of differences which define Asiatic/patrimonial societies, in particular the monopoly ownership of the land by the state and the subsequent subsumption of the land-owning class within it, are deduced from the absence of this fundamental factor in the East. Decentralized suzerain monarchies and centralized sovereign states are thus constitutive of Western feudalism and Eastern Asiatism respectively. The main function of the political conception of feudalism in Marx and in Weber is a definition of Asiatic/patrimonial society as an essentially static entity which, in contrast to the dynamic West, lacks the propensity to change and development.

The political conception of feudalism is central to all Asiatic definitions of Iranian society and history, serving as a model in contrast with which the Asiatic character of Iranian society and history is established. The fundamental differences between Asiatic Iran and feudal Europe are reduced to the institutional form and organizational structure of political power: a centralized sovereign state as opposed to a decentralized suzerain one. The functioning of centralized sovereign states in Iranian history, their monopoly ownership of land and control of mercantile activity and the merchant community, led to the underdevelopment of productive forces in agriculture and the backwardness of commodity circulation and exchange in urban centres. The result was the underdeveloped structure of the division of labour in both town and country which, in turn, prevented the accumulation of capital and the associated forms of class relations in Asiatic Iran.

The monopoly ownership of agricultural land by the state and the consequent absence of an autonomous land-owning class in Asiatic Iran meant that rural communes lacked the incentive to produce for sale in the market. Economic surplus over and above subsistence had to be remitted to the central treasury in lieu of taxes, to pay for the upkeep of the massive military and bureaucratic apparatuses of the state. Nor did the mercantile community have any security; mercantile wealth and profit were subject to usurpation and confiscation by the despot and his satraps. Trade and commerce were for the most part controlled by the state, and were directed towards outside and distant markets, with little effect on the underdeveloped structure of the division of labour in society. The insecurity of the mercantile community and its dependence on the goodwill of the despot is thus seen as being the major obstacle to the development of a modern bourgeoisie in Asiatic Iran.

A crucial issue in this respect, and a recurrent theme in the Asiatic definitions of Iran, is the specific character of Iranian towns and their particular relationship with the surrounding countryside. It is argued that Iranian cities, despite their developed urban structure and communication networks, lacked the political and administrative autonomy which was enjoyed by the less developed European towns in the Middle Ages. This, too, is related to the absence of the structural conditions which provided for the autonomous development of European towns: namely, the parcellization of sovereignty peculiar to feudal Europe. The prevalence of the centralized state in Asiatic Iran did not permit the development of politically autonomous urban centres. Iranian cities remained captive to the direct control of the central government, which shaped their administrative structure to suit the exigencies of its political and military apparatuses. They resembled 'princely camps', dominating the countryside and representing an absolutely central economic and cultural component of Iranian despotism.

Soviet and Asiatic historiographies of Iran thus share a common theoretical ground. They both interpret Iranian history in terms of the functioning and development of centralized states. The specificity of Iranian feudalism and the Asiatic character of Iranian society are both deduced from the institutional form and organizational structure of political power in Iran. The element of political essentialism central to both feudal and Asiatic definitions of Iran leads to an 'externalist' view of capitalism and capitalist development in contemporary Iranian history. Soviet and Asiatic historiographies both consider Iranian history as an evolutionary and 'natural' process of development, interrupted by the encroachments of capitalism from the outside. The history of modern Iran is thus explained in terms of the functioning of this external force, shaping and reshaping Iranian society in accordance with the rhythm and requirements of capitalist accumulation in the West.

It is interesting to note in passing that the political essentialism and the associated externalist conception of capitalism and capitalist development are also central to studies of contemporary Iranian history and society which are influenced by the 'Modernization Theory', which operates with the cosy assumption that there is a universal functional correspondence between the emergence and development of modern social, economic and political institutions on the one hand, and the gradual but inevitable dissolution of the old and traditional ones on the other. The correspondence between the two processes is established via the activity of the modern middle classes as the main agent of change in the process of transition from traditionalism to modernism. These classes are said to subscribe to modern and rational outlooks, values and norms of conduct in the spheres of the economy, the family and education, which are in conformity with the functional requirements of modern institutions in the transitional society.

Modernization theory is conceptually informed by the structural functionalist schools in sociology, and in particular by the works of Talcott Parsons, for whom broadly speaking there is a direct functional correspondence between the development of modern socio-cultural institutions and the requirements of industrial society. (*The Structure of Social Action*, New York, 1948.) As applied to Iran, modernization theory presupposes a field of modernity which is initially external to its traditional socio-economic structure, an assumption which entails a notion of traditional society as static, lacking social dynamics or any developmental force. The dynamics of development, therefore, must be imparted to it from the outside, through an increasing recourse to the West beginning in the late nineteenth and early twentieth centuries. The period is defined in terms of struggle between traditionalist and modernist forces, which acquire their respective designations by their orientation towards the Qajar State as the centre of opposition to modernism. The Constitutional revolution signifies the victory of the modernist over the traditionalist forces. The post-Constitutional State, notably the

Pahlavi regime (1925–79), thus becomes the agent of modernization in the struggle against the conservative forces of traditionalism. The functional correspondence between the development of modern and the dissolution of traditional institutions and processes is established through the agency of the state, which specifies the field of struggle between the forces of tradition and modernity. In fact, the shift of emphasis in the analysis from the middle classes to the state leads to a redefinition of social forces and the field of conflict between them in the post-Constitutional period. The traditional and modern forces are defined not so much by their real or alleged association with economic processes and institutions as by their political orientation towards the state. This may explain the failure of the modernization theory to understand the apparent paradox of the 1979 revolution: the active role played by the modern middle classes in the downfall of a modernizing state![39]

To return to the main theme of this discussion: according to Soviet historiography Iranian feudalism evolved out of a slave-based economy and was, in line with a universal and natural process of development, to evolve into an indigenous capitalist economy. But the natural process, and hence the conformity of Iranian history with the universal law, was suddenly interrupted from without by the impact of the encounter with capitalist relations. The result was a historical deformation, the unnatural birth of a dependent capitalist economy which dominates Iranian society to date. Soviet historiography, on the whole, viewed Iranian capitalism as an unnatural, illegitimate and morally undesirable child, artificially inseminated and raised by world imperialism. For the protagonists of Asiatic Iran, too, the advent of capitalism in Iran is an 'accident' of history. It was forced upon Iranian society from the outside and provided a new economic basis for the declining despotism.

The concept of an Iranian feudalism, elaborated by the Soviet historians, and the alternative Asiatic definitions of Iranian history define the terms of a controversy which has dominated historical writing on Iran in recent years. The controversy, despite serious theoretical and conceptual flaws and inconsistencies, signifies a new opening in historical writing on Iran. It attempts, for the first time in Iranian history, to relate historical argument to contemporary economic and political conditions, a need which has become more pressing after the unfortunate fate of the Iranian revolution.

2. THE CONCEPT OF THE ASIATIC MODE OF PRODUCTION AND DEFINITIONS OF PRE-CAPITALIST IRAN AS AN ASIATIC SOCIETY

In recent years the field of Iranian studies has witnessed a revival of interest in the concept of the Asiatic mode of production. The contention that pre-Constitutional Iran was an Asiatic society enjoys considerable popularity among social scientists, economic historians and political activists, both Marxist and non-Marxist. The popularity of this contention is due primarily to two factors: first, both the concept and its specific application to Iranian history have a long pedigree within Marxism, deriving from Marx himself; and secondly, it appears to avoid some of the major theoretical and empirical inconsistencies involved in the rival proposition that Iran was a feudal society—namely, the absence both of a landed aristocracy and of the institution of serfdom.

Marxist definitions tend to be more general, and often consist of an uncritical and *ad hoc* application of the concept to socio-economic and political conditions in Iran before the Constitutional revolution. They emphasize the significance of state ownership of the agricultural land and the prevalence of tax-rent, arising out of the general geographic and climatic conditions of the country.[1] The major problem facing these definitions, as was indicated in the introductory chapter, is empirical. State ownership of land was not the sole and universal category of land-ownership in Iran. It existed alongside the other forms of land-ownership, e.g. private and *waqf* lands, and varied in size and proportion from one period to another.[2] Nor was there any 'hydraulic project' of the type and significance capable of explaining the economic role of an otherwise essentially external state apparatus.

21

Non-Marxist definitions, by contrast, are more concerned with the correspondence, or lack of it, between the concept and Iranian history, and identify various real or alleged incompatibilities to stress both the scientificity and the originality of their analyses. Ashraf's 'Asiatic patrimonial despotism' and Katouzian's 'Persian despotism' and 'Aridisolatic society' are the two most serious and influential alternative definitions of this kind.[3]

Both authors refer to the absence of hydro-agriculture and relate it to the specific effect of aridity on the socio-economic structure of Iranian society. Ashraf, however, has a distinctly political view of Marx's concept of the Asiatic mode and identifies it with its political component as Asiatic despotism. For Ashraf the Asiatic state in Iran was based on 'bureaucratic landlordism' and 'state capitalism', which he explains using Weber's notion of 'Oriental patrimonialism'. Katouzian, on the other hand, relies almost exclusively on Marx's definition of the concept in *Grundrisse*, and emphasizes the significance of the 'isolated' and 'self-sufficient' peasant communities as the foundation of Persian despotism, characterized by arbitrary rule and a state of complete lawlessness. Unlike Ashraf, who considers Marx's 'Asiatic despotism' and Weber's 'Oriental patrimonialism' as the two essential and constitutive elements of his 'principle of historical specificity of Iranian society', Katouzian is reluctant to acknowledge his debt to Marx, insisting that his definition constitutes the 'rudiments of an original and scientific model' for understanding the specificity of the historical development of Iranian society.[4]

Katouzian's assertion amounts to more than a simple oversight or a means to promote an otherwise unfounded claim to originality. It is an intentional omission, necessary to sustain the opposition to Marxism which is the *raison d'être* of his study as a whole. But before assessing the theoretical status and validity of the 'Asiatic definitions' of pre-capitalist Iran, I shall briefly discuss Marx's concept of the Asiatic mode of production, examining the theoretical status and validity of the concept and demonstrating the manner in which it has directly influenced these alleged 'scientific principles' and 'original models' for the analysis of Iranian history.

The Concept of the Asiatic Mode of Production

Marx's concept of the 'Asiatic mode of production' signifies the economic structure of a predominantly agrarian society, constituted by the articulation of land-ownership and political sovereignty in the body of a centralized state. The Asiatic state, in its double capacity as landlord/sovereign, appropriates the economic surplus of the direct producers in the form of tax-rent. The relations of appropriation, therefore, do not involve class relations. They are effects of the exercise of sheer political coercion by the state, which is constitutive of the mode of production as a whole. The Asiatic state provides for and ensures the reproduction of the economy, while remaining essentially independent of economic relations. The absence of the institution of private property in land and an autonomous land-owning class are the defining characteristics of the concept and its various elaborations in Marxist theory.[5]

The concept itself has been the subject of a long and continuing debate in Marxist theory.[6] The strategic aim of the debate, however, has been to evaluate the concept within historical materialism; at issue is the existence of centralized sovereign states in the essentially classless societies of the Orient. Opponents of the concept have found the notion of state-class to be in stark contrast with the established tenets of historical materialism, and have viewed the concept itself as an unfortunate mistake on Marx's part—the result of an insufficient knowledge of Oriental societies, largely inherited from earlier Western political theory. Exponents of the concept, on the other hand, although they have sought to rectify the notion of state-class in various ways, have done so mainly by expanding on themes already present in Marx's remarks. Some have proposed a generalization of the idea of the hydraulic society and the associated conception of the Asiatic state as a functional necessity, hence ranking the concept on a par with the concepts of other pre-capitalist modes of production in historical materialism. Others have solved the problem by shifting the emphasis from the dominance of state ownership (*Capital*) to that of communal ownership (*Grundrisse*), as the foundation of social relations in Asiatic societies; this latter view, placing Asiatic societies in the context of an arrested transition from a classless to a class society, has been the main cause of the recent revival of interest in the concept of the Asiatic mode of production.[8] There are still others who have addressed the paradox simply by naming of the taxes as tributes, supplemented by the proceeds of state-controlled, long-distance trade in Asiatic societies. Hence the notion of the 'tributary mode of production' as the latest addition to the long list of new modes of production coined by the ardent but misinformed students of structuralist Marxism since the late 1960s.[9] These attempts, on the whole, fail to come to terms with the theoretical problems posed by the concept. They all presuppose particular forms of social relations generated by the functioning of the centralized states but cannot explain their existence in the specific context of Asiatic societies. This issue will be discussed later in some detail.

The conventional Marxist critique of the concept of the Asiatic mode of production has led to its rejection as a theoretical category signifying an autonomous mode of production within historical materialism. But 'Asiatism' as a discursive construct, denoting a distinct yet indeterminate social entity in the past and present, has continued to persist in most of the Marxist historical writing on Asian societies. This is because critics have consistently failed to come to terms with the theoretical and conceptual problems posed by the study of the historical development of non-European social formations. The dominant trends in Marxist scholarship—the sweeping generalization of the concept of the feudal mode of production and its opposite, i.e. the Asiatic definitions, which emphasize the essentially Eurocentric character of historical materialism—have achieved little more in relation to non-European societies than fragmented political histories.

Anderson's work on the 'House of Islam' is a case in point (Anderson 1974b, pp.361–397). This work is intended to serve a double purpose: it sets the historical ground for reaffirming, by way of contrast, the essentially Eurocentric character of the concept of the feudal mode of production on the one hand, and for refuting the concept of the Asiatic mode of production on the other. With regard to the former, Anderson is largely in agreement with the bulk of Orientalist writing, old and new, on the nature of the Ottoman polity and economy, despite its clear implications for the concept of the Asiatic mode of production. With regard to the latter, he attempts a powerful critique of the Orientalist literature in the context of a genealogy of the concept in Marx's discourse. The result of these two incompatible positions in Anderson's essay is not a synthesis but a paradox, which runs through his analysis, and is seemingly overcome by opting for scepticism as to the 'nature of the prevailing modes of production in Islamic social formation'. Anderson's scepticism however does not offer a way out of the dilemma. Rather, in his otherwise eloquent account of the development of Islamic civilization, Anderson falls back on the theoretical premises of the concept of the Asiatic mode of production.

Anderson is scornful of both the feudal and the Asiatic definitions of non-European societies. He finds both approaches erroneous, theoretically and empirically. In the case of the Asiatic mode, his critique invokes the terms of the conventional debate, rejecting the concept for its discursive incoherence. Although Anderson does refer to the theoretical inconsistency of the tax-rent couple, the point, which emerges only casually in his exposition, is too weak to overcome the enormity of the weight assigned to the state and political relations in the preceding and succeeding stages of the analysis. For as we shall see shortly, his analysis of the historical development of the 'House of Islam' is negatively determined by a political definition of the concept of the feudal mode of production which is central to his analysis of the origins and development of the absolutist state in Europe. The entire course of Ottoman history, too, is explained in terms of the military expression of the centralizing tendencies within the state.

Anderson takes up the central theme of Wittek's analysis of the Ottoman state,[10] which, according to him, is a 'subtle reversal of Ibn Khaldun's famous formula: the division of the Islamic history into alternating phases of nomadic *asabiyya* (characterized by religious fervour, social solidarity and military prowess) and urban *faragh* or *dia* (characterized by economic prosperity, administrative sophistication and cultural leisure), which he believed were mutually incompatible —urban civilization being unable to resist nomadic conquest, nomadic fraternity then being unable to survive urban corruption, producing a cyclical history of state formation and disintegration' (ibid. p.363).[11] Following Wittek, Anderson argues that 'in the Turkish state, the two contradictory principles of Islamic political development for the first time came into structural harmony' (ibid. p.363). Anderson's subsequent analysis, much influenced by the work of Gibb and Bowen (a classic of modern Orientalism),[12] makes it clear that it was the peculiar military organization of the Ottoman state and the associated fiscal institutions along with the *millet* system, its other creation, which provided for the structural harmony of the two contradictory principles in Ottoman society; thus setting straight the cyclical course of Islamic history.

Implicit in Anderson's analysis of the 'House of Islam' is the

Orientalist thesis of the uniqueness of the West, substantiated by his remarks on the nature of the agrarian relations and structures in Ottoman society. These remarks are prompted by the question which underlies his enterprise as a whole: why did capitalism develop in the West?—a question which is already an integral part of the Orientalist problematic. The answer, according to Anderson, lies in the specificity of feudal landed property with its particular scalar structure, which provided for an autonomous landed aristocracy in the countryside and an independent mercantile bourgeoisie in the developing towns. Islamic *iqta*, by contrast, lacked such a structure, and the associated forms of feudal hierarchy did not develop in Ottoman society. In seeking to explain the reason behind the failure of the *iqta* to develop into private property similar to feudal landed property, Anderson then invokes the Islamic *sharia*, and its alleged confusion on matters related to property rights and relations in land, in particular with respect to the question of inheritance (op.cit. p.505).

Reference to the retarding effects of the *sharia* on the development and consolidation of landed property in the Islamic societies is commonplace.[13] The most notable factor in this respect is the absence of primogeniture in the *sharia*, causing parcellization and non-consolidation of landed property. But this point, however significant, does not exclude the institution of private property in land. Further, it is a well known fact that, in practice, the rules of the *sharia* seldom applied to the grant of *iqta* to the soldiery in Ottoman and other Islamic countries, which was in fact subject to political rather than legal relations. The conditions governing the grant of *iqta* and the continuity of its possession by the assignee depended strictly on the relationship between him and the ruling sultan, itself an expression of their relative political and military strength.

These points, however, are for the most part implicit in Gibb and Bowen's conception of the Ottoman state, to which Anderson largely subscribes. Anderson, following these authors, treats the Islamic *iqta* as a political institution, an adjunct of the state's fiscal administration, and the *iqta*-holder as the state functionary subsumed within it. This conception of *iqta*, needless to say, contains the conditions of existence of tax-rent, as the form of exploitation associated with it. Anderson's repeated reservations, his scepticism about the character of the prevailing modes of production in Islamic societies, fall far short of solving the contradiction apparent in his essay: a contradiction between his critique of the concept of the Asiatic mode of production and his conception of the development of the Islamic society. For Anderson effectively reconstitutes the conditions of existence of the concept of the Asiatic mode of production and redefines them within an Orientalist framework.

The conventional Marxist critique of the concept of the Asiatic mode of production focuses on the question of the state-class, pointing to its discursive incoherence.[14] Although necessary, this is by no means sufficient for an effective critique of the concept. The incoherence can be rectified, at least formally, by invoking the economic functioning of the Asiatic state, already a familiar feature in the conventional defence of the concept,[15] since, as with the feudal mode of production, state power would suffice to ensure the non-economic (i.e. the juridico-political) relations of appropriation. The difference between the two lies not in the character but in the form of their respective relations of appropriation: feudal rent and tax-rent. They appear as the two variants of the same structure of social relations: the political relations of the appropriation of surplus.

This position is adopted by Balibar in his influential essay 'Basic Concepts of Historical Materialism' (Althusser and Balibar 1970, pp.199–308, esp. pp.209–224). Balibar locates the concept in the conditions of its formation in Marx's discourse, in which, he argues, it has a similar theoretical status to the concepts of all pre-capitalist modes of production. They all serve to highlight the specificity of the capitalist mode of production by retrospectively projecting the complex historical process of transformation in the dominance of non-economic to economic relations of appropriation (Balibar, op.cit. pp.218–20). Marx, Balibar further argues, focuses on the process of production of surplus value as opposed to surplus labour/product in pre-capitalist modes of production. The productive force of capital, here, is highlighted by contrasting it with the role played by the state in the Asiatic mode of production. They are both 'endowed with the power to set the labour force to work': a 'productive power' immanent both in the state and capital, which transforms labour to social labour. The productive power of the state in the Asiatic mode of production, maintains Balibar, results from the non-coincidence of necessary and surplus labour; the non-correspondence of the labour process and the process of production: a structural feature of all pre-capitalist modes of production, as opposed to the capitalist mode of production, which is characterized by the coincidence of the two processes in 'time and space' (ibid. pp.221–2).

Balibar conceives the coincidence/non-coincidence of necessary and surplus labour as the characteristic difference between the capitalist and pre-capitalist modes of production. It is, in his words:

> the essential point of the whole of Marx's analysis in *Capital* of the capitalist mode of production . . . another way of expressing the term by term coincidence of the labour process and the process of producing value. The distinction between constant capital and variable capital which defines the process of producing value will always be found to correspond to the distinction between labour power and means of production peculiar to the labour process. (ibid. p.222)

Coincidence/non-coincidence is determined by the forms of combination of the factors of the production process in capitalist and pre-capitalist modes of production: the forms of combination of property relations and the relations of real appropriation. Balibar thus concludes that in pre-capitalist modes of production there is an intrinsic 'disjunction' in 'time and space' between the processes of labour and production, resulting from the forms of combination peculiar to them; the dual form of property relations as 'possession' and 'property', in effect, means that surplus labour cannot be appropriated by economic coercion. The intervention of non-economic (political, legal and ideological) coercive relations in the process of production is therefore requisite (ibid. pp.221–2).

Balibar's analysis suggests that in pre-capitalist modes of production state power *directly* intervenes at the economic level, and the transformed social forms, i.e., the production relations, assume an economic form only *indirectly*. They are not 'directly economic, but directly and indissolubly political and economic', as he puts it. This paradoxical statement, in turn, is sustained by invoking the materialist thesis of 'determination in the last instance by the economy'. The economic level is thought to assign a dominant status to political relations in the structure of the mode of production. The dominance of the political is ensured despite the intrinsic disjunction between the labour process and the process of production; a disjunction which, in effect, means that the production relations have no effect on the functioning of the labour process and the latter is a virtually autonomous economic unit.

This point has serious implications for Balibar's reformulation of the classical Marxist concepts of the pre-capitalist modes of production. It means that the division of necessary and surplus labour, the central theme of his argument, is not a function of the structure of the mode of production, but a politically enforced deduction from the total product, extracted by an exploiter who is external to the process of production. The transformed social forms (i.e. feudal rent, tax-rent, tributes, etc) are no more than the effects of political relations, a point which, in turn, calls into question the form of the combination of relations and forces of production peculiar to the structure of these modes: the 'dual form' of pre-capitalist property relations which presupposes a distinction between 'economic property' and 'legal ownership'.

Balibar's conceptualization of pre-capitalist social relations essentially presupposes the materialist thesis of determination in the last instance by the economy. Without this thesis the economic role assigned to the state and the political in the structure of these modes cannot be sustained. 'Determination in the last instance' has been the subject of much scrutiny in contemporary Marxism, initiated partly by Balibar's essay itself; critics have found the thesis inconsistent and indefensible, for reasons which are largely beyond the immediate scope of this study.[16] But Balibar's response to the objections initially raised against his theorization of this thesis was to retreat from his earlier position and leave the outcome of the process to the determinations of the struggle between classes; an argument which can hardly escape the consequences of the points made in previous pages.[17] In the case of the Asiatic mode of production, Balibar's defensive move fares still worse, since there are, in this mode, simply no classes to wage war against one another, and no politics other than that emanating from a functionally necessary state apparatus.

Balibar's conceptualization, despite its sophistication, thus largely reproduces the major theoretical inconsistencies involved in the classical Marxist concepts of pre-capitalist modes of production. The dominant position he assigns to state power in his analysis of labour and production processes in pre-capitalist modes of production effectively reduces their structural differences to the modality of the distribution of political power in pre-capitalist social formations. Feudal rent and tax-rent, for instance, appear as two variants of the same structure of social relations. They are conceived as particular effects of two different forms of state power on agrarian economies characterized by the non-separation of the direct producers from the land—the very foundation of an 'anthropological conception' of property, which presupposes the separation of 'economic property' from 'legal ownership' in the structure of pre-capitalist modes of production.

Balibar's contribution, despite its shortcomings, occupies an important place in the contemporary debate on the status of the Marxist theory of modes of production. It shows clearly that a critique of the concept of the Asiatic mode of production, if it is to surpass the theoretical limitations of the conventional debate, must involve a problematization of the non-economic conception of pre-capitalist social relations of production. This conception has dominated classical and contemporary Marxist discourse on pre-capitalist social formations in the West and East alike.

In the array of criticism generated by Balibar's contribution to the theory of modes of production, the work of Hindess and Hirst stands out for its pioneering role in expanding and superseding the theoretical boundaries of Marxist discourse on pre-capitalist modes of production. Their problematization of the theoretical consistency of the tax-rent couple ultimately leads to the rejection of the classical Marxist concept of pre-capitalist relations of production. Adopting a mode of proof derived from the discourse of *Capital*, the authors argue that Marx's conceptualization of pre-capitalist production relations is not consistent with that discourse which, they further maintain, contains elements for the subversion and reconstitution of the concepts of pre-capitalist production relations. Marx's theorization of the structure and reproduction of the capitalist mode of production in *Capital* thus constitutes the main point of reference in their analysis.[18]

In Marxist theory, argue Hindess and Hirst, a mode of production is structured by a definite set of production relations, which determine both the distribution of the means of production to the unit of production and the distribution of product from the labour process. The relations of production, as such, structure economic agents as social classes, in accordance with their possession of and separation from all or part of the means of production necessary for the functioning of the labour process. This definition of the concept of the mode of production presupposes: first, a unity of economic property and legal ownership in its structure, hence a necessary correspondence between the relations of production and the labour process; and second, a mechanism for the appropriation of surplus which is economic in character and involves possession of and separation from all or part of the means of production.

At the root of this argument lies a rejection of the 'non-separation' of labour from the means of production, the foundation of the classical Marxist concept of pre-capitalist social relations. The notion of 'possession in separation' involves forms of class relations which depend strictly on the separation of the direct producers from the means of production, the necessary basis for relations of appropriation. The possessing and non-possessing agents are internal to the process of production and their status is a function of their relationship to the means of production. The process of transformation of legal ownership into economic property, ownership into possession, is economic. It involves forms of economic exchange which exclude the non-economic forms of appropriation of surplus.

The classical Marxist concepts of pre-capitalist social relations, maintain the authors, do not satisfy such a definition of productive relations. They have no structural status in the concepts of the pre-capitalist modes of production. They are political categories, resulting from the mode of distribution of political power in pre-capitalist societies, and incapable of affecting the functioning of the labour process, whether on a peasant holding or a rural commune. The classical Marxist concepts of pre-capitalist modes are thus characterized by a disjunction between production relations and the unit of production; a disjunction which is the effect of the conflation of the relations of production with the non-economic conditions of their existence. The concepts of these modes, conclude the authors, are theoretically inconsistent.

The theoretical inconsistency of the concepts of the pre-capitalist modes of production is secured by political relations: the incorporation of state power into the structure of the concept, whereby the political relations of appropriation of surplus secure the connection between the forces and relations of production. In the case of the Asiatic mode of production, nevertheless, the situation is somewhat different. Here, the insertion of a functionally necessary state apparatus into the structure of the concept falls short of securing the connection between the forces and relations of production. Since the tax-rent couple, the production relations of the Asiatic mode, does

not involve class relations, it is incapable of explaining the existence of
the state on which it depends. The concept of the Asiatic mode of
production is not only theoretically inconsistent but also discursively
incoherent (Hindess & Hirst 1977, pp.42–43).

The insertion of the state into the process of economic production,
argue Hindess and Hirst, provides only a formal solution to the
theoretical inconsistency of the concept. It secures the conditions of
existence of tax-rent, but is unable to provide for class relations other
than those determined by political/legal relations of domination and
subordination between two contradictory communities: a large
community of exploited composed of the mass of the direct
producers, and a small community of exploiters, a privileged minority
controlling the state apparatus and exercising state power in their own
interest. The unity of the two communities, that is to say, the
structure of the Asiatic social formation, is sustained by the
intervention of the state in the process of economic production. A
social formation characterized by such a structure excludes class
relations, and the notion of a centralized state in a classless society is a
logical impossibility (Hindess and Hirst 1975, pp.201–6).

In Marxist theory, it is further argued, the state is an instrument of
class rule and the organization of class domination. It presupposes a
definite set of production relations resulting from possession in
separation from the means of production. The concept of the Asiatic
mode of production does not entail such relations. The production
relations, here, are the effects of state power, and constituted by it.
The communities of the exploiters and the exploited are organized
around a mode of exploitation which operates through the agency of
the state. In Asiatic societies, therefore, social classes and relations of
production are effects of the functioning of the state. There is, in
these societies, no sphere of the economic or social independent of
the state. The despotic state is the essence of the Asiatic society
(ibid.).

Let us now return to Marx's writings on the Asiatic mode of
production, which, it should be noted, are not homogeneous in form
or content. They entail different conceptions of the relationship
between the political and the economic, and different views on the
origins of the despotic state. For example, his view of the relationship
between the political and the economic in pre-colonial India differs
radically from that implied in the case of hydro-agricultural society. In
relation to Indian peasant communities, Marx argues that 'the

dissolution and refounding of the Asiatic state' does not affect 'the economic elements of society'. This, he suggests, is due to the 'simplicity of the organization for production in these self-sufficing communities that constantly reproduce themselves in the same form'. 'This simplicity', concludes Marx, 'supplies the key to the secret of the unchangeableness of Asiatic societies ... The structure of the economic elements of the society remains untouched by the storm-clouds of the political sky' (*Capital* Vol.I 1970, p.358).

This theme first appears in his articles on 'British Rule in India' and is then reiterated in *Capital*. Marx argues here that in Asiatic societies there is no intrinsic relationship between the political and the economic structures. The economic structure, composed of small, isolated and self-sufficient peasant communities, reproduces itself independently of the political structure. The state is superimposed upon the economy and metamorphoses in the structure of political relations have no bearing on the functioning of the economic structure. Yet, with regard to the mode of exploitation, the state plays an active and essential role. It exploits the peasant communities by means of taxes in kind, often amounting to the entire economic surplus above subsistence level, leaving no incentive for the peasants to produce surplus and engage in exchange relations. The possibility of the creation of a market is thus limited by the state's use of peasant labour and by the absence of any economic limit to exploitation—the amount and level of taxes in kind being arbitrary, depending on the financial requirements of the state. Elsewhere in *Capital* Marx expands on the same theme. He argues that exploitation can be so intense as to hold back the development of productive forces for a long time (*Capital* Vol.III 1971, p.796).

Clearly, this conception of the state and economy in Asiatic societies entails a different form of the state and state power to that in hydro-agricultural society; one in which the state is not only external to the economy but also superimposed upon the society as a whole from the outside (e.g. as a consequence of the military conquest of a territory inhabited by a stateless people). It is constituted by relations other than those which structure the social formation. The relations of exploitation, the tax-rent couple, are ensured by extending the political domination of an already constituted state apparatus to a community of direct producers with no state relations.

In *Grundrisse* (1974, pp.472–3), we encounter a different definition of the concept of the Asiatic mode of production. Here Marx emphasizes the prevalence of communal/tribal property relations as opposed to state ownership stressed in *Capital* (Vol.I 1970, pp.357–8); these remarks, as indicated above, have been at the heart of the recent revival of interest in the concept of the Asiatic mode of production. Those favouring this altered emphasis tend to stress the transitional character of communal landed property, thus locating the concept in the context of a universal and evolutionary process of development: the transition from the primitive communal to the ancient mode of production. Broadly speaking, the general argument is that in the East, the universal process of transition was interrupted by the intervention of external forces, but above all by tribal wars and invasions, leading to the superimposition of strong centralized states upon the peasant communities and to their subsequent consolidation and stagnation. The existence of strong and war-like centralized states thus prevented the development of productive forces and barred the process of transition from a classless to a class society.[19]

The emphasis on communal landed property as the foundation of agrarian production in Asiatic societies provides the basis for certain forms of social relations in the context of the tax-rent couple. But the primacy of the notion of an external state apparatus in the structure of the concepts of these relations creates further insurmountable theoretical problems. First, as pointed out earlier, the conception of a social formation as a community of direct producers with external political/legal relations is a logical impossibility. The absence of political/legal relations in a social formation leads to its reduction to and identification with the economic structure. The Asiatic social formation and the Asiatic mode of production thus become identical concepts. Secondly, the set of production relations derived from the communal landed property does not involve economic class relations. Consequently the communal unit of production appears as an autonomous economic base, endowed with all the production and distribution functions of a mode of production proper; hence the identification of the unit of production with the mode of production which is a common characteristic of the studies emphasizing the primacy of the communal mode of production in Asiatic societies.

The Definitions of Iran as an Asiatic Society

Ashraf's 'Asiatic patrimonial despotism' and Katouzian's 'Aridisolatic society', also presuppose a state which is external not only to the economy but to the social formation as a whole. Thus the historical process depicted in their analyses reveals the continuous effects of this external force on the economic structure of Asiatic Iran. 'Asiatic patrimonial despotism' and 'Aridisolatic society' are both concepts designed to explain this one-sided relationship between the despotic state and the economy in Asiatic Iran in a period exceeding two and a half millenia.

Katouzian begins with a critique of the application of general and abstract models to the specificities of Iranian history, emphasizing the 'bizarre methodological similarities between protagonists of feudalism and those of Oriental despotism'. The two modes of analysis, he contends, are based on the 'universalization of abstract and general theories', and this is their 'great methodological weakness' (Katouzian 1981, p.9). He thus attempts to 'dispense with pragmatic benefits of intellectual complacency and take the trouble of looking for models and theories which may result in genuine addition to our knowledge of the world' (ibid. p.7). The outcome of this project is the twin concepts of 'Persian despotism' and 'Aridisolatic society', considered as 'rudiments of a model' capable of explaining the historical specificity of Iranian society without falling into the trap of 'unscientific generalizations' (ibid. p.309).

Katouzian's model, therefore, has two components: a political and an economic structure, defined as 'Persian despotism' and 'Aridisolatic society' respectively. The former refers to a centralized state characterized by a massive bureaucratic apparatus and the arbitrary exercise of power; the latter designates an agrarian economic structure composed of self-sufficient and isolated peasant communities. The two components of Katouzian's 'scientific model' are related through political coercion on the part of the state, which is also the source of the relations of appropriation of surplus. But these relations have no foundation in the economic structure. In fact, Katouzian insists on the complete autonomy of the economic from the political:

> Iranian agriculture and Iranian peasantry were *not* dependent on the state for the provision and regulation of water supplies, or for anything else. It was the state which depended on scattered and isolated village units for the agricultural surplus which it either directly requisitioned, or assigned to the landlords and tax-farmers. This is the likely origin of the despotic state, which, basing itself on urban centres and military outposts

linked together by a country wide transport system, dominated the scattered village *units* of agricultural production. (ibid. p.299)

This brief exposition shows the close resemblance of Katouzian's original model of Iranian history to Marx's concept of the Asiatic mode of production. They both presuppose a despotic state which is external to the society as a whole, hence asserting the complete autonomy of the economic from the political. In fact, Katouzian's view of the origin and the conditions of existence of Persian despotism, the political component of his original and scientific model, is a faithful reproduction of Marx's remarks and entails the same inconsistencies:

This material force [the despotic state] was originally provided by invading tribes, and thereafter both by the existing and further incoming nomads, who succeeded in setting up various urban states at different stages of history. The size of direct and indirect collective agricultural surplus was so large as to enable those despotic states to spend on transport, communications, military and bureaucratic organization, and so on, which both maintained their hold on the land and prevented the later emergence of feudal autonomy in agriculture and bourgeois citizenship in towns. (ibid. p.300)

Just as in Marx, here we encounter the state as an external force with no foundation in the structure of social relations in Iranian society. It is a centralized political entity superimposed upon the agrarian social structure from without, by means of military conquest, and reproduces its total domination and arbitrary rule over the local population by expropriating the 'collective economic surplus' of the subjugated Iranian peasants: a process which, in turn, prevents the emergence of feudal autonomy and bourgeois citizenship in Iranian society. That society, in Katouzian's view, lacked indigenous political relations and structures. They were imposed on it from the outside, by the invading tribes, which, as it were, either possessed them or simply created them in time to suit their immediate objectives: to dominate and exploit the stateless local inhabitants. We have here a conception of Iranian society which is identical with its economic structure; the community of the self-sufficient peasant producers, lacking political, legal and ideological relations of its own. This model, applied to the complexities of the historical development of Iranian society, may leave Katouzian with too little to answer too much.

Katouzian does acknowledge the relevance of Marx's concept of the Asiatic mode of production to Iran. He nevertheless insists that there were in fact fundamental differences between Iran and other Oriental societies, hence the originality of his model:

> It should be clear by now that many, though not all, of the features of life and labour that Marx, Engels and his precursors described as present in Asiatic society have indeed been present in the economic and social relations of the country ... the system was certainly despotic, and the country, by the wider definition of the term, Oriental ... It is true, too, the general aridity of the country, which made water scarce and artificial irrigation widespread, has been an important factor. (ibid. pp.20–21)

What are the fundamental differences between Iran and other Oriental societies, we may ask? Katouzian has little to say beyond pointing to the 'specific effects of aridity' on Iranian society (ibid. p.300). In fact, climatic conditions constitute the driving force of his analysis of Iranian history. On the specific effects of aridity, he writes:

> aridity did play a basic role in shaping the structure of the Iranian political economy, but in its own particular way: it served to create autonomous village units of production, none of which could produce a sufficiently large surplus to provide a feudal power base, but all of which taken together produced a collective surplus so large that, once appropriated by an organized external (regional or countrywide) force, it could be used to prevent the fragmentation of the politiconomic power. (ibid. p.300)

Central to Katouzian's argument is the notion of a collective economic surplus produced by isolated village communes and appropriated by the state whose total domination over society is thus perpetuated. This pattern, however, is far too general to be specific to Iranian society. As seen above, it is already present in Marx's comments on agrarian relations in Asiatic societies. Marx argues that isolated and self-sufficient village communities are the source of the collective economic surplus expropriated by the state as the external force standing above the society. The lack of marketable surplus, and of exchange relations, on the part of these communities leads to their reproduction on the same scale, thus perpetuating economic stagnation and social stasis. But while for Marx this phenomenon is the 'key to the secret of the East', in general for Katouzian it is the foundation of an original 'scientific' model of the historical specificity of Iranian society.

There is, however, a fundamental difference between Marx's and Katouzian's analysis of agrarian relations and structures. Marx in *Grundrisse* clearly emphasizes the predominance of communal (tribal) landed property in the Orient. Katouzian, by contrast, is highly ambiguous on the nature of property relations in Aridisolatic Iran, and this ambiguity is by no means accidental, since, of the two main forms of landed property associated with Asiatic despotism, neither can be incorporated into his model without raising insurmountable theoretical and conceptual problems. State ownership of agricultural land is incompatible with the alleged self-sufficiency and total independence of the village communities; while communal/tribal ownership undermines the dominant and determinant role assigned to aridity, which, in turn, justifies his conception of the village as the unit of production in Aridisolatic Iran. Property relations, conspicuously absent from Katouzian's scientific model of Iranian history, are replaced by climatic conditions.[20]

In Marx's definition, the collective economic surplus is appropriated by the relations of domination and subordination between the state and the direct producers. The intrinsic disconnection between property relations and the labour process is formally rectified by the incorporation of the state into the structure of the concept: political power provides for the existence of the tax-rent couple. Further, under the dominance of communal property relations, as suggested by Marx's remarks in *Grundrisse*, tax-rent may in fact provide the basis for certain forms of social relations other than the state-subject relations associated with the predominance of state property, a possibility impaired by the externality of the state to the social formation. In Katouzian's analysis, on the contrary, there is no mention of property relations and no provision, however formal, is made for the articulation of economic and political relations in the structure of his scientific model; a provision necessary if he is to account for the appropriation of the collective economic surplus by means and mechanisms other than sheer political-military violence. But Katouzian cannot dispense with the alleged autonomy of the economic structure, nor with the primacy of the climatic conditions in his model. They are central to his conceptualization of the structure and relations of Aridisolatic society.

According to Katouzian, the village was the unit of production in Iranian agriculture until the land reform of 1962. Peasant households, organized into communes known as *boneh* or *sahra*, carried out production communally. The conception of the village as the unit of production, however, raises a number of problems. The village, in Iran or elsewhere, is not an economic but a geographical entity, and as such no specific set of production relations can be deduced from it; thus it cannot be conceived as the unit of production. The village can only refer to the space where the economic agents—the various categories of peasants, landless labourers, agricultural wage-labourers, etc.—live and work. It can say nothing about the socio-economic relations governing their productive activities, any more than the notion of the city can explain the nature of the dominant industrial relations. Both terms denote the geographical location of economic activity, asserting only its rural or urban character.

Katouzian, however, claims that the Iranian village was an autonomous economic unit, with specific social boundaries determined by the 'internal socio-economic structures and relations and external (geographic as well as politiconomic) conditions'. He writes:

Therefore, both the internal socio-economic structure and relations and external (geographic as well as politiconomic) conditions made the Iranian village an independent unit of life and labour with few links with other (usually distant) villages, and little interest in the urban outsiders who came and left at the right time taking their appointed share of the village output. (ibid. p.299)

What are these 'internal socio-economic structures and relations' that constitute the village as the unit of production? For Katouzian, these relations all emanate from a single structure: the *boneh*, the Iranian peasant commune. The *boneh*, argues Katouzian, organized the supply of water to the production units, and thus determined the distribution of the production units in the Iranian countryside, ensuring an average equality of fertility for holdings of all cultivators.

Consequently, peasant holdings were usually open and scattered, and in general the more arid the location the stronger the *boneh* and the more scattered the holdings (ibid. p.299). Iranian peasant communes, contends Katouzian, characteristically ensured the uninterrupted existence and functioning of the Iranian village as an 'independent' unit of life and labour. Unlike other Oriental societies, agriculture and peasantry in Iran were not dependent on the state or any other agent for the provision and regulation of water or for anything else. The *boneh*, according to Katouzian, was responsible for preventing the development of Iran into a hydraulic society of the type defined by Wittfogel (ibid. pp.298–9).

It is interesting to note that in Katouzian's exposition of the role and functioning of the *boneh* in Iranian agriculture there is no reference to property relations. He does not specify the ownership of land and water, and the multitude of production and distribution functions attributed to the *boneh* appear as the effects of invisible causes. His argument can be sustained only if we admit that pre-reform Iranian agriculture was dominated by communal/tribal property relations. But this proposition, too, has implications which run counter to the premises of Katouzian's 'scientific model'. For the predominance of communal property relations means that the *boneh* and not the village was the unit of production in Iranian agriculture in the pre-reform era: a view widely held by Iranian populists, Marxist and non-Marxist.[21] Agrarian populists, who are characteristically in search of the 'people's production', find in the *boneh* a true expression of man's harmony with nature—a harmony disrupted by the intrusion of 'external' capitalist relations of production, pioneered and directed by the state apparatus. The populist myth of self-sufficient and autonomous peasant communal production, in Iran as elsewhere, rests upon a 'calculated omission' of property and exchange relations in the analysis of the unit of production. They are treated as 'external' to the process of production, having no place in the conceptualization of the agrarian relations and structures.

Katouzian, in line with the agrarian populists, argues for the 'self-sufficiency' and 'independence' of the *boneh*. These attributes, essential as they are to his model, are sustained at the expense of the property and exchange relations. A consideration of the prevailing forms of land-use and land-tenure in Iranian agriculture in the pre-reform era demonstrates the fallacy of Katouzian's argument.

The right to use the land, the *nasaq*, by definition presupposed forms of property ownership in agricultural land other than communal ownership. *Nasaq* was an individual right assigned to the direct producers—usually to the head of the household—by the landlord, whether Crown, State, charitable institution or individual owner (corresponding to the *khaleseh*, *divani*, *waqf* and *arbabi* categories of land-ownership respectively) in return for a share of the produce. These categories of land-ownership, though varied in size and proportion according to time and circumstances, dominated Iranian agriculture for centuries. The relationship between the landlord and the direct producers always involved a form of economic exchange; the exchange of the right to use the land for a share of the produce, resulting directly from the possession in separation from the land. *Nasaq* was, in this sense, an expression of the prevailing economic class relations in Iranian agriculture and inevitably involved forms of economic exploitation which cannot be deduced from the functioning of an 'independent' and 'self-sufficient' *boneh*.

Further, the dominant form of land tenure in Iran was share-cropping, an age-old form dating back to the pre-Islamic period. Fixed rent (in kind and in money) and labour-rent played secondary and marginal roles. Share-cropping, by definition, assumes contractual relations between the direct producers and the owner of the land which, in turn, provide a basis for relations of exploitation. The forms of the division of produce are regulated in accordance with the provision of the means of production by the agents of production: land, water, seed, draught animals and labour. In Iran the landlord usually received no less than two shares (two fifths) of the total produce for provision of the land and water, and three shares when the seed was also provided by him was not an uncommon practice. The point, however, is that share-cropping involved a form of division of produce which was a function of the total/partial possession of, and separation from, the means of production, by the economic agents involved in the process of production. The contractual relationship which specified the form of the division of produce involved forms of economic class relations which cannot be deduced from the institution of the communal ownership of the land attributed to the *boneh*. But Katouzian disregards both the property and the exchange relations associated with agrarian production in Iran. The former are replaced by climatic conditions and the latter are conveniently wrapped in the mysterious activity of the 'urban outsiders who came and left at the right time taking their appointed share of the village output' (ibid. p.299). From an expert economist such a definition of exchange relations is surprising.

A consideration of the prevailing forms of land-use and land tenure in pre-reform Iranian agriculture, therefore, undermines the populist conception of the *boneh* as the 'self-sufficient' and 'independent' unit of production. Share-cropping and *nasaq* both presuppose forms of landed property and ownership other than the communal form essential if the *boneh* is to be considered as the unit of production. They further show that it was in fact the peasant household which constituted the unit of production in Iranian agriculture. The peasant household was neither autonomous nor self-sufficient. It was constituted by and functioned under the dominant form of landed property and property relations in pre-reform Iran. The *boneh*, on the other hand, was no more than a production team and, whatever its origins in the distant past, it functioned as an adjunct of the dominant relations of production in Iranian agriculture.

It might be argued—as the agrarian populists claim—that *nasaq* was a communal rather than an individual right, and that it was assigned to the *boneh* rather than the individual peasant household. The household obtained the right to use the land by virtue of its membership of the *boneh*, and the produce was divided between the owning agent and the *boneh* on the basis of the provision of the means of production. This argument may justify the conception of the *boneh* as the unit of production, but it nonetheless cannot validate the theoretical presuppositions of Katouzian's scientific model, since, as was pointed out, the forms of property and exchange relations entailed in *nasaq* and share-cropping are incompatible with the 'self-sufficiency' and 'independence' he attributes to the *boneh*. On the contrary, they show that Katouzian's ideal *boneh* was neither independent nor self-sufficient; rather it depended strictly on the provision of the land and water from the outside by an owner, and was accordingly the site of the relations of exploitation in the Iranian countryside. The owner may, as Katouzian argues, have been an urban outsider. But the fact that he did not reside in the village makes no difference to the character and functioning of the production relations in agriculture. The landlord's control over the process of production results from his monopoly ownership of the land: 'absentee landlordism' is primarily a political concept, with little or no economic significance.

Katouzian insists on the centrality of the *boneh* to Aridisolatic Iran, attributing to it a multiplicity of production and distribution functions amounting to a mode of production. But in the absence of communal landed property in Iranian agriculture, his conception of the *boneh* amounts to a mode of production without property relations; a contradiction in terms in all accounts except Katouzian's, which replaces property relations by climatic conditions. The *boneh*, allegedly constitutive of the economic structure of Aridisolatic Iran, is ultimately the creature of aridity. According to Katouzian:

> The *boneh* must owe its origin to the fact that water is the country's most scarce agricultural resource, except in one or two small pockets of land: the scarcity of water encouraged communal cooperation for the construction and upkeep of underground canals (*qanat* or *kariz*), as well as the distribution of water among the cultivators, hence the peasant rank of *abyar* (*owyar*) or water assistant. (ibid. p.298)

Scarcity of water may indeed have encouraged communal cooperation. There is also little doubt that it was the main reason behind the construction of the *qanat* network in the Iranian countryside. But scarcity of water in itself cannot account for the assumed predominance of communal property relations in Iranian agriculture, which is essential to sustain Katouzian's claim about the production and distribution functions of the *boneh*. Although the scarcity of water can explain the existence and significance of the *qanat* network in the Iranian countryside, it cannot explain the existence of private ownership of water as an essential means of production in Iranian agriculture, still less its control and distribution through that network. The fact that almost everywhere in Iran the *qanat* networks were owned and controlled by the owners of the land and water casts serious doubts on Katouzian's argument about the specific effects of aridity on the socio-economic structure of pre-reform Iran. In fact the position assigned to the *boneh* in Katouzian's model can be maintained only if the predominance of communal property relations in Iranian agriculture is *a priori* assumed; it collapses when that assumption is challenged on theoretical and empirical grounds.

It is important to note that, in Katouzian's model, land and water are not conceived as 'economic categories'. Rather, they are conceived as 'natural categories', part of 'nature' and natural geographic conditions in Iran, and, as such, remain independent of the prevailing social relations. Their contribution to the process of production, too, is assessed only in terms of their quantity and quality (scarcity/ abundance and fertility/infertility): the effects of the natural geographic conditions on the process of production in agriculture. However, nature in itself is an empty category, and land and water, in so far as they are considered as part of it, as natural phenomena, are devoid of any social significance. They acquire social significance only in the process of economic production, when they are subjected to the effects of particular property relations. These relations constitute land and water as a means of production in the process of production, where they cease to be natural phenomena. The effects of variations in the quantity and quality of land and water as the means of production on the process of production appear only after they are filtered through existing property relations. Thus they are entailed in the mode of the combination of the forces and relations of production in the labour process and are reflected in terms of the variation in the size and the market price of the economic surplus. They cannot structure the labour process, nor can they determine the mode of appropriation of surplus. Thus, though the scarcity of water in Iran, emphasized by Katouzian, has undoubtedly had particular effects on the combination of the forces and relations of production in the labour process (e.g. the existence of the *boneh* as the production team) and those functions related to the technical division of labour enforced by the method of distribution of water (such as the peasant rank of *abyar* or *mirab*), it cannot account for the predominance of a communal mode of production structured by aridity, still less a mode of appropriation of surplus corresponding to taxation.

An economic model which intends to analyse agrarian relations and structures should begin with an investigation of the prevailing forms of property relations in the countryside. But Katouzian's model, on the whole, excludes these relations in favour of climatic conditions. It entails a conception of economy and economic relations as a 'natural process' of interaction between man and nature, whereby men act on nature and transform nature within the constraints of prevailing climatic conditions, such as the scarcity of water and the aridity of the land. This notion of the economy involves no concept of social labour except as an effect of the intervention of political relations of domination and subordination between the state and the producers, in an otherwise natural process of production; hence, a notion of surplus which is neither the difference between necessary and surplus labour nor a simple excess of production over consumption, but a politically enforced deduction from the total product, determined at will by the despotic state which deprives the producers of their natural right to it. Katouzian's naturalist conception of the economy correlates with his populist notion of Iranian politics as a process of 'natural opposition' between two homogeneous entities: the state (the *dowlat*) and the Iranian nation (the *mellat*). This correlation, explained in some detail by Katouzian, forms the basis of his otherwise curious notion of 'politiconomy' (ibid. pp.1–2).

However much Katouzian asserts the originality of his scientific model of Iranian history, there is nothing in his analysis to substantiate the claim. His notion of Persian despotism and his emphasis on self-sufficient villages as the foundation of agrarian production in Aridisolatic Iran both reproduce Marx's comments on the political and agrarian structures of the Orient, and inherit their theoretical errors *en bloc*. Climatic conditions, however, are the point on which he diverges from Marx's writing. Although climatic conditions, in particular aridity, occupy a significant position in some aspects of Marx's conceptualization of the relationship between the state and economy in Asiatic societies, they cannot be taken to replace the production relations which are variously deduced from the state and communal ownership of the land.

But even Katouzian's emphasis on aridity as constitutive of social relations can hardly be called original. The theme is already present in Wittfogel's *Oriental Despotism*, though in a somewhat different form. Wittfogel, like Katouzian, claims to have produced a general and scientific theory of the historical development of the Orient, whereby the historical differences between various Oriental societies can be reduced to their state structures as conditioned by climate. Nor is this the only common ground between Wittfogel and Katouzian. They also share a common sense of purpose: opposition to Marxism. Katouzian, unlike Wittfogel, has never been a Marxist, but like Wittfogel he is only too anxious to tell his readers that he knows Marxism well enough to refute its relevance to the analysis of historical phenomena, in particular in the backward societies of the Orient. Judging by his opening chapter on modes of production and his alternative scientific model of Iranian history, he should offer more convincing proof to demonstrate his claim. Katouzian's cynicism and dismissiveness of Iranian Marxists—especially the Tudeh party with which he often takes issue—is largely justified, and there are many who share his attitude; but when allegedly scientific alternatives to Marxist dogmatism so easily falter in the face of harsh reality, criticism should perhaps be more self-critical.

I now turn to Ashraf's notion of Asiatic 'patrimonial despotism', a notion developed as a means of inquiry into 'Historical Obstacles to the Development of a Bourgeoisie in Iran' (Ashraf 1975). This notion refers to a type of political domination which determines the specificity of the historical development of Iranian society. Ashraf contends that the effective control of agriculture and trade by the despotic state, and the subsequent domination of the economy by 'bureaucratic landlordism' and 'state capitalism', retarded the development of an autonomous bourgeoisie in Iran before the Constitutional revolution. Although the Constitutional period then witnessed a form of quasi-bourgeois development, the process was soon frustrated by the submission of the despotic state to foreign colonial rule, and the Iranian bourgeoisie, he maintains, remained weak and dependent on the state until the early 1960s, when it managed gradually to rid itself of this retarding influence.[22] According to Ashraf, therefore, the post-Constitutional state in Iran was a redeployed form of Asiatic patrimonial despotism (op.cit. p.313, pp.327–332).

Asiatic patrimonial despotism is, in Ashraf's words, 'the principle of historical specificity' of Iran. The notion is intended to 'forestall universalist theory and premature generalizations and leave open the space for a general theory of social change'. But the constituent elements of this general theory of social change bear little or no relevance to the specificity of socio-economic forces and relations in Iranian society. They are, in fact, deduced from Marx's notion of Asiatic despotism and Weber's concept of patrimonial domination. Ashraf's analysis is an attempt to establish a correspondence between these concepts and Iranian history (ibid. pp.307–309).

Marx's Asiatic despotism and Weber's patrimonial domination, though defining by and large similar conditions (i.e., the absence of the institution of private property in land and an autonomous land-owning class), entail different modes of causality. Their uneasy union in Ashraf's model forms a precarious structure sustained only by the fundamental importance of political relations—constitutive of both concepts. But Ashraf's mode of approach, and in particular his conception of the bourgeoisie and of capitalism, is strictly Weberian.

The centrality he gives these concepts renders Marx's Asiatic despotism completely marginal, if not irrelevant, to his analysis.

Ashraf's analysis is based on the Weberian thesis that the development of the bourgeoisie is the essential prerequisite for the development of capitalism. The development of the bourgeoisie, in turn, presupposes particular historical conditions, but above all the existence of a decentralized feudal state which enhances the 'free acquisitive activity' of the mercantile community. This thesis constitutes the basis for Ashraf's analysis of Iranian history. In Iran, he maintains, the existence of a centralized state apparatus and the arbitrary exercise of political power by reigning despots retarded and deformed the 'natural' process of capitalist development.

Clearly, such conceptions of the bourgeoisie and of capitalist development are alien to Marx's writings, in which, by contrast, social classes are effects of particular modes of production. They are sustained and reproduced by definite sets of social relations, which result from the ownership/non-ownership of the means of production. In Marx, the development of capitalism presupposes the separation of the direct producers from the means of production and the generalization of commodity production and exchange. These conditions cannot be deduced from the relationship between the feudal state and the mercantile community. It is true that the state and political power play an important role in the expansion of commodity production in the process of transition to capitalism. But, contrary to Ashraf's assumption, in Marx trade and commercial relations are not conceived as the 'organizing principle' of the capitalist economy.

Further, as indicated above, in Marx's concept of the Asiatic mode of production the relationship between political and economic structures is variously affected by taxation and by hydraulic projects. Taxation is constituted as social relations and the hydraulic projects establish the state as a functional necessity. Both forms, however, exclude trade and commerce as the primary locus of social relations. In Ashraf's concept of Asiatic patrimonial despotism, neither taxation nor hydraulic projects feature as prominent. The former is dealt with in passing and the latter considered as irrelevant to Iranian society; hence his rejection of the applicability of Wittfogel's thesis to Iranian history. There is, therefore, little in Ashraf's Asiatic patrimonial despotism that can be attributed to Marx. His 'principle of historical specificity', as we shall see, is based solely on Weber's Oriental patrimonialism.

According to Ashraf, Weber distinguishes Oriental patrimonialism from Western feudalism on the basis of the difference between two forms of landed property: fief and benefice (ibid. p.312). Ashraf's interpretation of this contrast, however, is incorrect: in Weber, fief and benefice indicate two distinct types of Western feudalism and not the difference between Oriental and Western models. Fief feudalism (*Lehenfeudalismus*) is a system based on the reciprocal contract between the king and the feudal lord. Benefice, on the other hand, is a grant of land revocable at the sovereign's pleasure (*Pfruendenfeudalismus*) (Weber 1974, pp.378–81). But this distinction, too, is only formal. Weber's exposition of modes of domination associated with the two forms of feudalism clearly shows that the two types of landed property are functions of the mode of distribution of political power in their respective societies. In the case of benefice feudalism, the organizational structure of the state is an extension of the ruler's household and the relationship between the ruler and his officials is based on paternal authority and filial dependency. Under fief feudalism, by contrast, this relationship is contractually fixed through reciprocal ties of fealty based on the provision of military service in return for land revenue (Weber op.cit. pp.373–8). In this case, the mode of distribution of political power presupposes a territorial basis (fief) which in turn provides for the articulation of economic and political relations in the form of feudal rent. In benefice feudalism, however, the situation is different. Here, the holding is an adjunct of the system of revenue administration, i.e., tax-farming, and lacks the status of an autonomous social institution. The crux of Weber's argument is that the dispersion of power under fief feudalism provides for the consolidation of the grant-holders into a cohesive social class, an autonomous political force, capable of restraining the powers of the feudal ruler; while the concentration of power associated with benefice suppresses this process and no independent landed aristocracy emerges. The ruler remains in total control of political power, which he exercises to utilize economic processes and practices in the sphere of both agriculture and trade. The ruler controls the main avenues of economic activity, leading to the predominance of 'bureaucratic landlordism' and 'state capitalism', which, in turn, serve to reinforce his domination over society. The term 'patrimonialism' is employed by Weber to designate this mode of political domination (Weber op.cit. pp.346–58).

Thus, in contrast with Ashraf's view, Weber's patrimonialism does not refer to a distinct social form. Rather, it is the form of domination associated with a variant of feudalism as a more or less universal phenomenon. There is, in fact, no conceptual analysis of patrimonialism in Weber. The notion is not even defined in any systematic way. It can be inferred, from various examples provided by Weber, that the term refers to a type of domination characterized by the absence of any form of institutional limitation on the exercise of power by the reigning monarch, who treats the entire territory and its inhabitants virtually as his own property, and rules through a state apparatus which is an extension of his own household, but Weber never gives a precise explanation of patrimonialism as a specific political form. It signifies a type of domination—the authoritarian power of command, to use Weber's own terms—rather than a particular form of state structure.[23]

Further, in Weber's writing the boundaries between feudalism and patrimonialism are not so rigid as Ashraf would like us to believe. Patrimonialism, in so far as it designates a particular social form, is a developed form of patriarchalism and can, if conditions permit, develop into feudalism. When the state functionaries increase in number and are organized into a disciplined and articulated form of bureaucracy and acquire some independence from the ruler, they may manage to limit his power and establish contractual and semi-contractual relations with him. Similarly, feudalism can be transformed into patrimonialism through a process of the concentration of power and the development of the state machinery. Neither of the two processes is irreversible, and they depend strictly on the concentration or dispersion of power within an initially primitive bureaucratic organization. In fact, in the light of Weber's writings, we can argue that most states in the recorded history of the pre-modern era were a mixture of patrimonialism, feudalism and hierarchy, and the developmental process of history appears as reversible changes in the relative weight of these ingredients, reflected in the modality of the institutional form of political power.

Ashraf, nevertheless, conceives patrimonialism as an autonomous social form. He generalizes Weber's rudimentary remarks into the outline of a general theory of history of the Orient. In Ashraf's analysis, Oriental patrimonialism designates a self-contained social totality with its own specific political and economic structure: despotism based on bureaucratic landlordism and state capitalism. Despotism is both the cause and effect of economic relations. In fact, in Ashraf's analysis, there is no economic explanation for the prevalence of bureaucratic landlordism and state capitalism. The economic processes and practices of Oriental patrimonialism are made intelligible only by contrasting them with a concept of capitalism defined by the activity of the subject endowed with rationality. Ashraf borrows this concept of capitalism from Weber, and following him differentiates the traditional and modern capitalist orders on the basis of the traditional and rational action of the subject. Patrimonial regimes are thus characterized by the predominance of a 'traditional attitude to economic activity', arbitrariness in financial activities, and above all the lack of a 'basis for the calculability of obligations' and the 'extent of freedom allowed to private acquisitive activity' (Weber op.cit. p.355).

These characteristics, in so far as they define traditional as opposed to rational economic action, are by no means specific to patrimonial regimes. They are the distinguishing features of all pre-modern (pre-capitalist) societies, Oriental and Occidental. They can tell us as much about the nature of the economic relations under patrimonial regimes as under feudalism or slavery. In this respect, Ashraf's principle of historical specificity can do no more than assert the traditional (pre-capitalist) form of economic relations in pre-Constitutional Iran. The actual character of the economy and of economic relations remains unexplained in Ashraf's analysis.

As mentioned earlier, in Weber the traditional/modern distinction entails a notion of rationality as the attribute of the economic subject. The transition from traditional to rational economic action is an internal process, the result of a change in the attitude of the subject to economic action (precipitated by the advent of protestantism in Western Europe) which institutes a gradual but total overhaul in the structure of norms and values determining subjects' attitudes to economic action; in particular, the maximization of profit becomes the universal norm for rational economic action. Once the bourgeoisie acquires this universal norm, the process of capitalist development begins to unfold, gradually undermining the foundation of the traditional social and political institutions in society.

In economic terms, however, the idea of maximization of profit —the principle of capitalist economic calculation—by definition pre-supposes the category of wage labour, imperative for measuring the rationality of economic action. In this sense Weber's notions of rationality and rational economic action presuppose the commoditization of labour power. Consequently, Weber's sociological categories of economic action founded on this notion of rationality and rational economic action are irrelevant to the conceptualization of economic relations in pre-capitalist societies. The economic structure of these societies is characterized by the absence of wage-labour, and the principle of capitalist economic calculation cannot be applied to the analysis of their economies, whether feudal or patrimonial.

Ashraf's analysis is dominated by the Weberian notion of rationality and rational economic action. Following Weber's functionalist conception of capitalist development, he argues that the traditional bourgeoisie, the assumed agent of capitalist development in Iran, failed to acquire norms of rationality, owing mainly to the retarding effects of patrimonial domination. Although this argument may throw some light on the complexities of the relationship between the state and the mercantile community in pre-Constitutional Iran, it certainly cannot explain the character of economic relations in pre-modern Iran. In Ashraf's analysis they remain simply as 'traditional' economic relations, a general descriptive term devoid of conceptual explanatory power.

The traditional/modern dichotomy on which Ashraf's concept of Asiatic patrimonial despotism rests, then, entails a notion of rationality and rational economic action which renders it irrelevant to the analysis of pre-capitalist economic forms. Just as Weber's sociological categories of economic action cannot explain the nature of economic forms and relations in pre-capitalist societies, Ashraf's model, too, fails to specify the character of these forms and relations in pre-Constitutional Iran. It falls far short of serving as the principle of the historical specificity of Iranian society, let alone a general theory of social change.

3. THE CONCEPT OF THE FEUDAL MODE OF PRODUCTION AND DEFINITIONS OF PRE-CAPITALIST IRAN AS A FEUDAL SOCIETY

Classical Marxism constitutes the social formation as the primary object of investigation. The concept of the social formation, however, is not adequately theorized in classical Marxist discourse. In Marx's writings it is often used to signify a social totality consisting of three distinct levels: an economic structure and two superstructural levels, political/legal and ideological. Marx maintains that the economic structure, the mode of economic production, is dominant in the social formation and determines the form and functioning of the two superstructural levels which rest upon it. Since the analysis of the social formation—that is the determination of social classes and class relations—should therefore necessarily begin with an analysis of the mode of economic production, it follows that the concept of the mode of production is the primary means of analysis in Marxist theory (Marx 1971, pp.205–6).

Marx's discourse entails a general concept of the mode of production, the constituent elements of which are derived from a notion of 'production in general'.[1] The latter, argues Marx, is an 'abstraction' common to 'all periods of production'. Its constituent elements—labourers, non-labourers, means of production and the object of labour—are common properties of all economic forms. Production becomes conceivable only through the combination of these elements, a combination which forms the structure of economic production within the social formation, and the variation in its forms is the basis for distinguishing one economic form from another (*Capital* Vol.II 1967, pp.36–37).

The combination is formed by means of two sets of relationships: the relations of appropriation of nature, and the relations of real appropriation. The former bring together the constituent elements of the structure in definite labour processes, where raw materials are transformed into products. The process of transformation pre-supposes the division of production into a series of specific functions so that the object of labour, the product, can be produced. The combination of elements and the division of production functions within each labour process may assume different forms, depending on the mode and degree to which a labour process is subsumed by the relations of real appropriation, property relations or the relations of production. These relations determine both the distribution of the means of production to the unit of production and the distribution of the products from the unit of production, and thus specify the relationship of the economic agents (i.e. the productive labourer and the unproductive non-labourer) both to the means of production and to the product of labour.

The relations of production, maintains Marx, result from the private ownership of the means of production by the non-labourer (the owning agent) and the correlative non-ownership of these means by the labourer (the non-owning agent) They determine the mode of appropriation of the surplus labour-product of the non-owning agent by the owning agent, and ensure the reproduction of the mode of production. The forms of the labour process and the relations of appropriation of surplus in a mode of production are thus determinate effects of its specific relations of production. For Marx, every mode of production has a specific form of appropriation of surplus which serves as an index for distinguishing it from the other modes (*Capital*, Vol.III 1971, p.791).

The structure of the mode of production is conceived in terms of a direct and necessary correspondence between the relations of production and the labour process, which is a consequence of the position of dominance assigned to the former in the structure of the concept.[2] The relations of production subordinate the labour process to their effects, hence providing for the subsumption of the labourer as the basis for the extraction of surplus labour, which, in turn, ensures the reproduction of the mode of production. The subsump-tion of the labourer within the relations of production is both the effect and the condition of existence of the relations of production; which means that the conditions of existence and the effects of the relations of production are given in the concept of the mode of production. They are essential to the definition of the concept of the mode of production in general.

The Marxist concept of the mode of production is intended as an abstract theoretical category; as the means of analysis of the concrete in its general form. The dominance of the relations of production in its structure entails a mode of causality which is reproduced in the order of the discourse, and which determines the analysis of the concrete real to which the concept is applied. The conceptualization of relations and forces, their combinations and connections, in the course of theoretical analysis is expressed in terms of the general determinations and effects of the relations of production, which are already specified within the concept. It can, therefore, be argued that the concept of the mode of production is not just an abstract theoretical category but is also capable of concrete historical existence.[3]

This mode of causality dominates the discourse of *Capital*, in which Marx constructs a concept of the capitalist mode of production in terms of the dominance of the relations over the forces of production. The conditions of existence of capitalist relations of production (i.e. possession in separation from the means of production), and their effects (i.e. the capitalist labour process), are both given in the concept of the mode. The relations of production subordinate the labour process to their effects, and there is a direct and necessary correspondence between the two, which means that the division of the product into necessary and surplus and the mechanism of appropriation are both effects of the structure of the mode of production.

The notion of property and property relations associated with Marx's concept of the capitalist mode of production rest essentially on the economic subsumption of the labourer within the relations of production. It entails forms of economic class relations which are based on possession in separation from the means of production, which, in turn, presupposes the unity of legal ownership and economic property in the structure of capitalist property relations. This, in effect, specifies the form and conditions of capitalist exploitation. Surplus value as the form of capitalist exploitation provides for and rests on the separation of the labourer from the means of production, and perpetuates it as the essential condition for capitalist production and exploitation. Thus the subsumption of the labourer, the foundation of capitalist property relations as relations of production, is ensured by forms and conditions of exploitation which are neither external nor accidental to the mode of production. They are both given in the concept of the mode, as 'effects' and 'supports' of the structure of capitalist relations of production.

The Concept of the Feudal Mode of Production

Marx conceives slavery and feudalism as autonomous economic forms, but mostly in the context of a theory of history as a process of the succession of modes of production. In theoretical terms Marx seldom considers pre-capitalist modes independently—that is, independently of the capitalist mode of production. As indicated in the previous chapter, concepts of pre-capitalist modes of production play a specific role in Marx's discourse. They are attempts to highlight the specificity of the capitalist mode of production which constitutes the main object of his investigation. The focus of Marx's remarks, it is further argued, is the specific relationship between the direct producer and the means of production—separation as opposed to non-separation—which characterizes the capitalist and pre-capitalist modes of production respectively. However, the concept of the feudal mode of production is discussed more often and in less general terms than the concepts of the other pre-capitalist modes. This is because, in the European context, feudalism precedes capitalism historically, and the process of the dissolution of the feudal mode of production is conceived simultaneously as that of the constitution of the structural elements of the capitalist mode of production: free wage-labour and money capital. This process is the pre-history of capitalism, in Marx's words, and is, as such, immediately relevant to his primary object of investigation.[4]

Marx's *Capital* is not a work of history; nor does it contain a theory of transition from the feudal to the capitalist mode of production. But the conditions under which he discusses the specificity of feudal relations of production presuppose a developmental process which makes it difficult to disentangle the theoretical from the historical discourse; that is, more difficult than is the case with the capitalist mode of production, where the process of the construction of the concept precedes a brief and largely fragmentary discussion of its pre-history. It is, nevertheless, justified to argue that Marx's writing, notably sections of *Capital* and *Grundrisse*, does contain a concept of the feudal mode of production.[5]

The specificity of the Marxist concept of the feudal mode of production can be summarized in the following terms. The concept signifies the articulated combination of the relations and forces of production specific to feudal economy. The characteristic feature of the feudal labour process is the non-separation of the direct producer from the means of production. The direct producer is in possession of the land and has the capacity to work it without the intervention of the non-labourer in the process of production. The reproduction of the unit of production, therefore, takes place entirely on account of the economic activity of the labourer. The non-labourer, on the other hand, is merely the nominal owner of the land, and his right to the economic surplus of the direct producer is sanctioned by political power, which he represents. The structure of feudal property relations, i.e. the separation of ownership from possession, requires the intervention of the non-economic, political instance in the process of production. Thus feudal relations of exploitation assume a non-economic character, and feudal rent is a non-economic category, a politically enforced deduction from the produce of an otherwise independent labourer (*Capital* Vol.III 1971, pp.790–91).

It should, however, be noted that this particular structure of property relations, and the subsequent non-economic mode of extraction of surplus, are by no means specific to the feudal mode of production. Rather, they are common characteristics of all pre-capitalist economic forms. Thus Marx writes:

> It is furthermore evident that in all forms in which the direct labourer remains the 'possessor' of the means of production and labour conditions necessary for the production of his own means of subsistence, the property relationship must simultaneously appear as a direct relation of lordship and servitude, so that the direct producer is not free; a lack of freedom which may be reduced from serfdom with enforced labour to a mere tributary relationship. (*Capital* Vol.III 1971, p.790)

Marx here subsumes all pre-capitalist economic forms under a general and indeterminate category: pre-capitalism, defined by the non-separation of the direct producer from the means of production. He further identifies pre-capitalist relations of production with legally/politically defined relations of subordination and domination between the direct producers and their overlords; hence a typology of the pre-capitalist modes of production based on their specific non-economic mode of appropriation of surplus. What, therefore, distinguishes the feudal mode from the other pre-capitalist modes of production, and feudal rent from the other pre-capitalist forms of appropriation of surplus, is the particular relations of domination-subordination associated with it; that is, the legally/politically defined relations of lordship and servitude.

This factor aside, there is, in fact, nothing specifically feudal about the classical Marxist concept of the feudal relations of production. Feudal landed property, like all pre-capitalist forms of landed property, is constituted by political relations. It is an expression of the status of the non-labourer in the hierarchy of political order in feudal society. The mode of distribution of political power (the downward flow of political authority from the suzerain monarch, the ultimate owner of the land, to his vassals, the lesser tenants, and the reciprocal relations between the two) presupposes a territorial basis whereby the right to land revenue is legally sanctioned in return for the provision of military service. But feudal property relations, as such, remain external to the process of production and fail to ensure the subsumption of the direct producer, whose possession of the land, *a priori* asserted in Marx's discourse, leaves no basis for economic subsumption. The landlords' right to revenue is reinforced directly by means of political coercion. Peasant bondage, albeit in varying degrees, is thus requisite for the extraction of rent, the economic condition of existence of the land-owning class. The mode of distribution of political power in a feudal polity is both constitutive of the feudal landed property and determinant of the form of exploitation. It defines the landlord's right to revenue and ensures its realization in the form of rent. Marx's definition thus equates feudal landed property with seigneurial power and property relations with intersubjective relations of domination and subordination. The term 'feudal' as such remains devoid of any economic content: it belongs to the sphere of political and constitutional history.[6]

Yet Marx argues that the non-economic relations of extraction of surplus in pre-capitalist modes are not external to the process of production, but emerge from the very process of economic production; and that the relations of lordship and servitude only signify the 'appearance' of pre-capitalist property relations, which are of quite a different (economic) 'essence'. This argument, much reiterated in different forms by contemporary Marxists, entails two inter-related assumptions. First, it is assumed that political relations provide for the intersection of legal and economic relations; that is, for the transformation of legal ownership into economic property by separating the direct producer from the land, his natural possession, and ensuring his subsumption within the relations of production. Secondly, that the dominant status of political relations in the structure of the pre-capitalist modes is not arbitrary but determined, in the last instance, by the economic (*Capital* Vol.I 1970, p.82).

However, as seen in the case of the feudal mode of production, Marx's conceptualization of the relationship between political and economic amounts to more than a simple relationship of appearance to essence, since economic and legal relations are the effects of the mode of distribution of political power, and are constituted by it. Feudal property relations and the mechanism of appropriation of surplus are both specified and determined by political relations: seigneurial power and the relations of domination and subordination between the landlords and the direct producers. These relations, as was seen, have no foundation in the process of production. Consequently, the feudal labour process is conceived as an autonomous economic base capable of self-reproduction without reference to external relations. In fact, in Marx's discourse, the landlord is merely the nominal owner of the land. He has no economic status and plays no role in the process of production. The legal and economic conditions of his existence (i.e. the feudal landed property and rent) are functions of his status in the hierarchy of political power. Marx at times comes close to considering the landlord as a parasite, completely superfluous, whose presence or absence would make no difference to the functioning of the process of production.

Despite some remarks to the contrary this conception of feudal landed property and the feudal lord, by and large, dominates Marx's discourse on the feudal mode of production. These isolated but often-quoted remarks, significant as they are, are inconsistent with the order of his discourse on the pre-capitalist modes of production; for example, a definition of the feudal landlord as 'the manager and master of the process of production and of the entire process of social life' (*Capital* Vol.III 1971, pp. 860–1) is incompatible with the concept of rent as a non-economic category. References of this kind, not infrequent in classical Marxism, are more in line with the discourse of *Capital* than the body of Marxist discourse, classical and contemporary, on the pre-capitalist modes of production. This point is often overlooked by the overwhelming majority of contemporary Marxist theorists, who seldom recognize the immense difference in the theoretical foundation of the two orders of discourse. Thus, for example, when Anderson suggests that Marx's remarks on the productive role of the feudal landlord should be made 'retrospective to the whole epoch before the advent of capitalism', he does not realize that their underlying logic would subvert the fundamental theoretical premises of the Marxist discourse on pre-capitalism (Anderson op.cit. 1974a, p.184).

Further, as was pointed out in the previous chapter, the dominance of political relations in the structure of the concepts of pre-capitalist modes of production cannot be explained by a simple reference to 'determination in the last instance by the economy', since it is the very absence of economic relations in the structure of these modes which makes the intervention of the political instance necessary for their reproduction. In Marx's discourse, this absence appears as a disconnection between property relations and the labour process whereby the subsumption of the direct producer is inconceivable without the incorporation of direct political coercion into the structure of the concept. But here, unlike the capitalist mode, the mode of causality generated by the dominance of political relations fails to establish the necessary connection between the relations of production and the labour process. It renders both property relations and the forms of rent ineffective with respect to the process of subsumption, the former becoming identified with the relations of lordship and servitude, and the latter an accidental appendage of the process of production lacking any basis within it.

In fact, Marx's conception of feudal landed property presupposes a direct and 'natural' link between economic property and the labour of transformation. It persistently asserts the non-separation of the direct producer from the land, hence the necessity of extra-economic coercion as both the form and condition of exploitation, which excludes the possibility of an economic instance, a process of production, other than that constituted by political relations. The notion of the non-separation of the direct producers from the means of production and the associated anthropological conception of economic property and ownership, as will be shown in the following chapter, are essential if the centrality of the labour theory of value in the analysis of the structure and functioning of the capitalist mode of production in *Capital* is to be maintained.

The political definition of the feudal relations of production has been central to Marxist historiography of feudalism and the transition to capitalism in Europe.[7] Marxist historians have seldom paid attention to the theoretical inconsistencies of the classical concept, and hence have reproduced the 'formal' definition of rent in their studies of particular feudal social formations. The works of Kosminsky and Anderson are two important, though quite different, examples.

Kosminsky begins his analysis of agrarian relations in medieval England with an intelligent restatement of the classical concept of feudal rent (Kosminsky 1956, p.vi). The merit of Kosminsky's analysis is his treatment of rent as a non-unitary category. The different forms of rent, he maintains, presuppose different conditions of existence and realization; namely, different forms of economic exchange which constitute the process of production as a process of exploitation. He nevertheless subordinates these forms to the non-economic relations of coercion as the principal mechanism of subsumption and exploitation of the direct producers in the process of production. In Kosminsky's analysis, just as in the classical concept, rent form, the expression of the relationship between necessary and surplus labour, appears as accidental to the process of production structured by the political relations of domination and subordination (Kosminsky, op.cit. pp.152–197).

Anderson's work, on the other hand, is perhaps the most important contribution to the vast domain of the historiography of Western feudalism and absolutism in recent years, and as such deserves a detailed examination. Anderson's study, as pointed out in the previous chapter, is 'Eurocentric' in character, and strives to establish the 'uniqueness of the West' in the context of a comparative historiography of Western and Eastern developments in the pre-modern era.[8] This element of Eurocentrism determines the conceptual structure of his analysis, and is largely responsible for his failure to achieve his stated objectives; above all, to construct a concept of the feudal mode of production which would surpass the theoretical limitations of the classical concept.[9]

The conceptual structure of Anderson's analysis rests on Weberian premises and addresses the question of why an indigenous capitalist economic form was a uniquely Western phenomenon. Anderson, following Weber, finds the answer in the complex structure and internal dynamics of the feudal mode of production in Europe; namely, an element of landlord autonomy *vis-à-vis* the feudal state constituted by the parcellization of sovereignty, the hallmark of Western feudalism as a whole. The non-European social formations, with the notable exception of Japan, did not experience a feudal epoch, hence no indigenous capitalist development took place outside the European continent.

The orthodox Marxist historiography of feudalism, contends Anderson, fails to appreciate fully the uniqueness of Western development, a failure which he argues is due to a 'narrow' definition of the concept of the feudal mode of production. The orthodox definition, which has dominated Marxist historiography, simply identifies feudalism with 'all traditional forms of landlordism'. Consequently, 'feudalism, in this version of materialist historiography, becomes an absolving ocean in which virtually any society may receive its baptism' (Anderson 1974b, p.402). The identification of feudalism with landlordism 'based on politico-legal relations of compulsion' leads to an unwarranted generalization and universalization of the concept, and 'all privilege to Western development is thereby held to disappear, in the multiform process of a world history secretly single from the start' (ibid.). The universalization of feudalism and its equation with landlordism, Anderson argues, reduces the uniqueness of Western history, in particular the emergence and the development of the capitalist mode of production in Europe, to the mere functioning of the superstructural levels. He thus attempts to construct a concept of the feudal mode of production which will fully render the characteristic 'complex unity of Western feudalism' and the dynamics of its development (Anderson 1974a, p.147).

Anderson therefore raises the question not of the theoretical consistency of the classical concept, but of its 'limitations'; that is, its real or alleged failure to correspond fully to the 'complex unity' of Western feudalism and grasp its 'internal dynamics'. This in turn is in line with the empiricist character of his approach as a whole. Anderson's identification of the theoretical limitations of the classical concept and his attempt to overcome them are both grounded in a particular reading of European history.[10] In fact, the structural elements of his concept are extracted from the histories of the two preceding modes of production, namely primitive and ancient, which, according to him, formed the economic structures of Roman and Germanic social orders. The feudal mode of production, argues Anderson, was a 'synthesis' produced by the 'final collision' of these two dissolving modes (Anderson 1974a, pp.144–153). This definition proceeds from his construction of the 'synthesis' (ibid. pp.128–142), which is systematically derived from the preceding historical analysis of classical antiquity and the transition to feudalism (ibid. pp.18–128). Neither the synthesis nor the concept is theoretically conceivable without the preceding historical interpretation. In this sense, his concept of the feudal mode of production, far from signifying the real-concrete, Western feudalism, is in fact identical with it. Anderson's empiricism leads him to equate the concept of mode of production with that of social formation in his historical discourse.

His critique of the orthodox Marxist concept of feudalism is outlined in *Passages from Antiquity to Feudalism* (1974a), in a chapter entitled 'The Feudal Mode of Production' (1974a, pp.147–153), where he maintains that it renders the complex unity of the feudal mode only partially, thus making it difficult to construct any account of its development (ibid. p.147). The classical concept as he characterizes it in *Lineages of the Absolutist State* (1974b) identifies feudalism with a 'combination of large-scale agrarian property controlled by an exploiting class, with small-scale production by a tied peasantry, in which surplus-labour was pressed out of the latter by *corvées* or dues in kind'. Such a combination, argues Anderson, 'was in its generality a very widespread pattern throughout the pre-industrial world. Virtually any post-tribal social formation that did not rest on slavery or nomadism revealed in this sense forms of landlordism. The singularity of feudalism was never exhausted merely by the existence of seigneurial and serf classes as such' (1974b, p.408).

The main plank in Anderson's critique of the classical concept is 'economism', which, according to him, undermines the specificity of the feudal mode of production by reducing its particular extra-economic sanctions to feudal economic relations (ibid. p.403). Consequently feudalism is identified with seigneurial and serf classes who respectively own and possess agrarian property as the foundation of small-scale production, the general characteristic of all forms of landlordism in the pre-capitalist era. In other words, although Anderson is in agreement with the orthodox definition in distinguishing pre-capitalist modes of production by their specific form of extra-economic sanction, he maintains that these forms cannot be 'read off from economic relations':

> The 'superstructures' of kinship, religion, law or the state necessarily enter into the constitutive structure of the mode of

production in pre-capitalist social formations. They intervene directly in the 'internal' nexus of surplus-extraction ... In consequence, pre-capitalist modes of production cannot be defined except via their political, legal and ideological super-structures, since these are what determine the type of extra-economic coercion that specifies them. The precise forms of juridical dependence, property and sovereignty that characterize a pre-capitalist social formation, far from being merely access-ory or contingent epiphenomena, compose on the contrary the central indices of the determinate mode of production dominant within it. A scrupulous and exact taxonomy of these legal and political configurations is thus a pre-condition of establishing any comprehensive typology of pre-capitalist modes of produc-tion. (1974b, pp.403–4)

Anderson's critique, however, does not signify a break with the orthodox concept. Rather, he retains its theoretical premises and attempts to redefine it in terms of the primacy of the superstructural forms. The result is a wholesale over-politicization of the concept, whereby its discursive coherency is subordinated to the exigencies of the central thesis of his analysis: the uniqueness of Western development.

According to Anderson, although 'serfdom provided ... the primary ground-work of the total system of surplus extraction', the specifically feudal character of the extra-economic coercion asso-ciated with it was determined by the 'specific organization' of the seigneurial and serf classes in a 'vertically articulated system of parcellized sovereignty and scalar property that distinguished the feudal mode of production in Europe'. 'It was', argues Anderson, 'this concrete nexus which spelt out the precise type of extra-economic coercion exercised over the direct producer' (1974b, p.408). These elements refer respectively to suzerain monarchy and the particular structure of the 'fief' combining 'vassalage, benefice and immunity'. Their articulation in the structure of the feudal mode of production, and the subsequent chain of contractual 'reciprocity' and dependent 'subordination', Anderson further argues, 'set a true feudal aristo-cracy off from any other form of exploitative warrior class, in alternative modes of production' (ibid. p.409).

The case in point, and the focus of Anderson's definition, is his conceptualization of the relationship between the political and economic instances in the structure of the mode of production. Central to Anderson's analysis here is his conception of feudal landed property. He argues that the specific mode of exploitation which defined the feudal mode of production was but an outward expression of the particular structure of feudal landed property, which provided for the fusion of the economic and political relations in the vertical structure of the feudal hierarchy. This argument, however, is an attempt to restore the determinant status of the economy in the last instance in the context of an otherwise avowedly political definition of the feudal mode of production: an apparent paradox which in Anderson's analysis is sustained by displacing the conditions of existence of the feudal ground rent.

According to Anderson, feudal landed property, typified by the fief, was the foundation of feudal relations of production. The feudal fief was 'an economic grant of land' and as such entailed '*personal* rights of exploitation and jurisdiction over the dependent peasants, consecrated in law' (1974b, pp.408–9). But the personal rights of exploitation —i.e. 'benefice' and 'immunity'—were conditional and dependent on 'vassalage', hence the scalar structure of feudal landed property. Vassalage, on the other hand, entailed a form of 'contractual "reciprocity" and "dependent subordination"' (ibid. p.409) which required the parcellization of sovereignty. The fief, Anderson thus argues, was in this sense 'an amalgam of property and sovereignty, in which the partial nature of the one was matched by the private character of the other: conditional tenure was structurally linked to individual jurisdiction' (ibid. p.408).

So far so good. However, what is left unexplained in this argument is the respective status of political and economic relations in the structure of feudal landed property. Anderson's exposition of the ownership rights associated with the fief in fact makes it clear that the political relations not only hold the dominant position, but are also constitutive of the 'economic land grant':

At the same time, the property rights of the lord over his land were typically of degree only: he was invested in them by a superior noble (or nobles) to whom he owed knight service— provision of a military effective in time of war. His estates were, in other words, held as a fief. The liege lord in his turn would often be the vassal of a feudal superior, and the chain of such dependent tenures linked to military service would extend upwards to the highest peak of the system—in most cases, a monarch—of whom all land could in the ultimate instance be in principle the eminent domain. (1974a, pp.147–8)

Here, just as in the classical concept, property rights are functions of the status of the holder in the hierarchy of political order; which in effect means that Anderson's economic land grant is actually constituted by seigneurial power, and the associated form of peasant bondage is the sole source of subsumption and exploitation. In other words, the discursive coherency of Anderson's definition depends on the incorporation of the legally/politically defined relations of lordship and servitude in the structure of the concept. This would lead Anderson back to the same narrow definition which allegedly failed to render fully the singularity of Western feudalism. But Anderson further qualifies his argument, though at the expense of the formal consistency of the classical concept:

The consequence of such a system [feudal land ownership] was that political sovereignty was never focused in a single centre. The functions of the state were disintegrated in a vertical allocation downwards, at each level of which political and economic relations were, on the other hand, integrated. This parcellization of sovereignty was constitutive of the whole feudal mode of production. (ibid. p.148)

Anderson thus conceives this 'parcellized sovereignty' as 'constitutive' of the feudal mode, the determinant of its 'transcendent success' and 'the only principle capable of explaining [its] differential development' (1974b, p.403). His comparative historical discourse, geared to establishing the uniqueness of Western development, is dominated by this conception.

Anderson's emphasis on the superstructural forms as constitutive of the feudal mode signifies a departure from classical Marxism. In classical Marxism the structural status of political relations is derived from the non-separation of the direct producer, and feudal property relations are effective through extra-economic coercion, which presupposes the political representation of the land-owning class by the feudal state. Feudal rent, the economic condition of existence of the land-owning class, depends on this form of political representation. In Anderson's definition, by contrast, the element of political representation is displaced in favour of the autonomy of the landlord *vis-à-vis* the feudal state, which both defines feudal rent and distinguishes it from other pre-capitalist forms of exploitation. Seigneurial power is constitutive of feudal landed property, and feudal rent rests exclusively on the entailed form of dependent subordination. This conception of feudal landed property not only invokes but in fact sanctions, in the most explicit manner, the thesis already present in the classical concept of feudal rent, that is, that the structural differences between the feudal mode of production and other forms of landlordism can be reduced to a single factor: the institutional form of state power.

Anderson admittedly does not read off the extra-economic relations of exploitation from the feudal economic relations. But nor does orthodox Marxism. In fact the charge of 'economism' which he levels at the classical concept is, at best, a grave misconception associated with his empiricist approach. The classical concept, as I have shown, assigns a structural status to political relations by conflating feudal relations of production with their non-economic conditions of existence, and feudal property relations with the political representation of the land-owning class by the feudal state. This, it was further shown, provides a solution, however formal, to the discursive incoherency of the classical concept, which can be sustained in so far as the determination in the last instance by the economy is not questioned. In Anderson's definition, on the other hand, feudal economic relations are mere effects of the feudal political structure, which is determinant of the mode of production as a whole. The primacy of parcellized sovereignty in Anderson's discourse involves a displacement in the conditions of existence of the feudal property relations, whereby the political representation of the land-owning class by the feudal state is replaced by the autonomy of the landlord in relation to the feudal state. This, in effect, excludes any form of class representation at the political level, thus leaving no basis for the intervention of the economy in the last instance. There remains, in Anderson's definition, a chronic disconnection between political and economic relations which, unlike the classical concept, cannot be rectified by the mode of causality, generated in the order of his discourse by the primacy of political relations.

Anderson's definition of the concept of the feudal mode of production is theoretically inconsistent. The condition of existence of feudal property relations, the element of landlord autonomy entailed in parcellized sovereignty, is not given in that concept. The non-separation of the direct producer from the means of production posits political relations as the condition of existence of feudal landed property, but by no means specifies their institutional form. The latter cannot be deduced from the specificity of feudal forces and relations. In fact, its relevance to the concept is historical rather than theoretical. In Anderson's discourse, too, the primacy of parcellized sovereignty is derived not from the specificity of feudal forces and relations, but rather from a specific reading of the history of pre-feudal Europe which precedes the definition of the concept. He is nevertheless at pains to establish that there is, in his definition, a structural relation between feudal landed property and parcellized sovereignty, reflected by the conditional character of the former and partial form of the latter. But these characteristics, significant as they may be, are all entailed in seigneurial power, which is already conceived as the essential condition of existence of feudal landed property. The scalar structure of feudal landed property thus falls flat on a single level, and is unable to fulfil the function assigned to it in Anderson's discourse, namely to provide for the fusion of the political and economic relations in the vertical structure of the feudal order. On the contrary, in fact, it is feudal political relations which provide for the fusion of legal and economic relations. For a conception of landed property resting on seigneurial power alone can produce economic effects only on the assumption that state power is an essential condition of production.

Anderson's definition signifies a departure from the whole tradition of historical materialism and ranks him conveniently alongside the institutional historians of feudalism. The theoretical limitation of his definition is encountered in his attempt to conceptualize the absolutist state, when the element of feudal autonomy gradually gives way to a centralized political structure controlled by the land-owning class which employs state power to consolidate its economic position in relation to the emerging bourgeoisie. Anderson defines the absolutist state as a 'redeployed feudal state'; a centralized political structure representing the land-owning aristocracy, but all in the wake of the disappearing autonomy of a previously distinct feudal nobility. The feudal character of the absolutist state, here, does not rest on the parcellized sovereignty, but on its capacity to represent the land-owning class and ensure the continuity of the feudal mode of exploitation. Anderson's definition of the absolutist state signifies a retreat to the 'narrow' concept of orthodox Marxism, the object of his sustained criticism.

Anderson's conception of feudal landed property will be considered in more detail in the following chapter, in the context of his theoretical reflections on the nature of *iqta* and the associated forms of property relations. It will be shown that, in Anderson's analysis, the sole factor distinguishing *iqta* from feudal landed property in the West is the element of seigneurial power and the autonomy of the landlords *vis-à-vis* the feudal state. This element also features prominently in Marxist definitions of Iran as a feudal society, which for the most part subscribe to the classical concept, but which fail to ascertain its correspondence to Iranian conditions. The major problem for such definitions is the existence of strong centralized states in successive periods of Iranian history. In order to overcome this difficulty, Marxist historians tend to locate their analysis in the context of successive periods of centralization and decentralization of the state structure in pre-Constitutional Iran, whereby the formation and development of the feudal structure is theorized in terms of a conflict between the *iqta*-holders and the central state. The decline in the power and control of the central government and the correlative increase in the autonomy of the *iqta*-holders is thus conceived as the essential condition of the existence of feudal landed property. In this case, too, the predominance of the rent form in the agrarian economy of Iran is established with reference to the growing autonomy of the *iqta*-holders in relation to the central state. It is to the analysis of these definitions that I shall now turn.

The Marxist concept of Iranian Feudalism

The Marxist concept of Iranian feudalism is a product of the Soviet historiography of Iran. Soviet historians have been unanimous in their adherence to a political definition of the concept, but their definitions of the conditions of existence of the feudal relations of production in Iran vary according to their view of the conditions of existence of rent in feudal Europe.[11] The work of Petrushevsky, *Agriculture and Agrarian Relations in the Mongol Era* (Tehran 1966), is the most serious attempt on the part of the Soviet historians to conceptualize feudal social relations in Iranian history. Among Iranian Marxists, on the other hand, Nomani's *The Development of Feudalism in Iran* stands out for its detailed empirical and theoretical analysis of feudal economic and political relations and structures in Iran.

These authors pursue a similar aim and employ a similar mode of analysis. Both locate Iranian history in the context of a universal and evolutionary schema, and argue that feudalism in Iran, just as in Western Europe, emerged from within an economy based on slave-labour and gradually evolved into one based on free wage-labour. Although Iranian feudalism assumed a particular form in the course of its development, its structural elements and internal dynamics for them are identical with those of the 'classical case' in Western Europe, signified by the Marxist concept of the feudal mode of production. Petrushevsky and Nomani thus take the concept of Iranian feudalism to be a variant of the general concept of the feudal mode of production, and attempt to theorize it with reference to the specifity of the relations and forces of production in Iranian agriculture. It is therefore necessary at this stage to consider briefly the notion of the variant of the mode of production in general, and the feudal mode of production in particular, as a means to assess the theoretical status and validity of the Marxist conceptualization of pre-Constitutional Iran as a feudal social formation.

The concept of the mode of production entails variations, as theoretical possibilities, resulting from the modality of the articulation of the relations and forces of production in its structure. A variant of a mode of production is constituted by the forms and outcomes of class struggle, economic and political, between labourers and non-labourers in the process of production and in the social formation at large. The struggle between the two classes assumes different forms with different effects on the organization and process of production in different social formations. Hence the variations in the complex unity of the structure of a mode of production in different social formations.

Class struggle between labourers and non-labourers has as its primary object the relations of exploitation, through which it affects both the organization and process of production. The conceptualization of the variant of a mode of production in a given social formation should, therefore, begin with the analysis of variations in three different levels of its structure:

(i) variations in the level of the subsumption of the labourer;

(ii) variations in the differential relationship of the labourers and non-labourers to the forces of production;
(iii) variations in the form and organization of the forces of production.[12]

The conceptualization of the variants of the feudal mode of production, however, entails a number of insoluble theoretical problems. In the case of the feudal mode, as seen above, the conditions of existence of classes are not given in the concept of the mode; they are secured by incorporating political relations into the structure of the concept. Political relations in turn form a basis for the analysis of the forms of class struggle and their differential effects on the structure of the mode of production, that is, for the conceptualization of the variation in the complex unity of its structure. In this sense, the variant of the feudal mode is conceived in terms of the variation in the mode of distribution of political power in feudal social formations.

The conceptualization of the variant of the feudal mode in non-European social formations, moreover, leads to further difficulties of which the most important arises from the absence of decentralized states, the assumed constitutive of feudal relations of production in feudal Europe. This is the theoretical problem addressed by Nomani and Petrushevsky, who both begin with a discussion of the conditions of existence of feudal ground rent in Iran, that is, the forms of feudal landed property and the relations of lordship and servitude; they then attempt to specify the particular effects of these conditions on the organization and process of production in terms of economic and political struggle between the landlords and the direct producers. I shall examine their conceptualizations of Iranian feudalism in some detail, in an attempt to show that: first, their analysis of the conditions of existence of rent in Iranian agriculture is not consistent with the classical concept of feudal rent; and second, that the difficulties involved in the conceptualization of pre-Constitutional Iran as a feudal social formation arise mainly from the inconsistencies inherent in the Marxist theory of feudal ground rent in general.

Petrushevsky, then, traces the origin of Iranian feudalism to the early Sassanian period in the third century A.D. Iranian feudalism, he maintains, underwent substantial changes under Arab rule and the succeeding dynasties. The result was a wide variation in the pattern of feudal ownership in Iran which, in effect, led to a variation in the mode of extraction of surplus from the direct producers. This argument is the starting point in Petrushevsky's conceptualization of the conditions of existence of rent in pre-Constitutional Iran.

Petrushevsky proceeds with a classification of land-ownership and argues that agricultural land in Iran was divided into two general categories: state lands and private holdings, each containing a few sub-categories (op.cit. Vol.II, pp.1–83). State lands, he asserts, resulted mainly from conquest and confiscation, or, as in climatically arid areas, from the state's capacity to organize and manage public irrigation works. The state was the sole owner of these lands, where the extraction of economic surplus assumed the form of tax-rent; an effect of the articulation of land-ownership with political sovereignty. Thus he writes:[13]

> [under feudalism] it was not necessary for an individual directly to own land and water. Rather, in certain periods, especially in the early stages of feudalism, the state, which was controlled by the feudal lords, could be the owner of the land and water. In this case, state lands were the common property of the ruling class and under their jurisdiction, and tax-rent was extracted from the peasants by the state. This phenomenon has been observed in several Eastern societies. The specificity of the state's ownership of agricultural land is that the state, through its fiscal officers, directly exploits the land possessors, i.e. the rural communities. Thus taxes and rents coincide. Tax-rent, extracted in money or in kind, was distributed among the ruling class in the form of salaries, subsidies and gifts. (op.cit. Vol.II p.7)

On private lands, on the other hand, different conditions prevailed. They were held by individuals (private holdings) or by institutions such as religious shrines, seminaries and mosques (*waqf* lands). In both cases, however, ground rent and not tax-rent constituted the dominant mode of exploitation (ibid. pp.26–45). Petrushevsky further maintains that the ratio of state to private lands, hence of tax-rent to rent, in the structure of feudal production in Iran varied in accordance with the variation in the organizational form of state power. Tax-rent was the dominant mode of extraction of surplus in feudal Iran prior to the tenth century A.D., when another and a completely reverse trend emerged in Iranian history.

The period covering the tenth and eleventh centuries, he contends, witnessed a powerful tendency towards political decentralization which reached its climax under Saljuq rule. The decentralization of political power, pursued by political notables and military magnates, was fuelled by a tendency towards parcellization and privatization of the land among the ruling class, and resulted in the emergence of various types of *iqta* (land assignments, resembling fief and benefice), along with the expansion of *waqf* lands and private holdings, all at the expense of the state-owned/controlled lands. Petrushevsky argues that from the twelfth century onward Iranian society became the field of conflict between these two opposing trends, and the Mongol invasion and subsequent domination in the thirteenth century shifted the balance in favour of decentralizing forces. Under Mongol rule, Iranian feudalism underwent substantial structural transformations, and feudal rent proper became a permanent feature of Iranian feudalism. Although tax-rent continued to exist, it played a secondary and steadily diminishing role as a mode of exploitation. It prevailed only in the state-owned/controlled lands, whose size and significance in the overall structure of feudal ownership had substantially decreased compared to the pre-Mongol period.

Iranian feudalism, Petrushevsky argues further, underwent another important transformation under Mongol rule. This was the institutionalization of the hitherto politically-defined relations of lordship and servitude in the Iranian countryside. Iranian peasants were now effectively tied to the land, and legal restrictions were imposed on their free movement. This transformation, too, had a lasting effect on agrarian relations in Iran. Although legally-defined relations of lordship and servitude did not become a permanent feature of Iranian feudalism, peasant dependency on the land continued more or less uninterrupted in the course of the following centuries.

Petrushevsky's concept of Iranian feudalism contains a number of important theoretical and conceptual defects. Firstly he fails to make a conceptual distinction between tax-rent and feudal rent, treating the former as the centralized variant of the latter (ibid. p.10). Consequently, his notion of Iranian feudalism incorporates two distinct sets of production relations: tax-rent and rent, as production relations of concepts of Eastern feudalism and feudalism proper, defining Iranian history respectively before and after the Mongol invasions in the thirteenth century. But clearly a concept of Iranian feudalism structured by tax-rent as the dominant mode of appropriation of surplus is inconceivable within the Marxist theory of the modes of production. The concept of tax-rent as the relations of appropriation of surplus presupposes the articulation of land-ownership with political sovereignty in the structure of a centralized state. Thus, a notion of feudalism based on these relations involves no more than a single and unitary political institution superimposed upon a community of otherwise free and self-sustaining direct producers by means of sheer violence. In fact, Petrushevsky's notion of Eastern feudalism involves all the characteristic features of the concept of the Asiatic mode of production; but he refuses to use this concept to define Iranian society before the thirteenth century. This refusal, however, is more a result of ideological considerations than a genuine concern for historical interpretation, and his rather thinly disguised notion of Eastern feudalism has the effect of reinforcing Asiatic definitions of Iranian society considered in the previous chapter.[14]

Secondly, Petrushevsky's analysis of the transition from the dominance of tax-rent to that of feudal rent, and the eventual constitution of the feudal mode of production proper in Iran under Mongol rule, is equally erroneous. The transformation in the mode of appropriation of surplus, argues Petrushevsky, involved a change in the form of feudal property relations: a change from state ownership to feudal ownership proper. He then proceeds to analyse this process in terms of a transformation in the institutional form of state power, induced by an on-going conflict between centralizing and decentralizing forces and tendencies within the state structure. But Petrushevsky's conception of Eastern feudalism in fact undermines his analysis. The predominance of tax-rent in the structure of the concept means that the decentralizing forces are subsumed within the state structure and have no independent economic existence. They have no autonomous class identity, economic or political, and their struggle against the centralized state, i.e., the process of the constitution of feudal landed property proper, cannot be explained by structural categories, but only by their subjective action to dominate the state apparatuses. Petrushevsky's analysis, in effect, constitutes the landlords' autonomy *vis-à-vis* the centralized state as the essential condition of existence of feudal landed property in Iran.

We have already encountered this crucial displacement of the conditions of existence of feudal landed property in Anderson's over-politicized concept of the feudal mode of production. Although Anderson and Petrushevsky subscribe to two entirely different definitions of the concept of the feudal mode of production, their analyses of the conditions of existence of feudal landed property are remarkably similar. Petrushevsky (op.cit. Vol.II, pp.1–5) subscribes to the classical definition criticized by Anderson, but his analysis of the conditions of existence of feudal landed property in Iran (ibid. Vol.II, pp.7–9, pp.83–93) signifies a radical departure from the theoretical premises of his declared position.

Petrushevsky argues that the Mongol period constitutes a turning point in the history of Iranian feudalism. The economic transformation that followed the Mongol invasion, and the social policies and reforms that it precipitated, led to the long overdue triumph of the decentralizing forces within Iranian feudalism. Private ownership gained dominance over state ownership, and the institutionalization of peasant bondage laid the foundation for the appropriation of surplus in the form of feudal rent proper; hence his concept of Iranian feudalism. The most likely underlying reason for this process, according to Petrushevsky, was the growing pressure for decentralization exerted on the centralized state apparatus by the *iqta*-holders, who sought economic independence and territorial autonomy; and he repeatedly invokes this argument in order to establish the classical conditions of the existence of feudal landed property (i.e. seigneurial relations) in Iran during the thirteenth and fourteenth centuries. But as indicated earlier in this section, Petrushevsky's argument falls short of this intended purpose. The predominance of the notion of the state-class associated with his concept of Eastern feudalism effectively excludes the forms of political class relations entailed in seigneurial power. Political class relations, we have seen, are essential to secure the intrinsic disconnection between feudal property relations and the forms of the labour process and to rectify the discursive incoherency of the classical concept. The absence of political class relations and their subsequent replacement by state-subject relations in Petrushevsky's analysis means that his concept of Iranian feudalism is not only discursively incoherent but also theoretically inconsistent.

This theoretical inconsistency can best be illustrated with reference to his attempt to conceptualize the conditions of the institutionalization of relations of domination and subordination between landlords and the direct producers under Mongol rule. Soviet historians, argues Petrushevsky, have failed to come to terms with the question of serfdom in Iran, treating the issue in a general and superficial manner. He summarizes the Soviet view as follows:

The question of serfdom [in Iran] has been interpreted by the

Soviet historians in two distinct ways. Some have conceived serfdom as all forms of peasant dependency on the landlord, even identifying the formation of feudal relations with serfdom. Others, by contrast, have viewed serfdom only as one among many forms of peasant dependency, that is, the most extreme and complete form of feudal dependency. (op.cit. Vol.II, p.154)

Petrushevsky rejects the popular but erroneous view that identifies serfdom with feudal relations of production. Serfdom, he maintains, is the legal/political condition of existence of feudal relations of production and as such may assume different forms in different feudal social formations (ibid. p.155). He is also aware that the conceptual difficulties in the relations of lordship and servitude lie not so much in the absence of any legal definition of serfdom as in what these relations actually involved in practice; namely, the forms of bondage in which the direct producers were tied to the land and the juridical restrictions on their mobility.

Prior to the thirteenth century, in Petrushevsky's reading of the historical evidence, Iranian peasants enjoyed freedom of movement, and there was no legal restriction on their mobility; and he maintains that this historic absence of serfdom in Iran was a direct result of prevailing economic and political conditions, which he then proceeds to explain in some detail (ibid. pp.163–166).

According to Petrushevsky, in Iran, unlike Western Europe and Russia, demesne production did not assume a dominant position in feudal agriculture. It always remained subordinate to other forms of production and played a very marginal role in the economic structure of Iranian feudalism. There was, therefore, no pressing need for forced labour on a massive scale, and the exploitation of the direct producers was secured without legal forms of bondage (ibid. pp.93–96). This absence of demesne production, Petrushevsky contends, was the specific and common feature of feudalism in the East: namely, Iran, central Asia, the Arab Middle East and Afghanistan (with the notable exception of Armenia, where it prevailed). His further contention, however, that there is no known explanation for the absence of demesne production in the East (ibid. p.90), cannot be sustained if we bear in mind his conception of Eastern feudalism; for the alleged prevalence of tax-rent and the associated subsumption of the land-owning class within the state apparatus, by definition, exclude demesne production and legal forms of peasant bondage.

Petrushevsky is not discouraged by such paradoxical statements. The absence of legal forms of bondage before the thirteenth century, he argues, should not be taken to mean that Iranian peasants were free of any form of feudal dependency. On the contrary, the prevailing economic and demographic conditions in the countryside (specifically the dominant form of land tenure, a surplus peasant population, and state taxation) sufficed to tie Iranian peasants to the land. The prevalence of share-cropping in the context of a surplus peasant population, he maintains, further reinforced the already insecure conditions of tenancy. This, coupled with the immobilizing effects of the heavy financial burden placed by the state on the peasants, effectively tied them to the land. Petrushevsky thus concludes that the feudal state in Iran did not deem it necessary to institutionalize peasant bondage in the manner which prevailed in various parts of feudal Europe (ibid. pp.155–68).

The restrictive effects of the factors cited by Petrushevsky could hardly be disputed. Nevertheless their capacity to constitute and sustain a form of non-economic mechanism necessary for the appropriation of surplus depends strictly on the character of the dominant relations of production. This argument thus leads us to a consideration of the forms of landed property and ownership in Iran before the thirteenth century. It is interesting to note that Petrushevsky's analysis of the economic and political restrictions on peasant mobility, like his detailed account of the absence of serfdom, lacks any reference to the prevailing forms of property relations in Iran. This, as was pointed out, is not an accidental oversight, but an omission which has its roots in his concept of Eastern feudalism. The concept presupposes state ownership of agricultural land, and a mode of appropriation of surplus based on direct political coercion inscribed in the state-subject relations. It excludes forms of domination and subordination between the landlords and the direct producers, and renders superfluous Petrushevsky's otherwise elaborate account of political and economic restrictions on peasant mobility in pre-Mongol Iran.

Petrushevsky's account of the institutionalization of the relations of lordship and servitude under Mongol rule is no more consistent. He seeks to explain this process with reference to the 'social policies' of the Mongol rulers, precipitated by the prevailing economic conditions in the countryside in the aftermath of the invasion: a sharp decline both in the area of arable land and in the size of the active peasant population, leading to a substantial decrease in the amount of extractable peasant surplus (ibid. p.165) The initial reaction of the Mongol rulers to this situation, states Petrushevsky, was to intensify peasant exploitation by increasing the level of labour-service (*bigari*) on their holdings, which led to mass peasant flight from the land and further decline in the conditions of production. The solution was thus sought in tying the peasants to the land.

The Mongol rules, however, introduced no new legislation to this effect; they simply extended the rules of Chenghiz Khan's *yasa* to the Iranian peasants (ibid. p.169). This was a set of rules governing the military organization of the Mongol tribes within the tribal confederacy, and included punitive measures to prevent the tribal soldiery from deserting their designated ranks and units within the Mongol army.[15] For this reason, writes Petrushevsky:

> the state, the feudal class, and in particular the group of desert-dwelling military notables were interested in imposing restrictions on the free movement of the Iranian peasants, and returning the fleeing peasants forcibly to their dwellings. This led to the Mongol policy of tying the peasants to the land. They [the Mongols) did not introduce new rules, but extended the rules of Chenghiz Khan's *yasa*, concerning the prevention of the nomadic soldiery from leaving their designated military units, to peasants and non-nomadic people. But the application of the rules of *yasa* to the non-nomadic population in Iran and the neighbouring countries was not a simple matter; it was made necessary by the changes that had taken place [since the invasion] in the feudal economy and by the fiscal interests of the state and the highest ranks of the feudal order. (op.cit. p.169)

The extension of *yasa* to the Iranian peasants, however, resulted in a specific form of dependency. Iranian peasants, unlike European serfs, were tied not to the land but to the person of their Mongol overlords; they were (as noted by some historians) the personal property of the Mongol landlords, their status resembling that of chattel slaves rather than serfs. Although Petrushevsky notes this point, he does not accept the view that the Iranian peasants were effectively reduced to the status of chattel slaves (ibid. Vol.II, p.177). Their dependency, their absolute lack of freedom, he argues, was a temporary phenomenon, which lasted only for the short period during which Iran was ruled by the Ulus Khans—Chenghiz (1219–1227) and the first four Mongol rulers (1229–1294). Under the first Ilkhans (1265–1295) the form of peasant bondage changed, and the Iranian peasants, like the European serfs, were legally tied to the land; and this change in the legal status of the Iranian peasants, he maintains, followed Ghazan Khan's conversion to Islam in 1303 whereby the long-apparent contradiction between the rules of *yasa* and Islamic principles could no longer be sustained. Ghazan attempted to reconcile the two by reforming agrarian relations. Petrushevsky here refers to Ghazan's *yerlik* (reform) in 1303 concerning the assignment of *tuyuls* to the Mongol military notables:

> From our point of view Ghazan Khan's *yerlik* was an attempt to reconcile Chenghiz Khan's *yasa* with Islamic *sharia*. That is, although *yasa's* restrictions on mobility were retained, the peasants, in line with Islamic *sharia*, were considered as legally free persons. The *yerlik* stated explicitly that landlords have no right to move their peasants from one village to another or to decide their fate in an arbitrary manner. They must not mistake their serfs for slaves. The *yerlik* further stated that peasants were dependent not on their overlords but on the land in whose register their names are mentioned. (op.cit. Vol.II, p.180)

The agrarian policy of the Ilkhans is thus said to have transformed the legal status of Iranian peasants, who were no longer tied to the person of their overlords but instead to the land that they worked.[16] Unlike the Russian and Georgian serfs, Iranian peasants legally remained free persons who could be bought and sold only as part of the land on which they lived and worked. Petrushevsky, nevertheless, maintains that the legal freedom of the Iranian peasants was merely a 'fraud' made necessary by the formal recognition given by the ruling class to the principles of Islamic *sharia*. In reality, he thus states, the Iranian peasant remained a 'dependent creature without any rights' (ibid. p.181).

Historical evidence suggests that during the thirteenth and fourteenth centuries certain legal restrictions were imposed upon the mobility of the Iranian peasants (Juwayni op.cit. p.24, Morgan op.cit. pp.158–170); but it is difficult to ascertain whether these restrictions actually amounted to the institutionalization of peasant bondage to a point resembling serfdom in Europe. However, my concern here is to evaluate not the historical validity of Petrushevsky's analysis but its theoretical status; that is, the manner in which he conceptualizes the conditions of the constitution of relations of lordship and servitude in Iranian feudalism.

Petrushevsky's analysis of the constitution of the relations of lordship and servitude under Mongol rule seems to escape the inconsistencies involved in his account of the absence of these relations in the preceding period. This analysis precedes the discussion of the universalization of feudal landed property and the extra-economic relations of appropriation of surplus entailed in political class relations, which appears to bring Petrushevsky's analysis in line with the theoretical premises of the classical concept of the feudal mode of production, and enables him to assign a form of class representation to the agrarian policies of the Ilkhan state. Hence he derives the argument that the institutionalization of relations of domination and subordination by the Ilkhan state was a measure to protect the economic interests of the land-owning class and to enhance their position in the struggle against the mass of Iranian peasants. Petrushevsky's analysis, consistent as it may seem, entails a number of theoretical errors which stem mainly from his conceptualization of the process and condition of the constitution of feudal landed property under Mongol rule.

The theoretical consistency of Petrushevsky's concept of Iranian feudalism (hence its correspondence with the classical concept) depends entirely on the forms of political class relations ascribed to the social policies of the Ilkhan state. Petrushevsky tends to deduce these relations from his analysis of the conditions of the constitution of feudal property relations. But his analysis, as we have already seen, does not in fact involve political class relations. Rather it rests precisely on the displacement of these relations in favour of state-subject relations—the basis of the conflict between the central state apparatus and the decentralizing forces, whereby the autonomy of the landlords *vis-à-vis* the state is conceived as the essential condition of the emergence and development of feudal landed property. This subjectivism underlying Petrushevsky's conception of feudal property relations undermines his elaborate historical account of the institutionalization of peasant bondage in the Mongol era.

Further, the host of economic changes charted by Petrushevsky cannot sufficiently account for the transformation in the organization of agricultural production under Mongol rule. In fact, he maintains that, despite a sharp decline both in the area of arable land and in the size of the active peasant population, share-cropping continued to prevail in the countryside—which, in effect, means that the organization of labour and production remained fundamentally unchanged in the aftermath of the Mongol invasion. This point is particularly significant in view of Petrushevsky's initial argument concerning the absence of serfdom in pre-Mongol Iran. Petrushevsky clearly relates the absence of serfdom to the marginal status of demesne production and labour-rent in Iranian agriculture; an argument which, in effect, implies that the institutionalization of peasant bondage must be accompanied by a transformation in the processes of labour and production. Although Petrushevsky fails to account for the transformation he continues to assert its implications by equating labour-service with labour-rent, and using the two as interchangeable concepts.

In fact, in the context of Iranian agriculture, labour-service (*bigari*) is clearly distinguished from labour-rent (*bahreh-e mālekaneh-e kari*). Theoretically, the former is an adjunct of the dominant relations of production, while the latter constitutes those relations. Changes in the quantity and duration of labour-service can be subject to factors other than production relations (e.g. the exercise of political power), but cannot alone induce or account for structural transformations in the organization of labour and of production. In Iran, as elsewhere, labour-service existed alongside dominant modes of exploitation, whether share-cropping, fixed rent or labour-rent; and there is no evidence to suggest that under Mongol rule share-cropping was replaced by labour-rent. The intensification of labour-service, significant as it was, can hardly be said to account for the transformation in the organization of agricultural production, a process necessary if Petrushevsky's analysis of the institutionalization of peasant bondage is to be retained.

Petrushevsky's notion of Iranian feudalism, I have argued, signifies a departure from the theoretical premises of the classical concept of the feudal mode of production. However, unlike the classical concept, it is not only discursively incoherent but also theoretically inconsistent. For it presupposes forms of landed property and extra-economic coercion, with conditions of existence and reproduction which are external to the concept. Their relationship with the concept is only historical; it is established by a particular interpretation of Iranian history in the Mongol era, which sets the ground for his conceptualization of Iranian feudalism. Petrushevsky's concept of Iranian feudalism is inconceivable independent of such an interpretation.

Nomani's work, unlike Petrushevsky's, is not confined to a particular period in Iranian history. It is a general history, offering a genealogy of the structural elements of the feudal mode of production in Iran: the development of feudal landed property (op.cit. pp.145–237) and the formation and evolution of the forms of peasant dependency on the land (op.cit. pp.237–257) from the Sassanian to the Safavid period in Iranian history. Nomani's history is fragmentary and lacks a unified structure. The origins and development of the structural elements of the feudal mode of production in Iran are traced independently of one another, and the study leaves out the analysis of their articulation, i.e. the formation of the structure of the feudal mode of production in Iran. Nonetheless, it entails a concept of feudal structure which informs his discussion of the dynamics of the development of the feudal mode of production in Iran (op.cit. pp.285–327). This concept pre-exists the genealogy of its constituent elements, and is derived from a detailed discussion of European feudalism (op.cit. pp.95–143). Nomani, in line with the Soviet historians, treats European feudalism as identical and interchangeable with the Marxist concept of the feudal mode of production. He thus attempts to establish a correspondence between Iranian conditions and Marxist concepts through the history of feudalism in Western Europe.

Nomani begins with an exposition of the Marxist concept of the feudal mode of production which serves as a point of reference in his genealogy of the structural elements of Iranian feudalism. Modes of production, he maintains, are distinguished by their specific mode of appropriation of surplus. Under the feudal mode, surplus is extracted in the form of ground rent. Feudal ground rent he describes as an expression of the monopoly ownership of the land by the landlord, constituting the object of the reproduction of the feudal mode of production (op.cit. pp.82–83). Nomani further maintains that feudal rent presupposes relations of domination and subordination between the landlords and the direct producers, resulting, he stresses, from the non-separation of the direct producers from the means of production, in particular the land. Thus some sort of extra-economic coercion is necessary for the extraction of rent and the reproduction of the mode of production (ibid.).

Nomani's exposition here is a reiteration of the classical Marxist position, in which rent is conceived as a non-economic category resulting primarily from the non-separation of the direct producers from the land. But he soon diverges from this position by assigning a transitional character to feudal rent. Feudal rent, he argues, 'represents a middle way in exploitation and expresses a combination of economic and non-economic coercion':

> Despite [the existence] of various forms of exploitation of man by man, two forms generally prevail. The first form is exploitation by means of 'economic coercion' which in the feudal order takes the form of rent; labour-rent, rent in kind and in money. The second is exploitation by means of 'non-economic coercion' or 'direct coercion'. Each one of these two general forms of exploitation contains variations, resulting from the specific relations between the producer and non-producer, and also from a definite level in the development of man's struggle against nature. Under slavery, the appropriation of surplus from the producer takes the form of direct coercion, in a naked manner. But under feudalism the lord is not the absolute owner of the peasant. Feudal dependency, therefore, represents a middle way in exploitation and expresses a combination of economic and non-economic coercion, although, in this system, exploitation by means of direct coercion [non-economic] still holds the dominant position. In a market economy, on the other hand, economic coercion is the dominant form of relations of distribution, since in this order, the producer sells his labour power in the market in order to provide for his subsistence. (op.cit. p.83)

Nomani's definition of the concept of feudal ground rent is clearly at odds with Marxist theory. In Marxist theory, rent is a consequence of the monopoly ownership of the land by the land-owning class, which, on account of the non-separation of the direct producers from the land, is extracted by means of non-economic coercion. A form of peasant dependency on the land is thus considered essential for the reproduction of the feudal mode of production. In Nomani's definition, by contrast, the feudal mode corresponds to two distinct sets of production relations, rent and non-rental relations, each presupposing a distinct mode of appropriation of surplus, economic and non-economic respectively. Non-economic coercive relations, it is further stressed, hold the dominant position in the structure of the mode of production. Nomani's definition thus implies that the feudal mode of production is basically structured by non-rental rather than rental relations.

Further, Nomani's conception of feudal rent as an economic relation lacks the requisite conditions of existence. Clearly an economic concept of rent presupposes the total or partial separation of the direct producers from the means of production; hence a conception of feudal landed property which rests on the economic subsumption of the direct producers in the process of production. Although Nomani refers to this partial separation, his conception of feudal landed property shows that the reference is to means of production other than land. He is in fact quite emphatic about the non-separation of the direct producers from the land, which is the basis of non-economic coercion in his definition of the feudal mode of production. In the absence of these conditions, an economic concept of feudal rent can be retained only if it is conceived not as *relations of production* but as *relations of distribution*, identical with capitalist ground rent. In fact, Nomani not only identifies feudal rent with the relations of distribution, but also fails to distinguish the latter conceptually from the relations of production. His definition of the economic coercion specific to the capitalist mode of production clearly illustrates this basic theoretical error. 'In a market economy', he argues in the same passage, 'economic coercion is the dominant form of the relations of *distribution*'. This identification of surplus value, i.e., capitalist relations of production, with relations of distribution, is an error which casts serious doubt on the Marxist credentials of his analysis.

Nomani's conceptualization of Iranian feudalism opens with a detailed discussion of the nature and forms of land-ownership in Iran (op.cit. pp.143–237). The forms of ownership associated with *iqta* constitute the central point of his analysis, and the rights of such ownership, he contends, were similar to those which characterized feudal landed property in the West: they were 'conditional rights', tied to the performance of specific duties on the part of the assignees (ibid. pp.201–229; Nomani 1972, pp.5-62). Whether *iqta* or *tuyul*, the form of land assignment varied widely, regionally and country-wide. After a detailed and interesting account of these variations in different periods of Iranian history, based on primary sources, Nomani concludes that, in general, any variation in the form of land assignment was a function of the conditions which governed the grant of land in the first place. That is, it was determined primarily by the type of service to which the assignment was bound, from the provision of soldiery to the administration of revenue, or a combination of the two (ibid.).

Nomani, nevertheless, notes a major difference between *iqta* and fief. He agrees with Lambton that *iqta* 'lacked the practice of commendation and therefore the main principle of vassalage' (op.cit. 1972, p.42). But, unlike Lambton, he believes that:

> The lack of any contractual relationship is not a 'fundamental difference' between *iqta* and fief, but a difference in form. After all, the practice of commendation became widespread in Europe only from the eighth and ninth centuries onward . . . Besides, in the case of the Islamic countries there was no special need for any contractual relationship, as the grantees were in any case pledged to obedience and loyalty to the caliph as the secular and spiritual guardian. The same, of course, was true of the ecclesiastical benefice and fief in Western Europe. However, the grantees in both cases were granted *iqta* or fief on the condition that they would perform military service for the lord; and in both cases the land had several claimants, who were dependent on each other in a hierarchical chain. (op.cit. 1972, pp.43)

Nomani thus argues that the formal difference between fief and *iqta* is not as important as their 'historical function': their contribution to the formation of a feudal class (ibid.). However, as will be shown, Nomani's argument remains an assertion, and the absence of seigneurial relations undermines his conceptualization of feudal relations of production in Iran.

Nomani distinguishes two types of *iqta*: *iqta al-tamlik* and *iqta al-istiqlal*, military and administrative *iqta* respectively.[17] The former was a 'grant of land' and the latter a 'grant of revenue'. In theory, he further argues, *iqta al-tamlik* was viewed as 'hereditary property', and in practice became hardly distinguishable from private property. *Iqta al-istiqlal*, on the other hand, was not hereditary, nor even tenure for life, and there were periodic changes in its distribution (ibid. p.34). Further, Nomani seems to suggest that *iqta al-tamlik* was exempted from state taxation, while *iqta al-istiqlal* was subject to various tax regimes at different times, and revenue derived from the land was in part remitted to the central treasury in lieu of taxes and other dues. This difference, too, seems to have arisen from the type of services to which the assignment was bound (ibid.). Nomani concludes that the ownership rights associated with *iqta al-tamlik*, the military *iqta*, were in conformity with feudal ownership in Europe, and thus that the conceptualization of feudal relations of production in this case does not present a problem. The difficulty, he concludes, lies in the conceptualization of *iqta al-istiqlal*, the administrative *iqta*.

The absence of hereditary rights of ownership clearly poses a problem for the conceptualization of feudal relations of production in the context of the classical Marxist concept, since it amounts to the absence of seigneurial relations as the condition of existence of feudal landed property and the basis for the consolidation of the assignees as a cohesive social class. This problem has been the most important obstacle by far to the conceptualization of feudal relations in pre-Constitutional Iran, and the most potent weapon in the arsenal of those criticizing the concept of Iranian feudalism, both Marxist and non-Marxist. The argument is that *iqta*, unlike fief, was not a form of landholding but an administrative unit, an adjunct of the fiscal apparatus of the centralized state, and the *iqta*-holder a revenue administrator, a tax-farmer appointed by the king who was the sole owner of agricultural land.

Nomani attempts to overcome this obstacle by arguing that the absence of hereditary rights of ownership was a theoretical rather than a real problem. In reality, the continuity of ownership rights depended not so much on the legal relations as on the actual balance of power between the assignor and the assignees, the king and the *muqtas*. The decline in the authority of the central government often coincided with a correlative growth in the local autonomy of the assignees. In most cases, though not as a general rule, this trend was followed by the merging of the 'functions of provincial military commander, tax-collector and *muqta*'. They were 'combined in one person', and 'the process led to the emergence of large, seemingly feudal properties which were substantially independent of the central government' (op.cit. 1972, p.35). The result was, more often than not, the emergence of assignees with local and regional power bases who used their growing independence to convert their *iqtas* into *de facto* private property. In most cases the assignees retained their allegiance to the central government, and the administrative *iqtas* were converted to military oncs which carried hereditary rights and were generally exempt from state taxation.

Nomani here invokes Petrushevsky's argument by deducing the conditions of existence of feudal relations of production from the transformation in the organizational form of state power, consequent on an inbuilt conflict between the state and the *iqta*-holders. The problems involved in this mode of analysis have already been discussed in some detail. Nomani, like Petrushevsky, adheres to the classical concept of the feudal mode of production, but fails to substantiate his own definition of Iranian feudalism in the absence of seigneurial relations. Although aware of the difference between the conditions of existence of *iqta* and those of feudal landed property, Nomani, as noted above, considers the absence of seigneurial relations as merely a formal difference, not affecting the historical function of *iqta* as a variant of feudal landed property; and he attempts to remedy this theoretically by substituting the landlord's autonomy from the central state for seigneurial relations, in much the same manner as Petrushevsky.

There are notable differences in the conceptualizations of feudal relations of production by the two authors. These differences correspond to their definitions of the classical concept of the feudal mode of production, and show clearly that their deviation from the theoretical premises of the concept is not arbitrary. Rather it is predetermined by the order of a discourse which in both cases is concerned to establish a correspondence between Iranian history and the general concept of the feudal mode of production as a universal historical phenomenon.

The specificity of agrarian relations in Iran, and their real or alleged differences from the conditions of existence of feudal relations in the classical concept, as shown above, leads Petrushevsky to argue for a notion of 'Eastern feudalism' characterized by the landlord's subsumption within the state. This notion reduces the difference to a single element, i.e., the landlord's relationship with the central state, and constitutes it as the focus of the struggle for the constitution of feudalism proper, characterized, above all, by the landlord's autonomy from the state. Petrushevsky's notion of Iranian feudalism, it was further shown, is sustained at the cost of an over-politicization of the classical concept, whereby political class relations are replaced by state-subject relations as constitutive of feudal landed property.

Nomani pursues the same mode of analysis, but his particular notion of agrarian relations in Iran gives a further twist to the over-politicization of the concept. Unlike Petrushevsky, he does not argue for a notion of Eastern feudalism and the predominance of tax-rent prior to the thirteenth century. Rather his conception of Iranian feudalism refers to a developmental process beginning in the third century, and the supposed predominance of feudal relations of production in the absence of seigneurial power is justified by a redefinition of the political concept of the feudal mode. Nomani's definition of feudalism as a transitional mode operating with two distinct economic and extra-economic relations of appropriation of surplus, already discussed in this section, is precisely an attempt to come to terms with this persistent problem. The two modes of appropriation of surplus correspond to the property relations associated with administrative and military *iqtas*, distinguished on the basis of the absence and presence respectively of hereditary rights. When, as a result of the increasing autonomy of the *iqta*-holders, the administrative *iqta* is eventually transformed to the military *iqta*—*de facto* private property—the extra-economic mode of appropriation becomes dominant in the structure of Iranian feudalism.

This detailed examination of the work of Petrushevsky and Nomani serves to illustrate a number of points. First, the Marxist definitions of Iranian feudalism, which take the classical concept of the feudal mode of production as their point of reference, fail to account for the conditions of existence of feudal landed property and property relations in Iran. Compared to the classical concept, they are not only discursively incoherent but also theoretically inconsistent. The Marxist definitions of Iranian feudalism, dependent entirely on a particular reading of Iranian history, have no independent discursive existence. Second, the real/alleged absence of seigneurial power, and the legally defined relations of domination and subordination between landlord and peasant, are the main obstacles to the conceptualization of Iran as a feudal social formation. These obstacles will persist in so far as the primacy of political relations in the structure of the classical concept and the mode of causality thus generated are retained.

This analysis has argued that the dominance of political relations in the structure of the classical Marxist concept is a consequence of its discursive incoherency: that is, the intrinsic disconnection between the relations of production and the labour process generated by the non-separation of the direct producer from the land, and the associated anthropological conception of economic property and legal ownership. It thus follows that any concept of Iranian feudalism should be grounded on an economic concept of feudal rent. Such a concept requires a notion of feudal landed property based on the subsumption of the direct producer in the process of production, and a mechanism of appropriation of surplus based on the exchange relations entailed in rent-form.

PART II

4. AN ECONOMIC CONCEPT OF FEUDAL RENT

In the previous chapter I argued that the the difficulties involved in the conceptualization of Iranian feudalism arise primarily from the inconsistencies of the classical Marxist concept of the feudal mode of production. The discursive incoherence of the concept, and its consequent political essentialism, effectively prevent any conceptualization of forms of landed property and property relations in terms of the prevailing economic structures and relations, independently of comparative political historiographies of pre-constitutional Iran and feudal Europe. In fact, as was shown, Marxist definitions of Iranian feudalism are inconceivable without such comparative historical frameworks, which specify at once the boundaries and the terms of theoretical discourse on agrarian relations in pre-constitutional Iran. If the analysis is to surpass the theoretical limitations and ideological consequences of the Orientalist discourse outlined in the opening chapter of this study, the conceptualization of Iranian feudalism should be preceded and informed by an economic concept of feudal rent, constructed on the basis of the specificity of feudal relations of production. It is thus the theoretical requisites of an economic concept of rent that we shall now consider.

Marx's writings, as I have indicated, present a dichotomy of capitalism/pre-capitalism based on the separation/non-separation of the direct producer from the means of production, and the notion of non-separation is then proposed as the foundation of pre-capitalist relations of production in general. This notion, in effect, assigns a particular character to the structure of the pre-capitalist forms of property, whereby legal ownership and economic property are separated from one another, and the appropriation of surplus assumes a non-economic form. The non-economic forms of appropriation of surplus constitute the basis for a typology of the pre-capitalist modes of production which expresses the modality of the organizational structure of political power in pre-capitalist social formations.

In what follows I shall attempt to problematize the status of the notion of non-separation in Marx's discourse. It will be argued that the non-separation of the direct producers is not a coherent theoretical construct but a necessary assertion, resulting from the discursive primacy of the category of labour and the associated anthropological conceptions of property and ownership in Marx's theory of the modes of production. The notion cannot be sustained if the nature of control over the means of production is problematized. A consideration of the economic role of the agents in the process of production presupposes conceptions of property and ownership which rest precisely on the *separation* of the direct producer from the means of production; and in fact, such a separation is essential for the definition of the relations of production, if the latter is to structure the process of production and to specify the mode of exploitation. The theoretical propositions entailed in this argument will then be used to construct an economic concept of feudal rent. This section will draw largely on some recent 'revisions' of Marx's *Capital*, as will be indicated in the course of the analysis.

The theory of the modes of production, it was pointed out earlier in this study, entails a concept of 'production in general', indicating a relationship between man and nature as the material basis of production, common to all economic forms.[1] The relationship is established through the agency of human labour, the essential property of man, which transforms nature and creates wealth; and this labour of transformation is then given as the source of property and the foundation of the economy. The notion of production in general thus excludes forms of property relations other than those emanating from the labour of human subjects in the labour process. The non-labourer, on the other hand, is thought to secure access to the means and conditions of production by means external to the process of production.

Although Marx considers 'production in general' as an 'abstraction', the intrinsic relationship between man and nature, and the status of the category of human labour as the source of economic activity and property, remain central to his theory of the modes of production. The theory, it has been pointed out, entails conceptions of economy and property which are founded on the 'anthropology of the subject'.[2] In fact, Marx, more often than not, deduces the rational organization of the economy and the conditions of the formation and appropriation of property from the needs and functions of human subjects, a notion which both 'informs' and 'deforms' his conceptualization of the relations of production in *Capital*.[3]

The origins of this economic humanism in Marx's discourse have been traced to his early reading of classical political economy.[4] Rancière points out that Marx initially confronted classical political economy through a Feuerbachian materialism; this, he states, was a confrontation between a discourse whose object was the structure of the capitalist economy, and one centred on man as the 'original producer'. The result, according to Rancière, was a displacement in Marx's early writings of the terminology of classical political economy, whereby an analysis of the structure of capitalist production is displaced in favour of a moral critique of capitalism in the name of man as the original producer and the only legitimate owner of the fruit of his labours, seen as his essential property. Economic property is thus transcribed as 'human essence' and exchange is transformed into 'species activity' (Rancière 1971, pp.40–44). Rancière's argument, however, is largely founded on Marx's early writings, in particular on the *Economic and Philosophical Manuscripts* of 1844, with an implicit refusal to extend it to the discourse of *Capital*. His position here is informed by the concept of the 'epistemological break' (a central tenet of structuralist Marxism, with which he was closely associated). This notion argues for a radical transformation in the conceptual structure of Marx's discourse, from human nature and the moral critique of capitalism to the structural categories of class and the relations of production, characteristic of his writings before and after 1848.[5]

Although there is some justification in the notion, to term it a 'break' overstates the case. For although the problematic of human nature and the associated moral critique of capitalism characteristic of Marx's early writings are largely displaced by structural categories in *Capital*, philosophical anthropology, the legacy of Feuerbachian materialism, continues to deform Marx's conceptualization of the relations of production, mainly through the operation of the category of value and the conceptions of property and ownership that it entails. This is most clearly manifest in Marx's treatment of the conditions of the formation and appropriation of economic property in *Capital*.

These conditions, in *Capital*, are not given, but are constituted by the relations of production—that is, by a series of exchange relations which are presented as the effects of the structure of possession in separation from the means of production. Thus the conditions of the formation and appropriation of property as such cannot be reduced to mere legal relations of ownership. They presuppose effective possession in separation, that is, separation of the labourer from the means of production and his subordination to capital in the process of production. In this sense, however, the conditions of the formation and appropriation of property are identical to those which constitute the process of production as a process of exploitation.[6] They are structural conditions and cannot be reduced to the activity of human subjects, i.e., to the mere consequences of the labour of transformation. The mechanism of the formation and appropriation of property —the exchange relations—is essentially economic, but presupposes non-economic juridico-political conditions of existence: juridico-political rights of ownership. The legal rights of ownership, as rights of appropriation and disposal vested in the owning subject, provide a basis upon which the appropriation of economic objects (the economic process of appropriation) is constructed.

But although 'structural' conceptions of economic property and ownership remain central to the discourse of *Capital*, this by no means signifies a total break with the economic humanism and the philosophical anthropology of the pre-1848 period; they find their way back into the analysis of the processes of production and distribution primarily through the category of value. Value reasserts the primacy of human labour as the source of economic property, the sole means of validating possession and appropriation of economic objects. Economic objects are thus so defined by virtue of being products of human labour, bearers of value, which justifies acts of exchange as economic exchange: this is the concept of the commodity in *Capital*.[7]

The pre-eminence of the labour theory of value—and the subsequent reassertion of economic humanism in the discourse of *Capital*—has a number of important consequences for the conceptualization of the forms and conditions of the formation and appropriation of economic property. First, it leads to the conflation of the economic process of the formation and appropriation of property with its juridico-political conditions of existence, since the capitalist commodity is conceived not as an object of 'possession' but as a 'possessed' object, and its appropriation by the non-labourer requires no more than the juridico-political relations of ownership already vested in him as the owner of the means of production. These relations then, initially conceived as supports of the structure of property relations, as non-economic conditions of existence of the economic processes of the formation and appropriation of property, are at the same time the very mechanism which ensures these processes.

Secondly, the concept of value and the associated conceptions of commodity and exchange entail a notion of the economic subject as the human subject. This identification of the economic subject with the human subject, and the invariant position of the latter as the owning agent in the context of property relations, imposes serious limitations on the conceptualization of the forms of property in which the rights of ownership are appropriated by non-human subjects, such as religious institutions and modern enterprises.[8] The analysis of the forms of property in *Capital* illustrates this point clearly. Marx here allows for two forms of property only: private and common. In the former the object of possession is assigned to a single possessor, a human individual (private ownership) who appropriates the rights of ownership; while in the latter the object of possession is assigned to an aggregate of possessors, human individuals, who commonly appropriate the rights of ownership (common ownership). The human subject thus occupies an invariant status within the forms of property considered by Marx. It is the only conceivable agent of appropriation (*Capital* Vol.I 1970, pp.761–764). These conceptions of economic property and ownership, as pointed out earlier, are derived from the 'anthropology' of the subject whose labour is the only legitimate source of economic property and the foundation of the economy in general.

Thirdly, the pivotal role of human labour in the conceptualization of property and possession leads to insurmountable problems when the object in question is not a product of human labour. Such objects (e.g. land) fall outside the domain of the labour theory of value and its determinations. Thus the forms of exchange pertaining to these 'natural' objects cannot be conceived as economic. They are juridico-political relations, constituted and sustained by these relations. The point is that political power alone is constitutive of property in natural objects and ensures their appropriation by the non-labourer. Here, therefore, the forms of access to surplus product, the relations of appropriation, altogether exclude any reference to the sphere of the economy, and the conditions of existence of the land-owning class is sustained exclusively by juridico-political relations of ownership. The result is the overall conflation of the relations of production with their non-economic conditions of existence; a complete identification of the economic processes of the formation and appropriation of property in land with their juridico-political conditions of existence, the identification of possession with ownership. Marx's theorization of the forms of economic property and ownership associated with the concept of capitalist ground rent is particularly instructive in this respect.

Marx's treatment of capitalist ground rent in Volume III of *Capital*, where he makes largely inconsistent and often paradoxical theoretical statements on the nature and the conditions of existence of rent, tends to cast serious doubt on the possibility of resolving the problems posed by the existence of rent and a land-owning class in a predominantly capitalist social formation (*Capital* Vol.III 1971, pp.614–678). In this case, it will be shown, the notion of exchange entailed in the labour theory of value seriously hinders the conceptualization of landed class relations in terms of the prevailing structure of economic relations; that is, in terms of the forms of possession in separation from the means of production which underlie his conceptualization of the conditions of existence and reproduction of the capitalist and working classes in *Capital*. The result is the persistence in Marx's writings on capitalist rent of two contradictory and competing forms of discourse operating side by side, whose paradoxical effects tend to cancel out each other.

For Marx, capitalist ground rent is a consequence of the monopoly ownership of land by the land-owning class. It is a 'price' paid by the capitalist to the landlord in return for the use of the land in the process of production. In this sense, capitalist ground rent consists of a portion of surplus value produced in the process of production, which accrues to the landlord owing to his monopoly ownership of the land as a necessary means of production. The mechanism of appropriation is thus juridico-political rather than economic, arising from the right of exclusion entailed in the institution of private property in land supported by political power, i.e., by the capitalist state. Marx further points out that the institution of private property in land, hence the existence of a land-owning class, is not a structural requisite of the capitalist mode of production, but a juridico-political phenomenon, a legacy of the pre-capitalist past which continues to assert itself in capitalist social formations for mainly 'historical reasons'. In other words, according to Marx, there is no 'economic reason' for the existence of rent and a land-owning class in capitalist social formations.

According to this general definition, the sole difference between capitalist and pre-capitalist forms of rent lies in the nature of the object of appropriation: *surplus value* and *land revenue* respectively. Yet Marx's treatment of the mechanism of appropriation and the conditions of existence of capitalist rent renders the distinction largely insignificant. The politically/legally defined mechanism of appropriation arising from the monopoly ownership of agricultural land by definition excludes the forms of economic class relations which underlie the process of production and distribution of surplus value. To be more precise, Marx's analysis here runs counter to the dominant order of discourse in *Capital*, and the form of possession in separation which sustains the relations of appropriation of surplus is replaced by the juridico-political relations associated with the institution of private property in land. The analysis is supported by the argument that capitalist rent, though a portion of surplus value produced in the process of production, constitutes *relations of distribution*—an argument signifying Marx's retreat to the philosophical anthropology of his early writings, and tenable within such a context alone.

Evidently, a conception of capitalist rent as payment for land-use, by definition, excludes the economic conditions of existence of surplus value as specified in *Capital*. The production and realization of surplus value in the form of rent requires, above all, the effective possession of the land by the land-owning class, and an economic mechanism of appropriation structured by capitalist exchange relations. These conditions are essential components of and internal to the definition of rent, if rent is to be conceived as a portion of surplus value produced in the process of production. However, capitalist rent conceived in this way no longer signifies relations of distribution arising from juridico-political relations, but *relations of production* arising from the effective possession of the land, as a means of production, by the land-owning class. Juridico-political relations of ownership are therefore external to the definition of the concept, which signifies the relations of production and their *economic* conditions of existence; i.e. the relations which determine the distribution of the land to the unit of production and the capitalist exchange relations which specify the mechanisms of appropriation of rent. It is, in fact, capitalist exchange relations which define the character of the rent as capitalist. The concept of capitalist rent, so defined, presupposes an *economic* role on the part of the land-owning class tantamount to its effective possession of the land and corresponding *partial* control of the process of production. Capitalist rent as the economic condition of existence of the land-owning class rests on the economic subsumption of the wage-labourers in the process of capitalist production. This point has wider implications for the main subject of discussion in this chapter, the conceptualization of feudal rent as an economic category, to which we will return in the final section of the chapter.

Marx's theorization of capitalist ground rent, in particular his analysis of the conditions of existence and reproduction of the land-owning class in capitalist social formations, clearly shows the effective presence of his early economic humanism in the discourse of *Capital*. The anthropological conception of property asserted by the category of value leads to the exclusion of capitalist exchange relations from the definition of the concept of capitalist rent. The result, as was noted, is the conflation of the relations of production with their non-economic juridico-political conditions of existence. This conflation, however, is theoretically necessary if the status of the human subject as the source of economic property and activity is to be restored and sustained in the discourse; a status achieved only by the subordination of economic class relations to intersubjective relations (between intentional human subjects) defined at the juridico-political level. The land-owning class thus ceases to be a structural category. It is an aggregate of individual owners whose economic existence cannot be defined in terms of the prevailing relations of production.

Economic humanism is thus at the root of the paradox of which Marx speaks, a paradox manifest in his treatment of the conditions of existence of the land-owning class in capitalist society.[9] In Marx's analysis of these conditions of existence we encounter a concept of possession which is devoid of economic content: it neither provides an economic role for the landlord, nor assigns him a corresponding capacity to control the process of production. The concept of possession here signifies not economic but rather juridico-political relations, synonymous with ownership. In fact, the notion of monopoly ownership is crucial to Marx's concept of rent as relations of distribution; for it ensures the distribution of rent—the portion of surplus value which assumes the form of rent—and as such enables Marx to explain the monopoly pricing of land and agricultural products without developing concepts of pertinent forms of exchange. Consequently, the processes of the formation and appropriation of rent are explained without reference to the categories of the commodity market, exchange and competition, and rent is presented not as an integral part of the price of production but as a component external to it.[10]

The monopoly ownership of land which is held to constitute the economic condition for the existence of the land-owning class in capitalist society, however, is a purely historical phenomenon, inexplicable by reference to capitalist relations of production. It is a consequence of 'historical circumstances', of the specific articulation of feudal and capitalist relations in the process of the transition to capitalism; hence Marx's assertion that the land-owning class is a 'remnant of the past', and that its present status as one of the three classes of modern society is to be attributed to 'historical' rather than 'economic' reasons. Capitalist relations of production do not in themselves presuppose a land-owning class, and in fact the monopoly ownership of the land by such a class may retard rather than enhance the development of capitalism.

This brief account of Marx's conceptualization of capitalist ground rent is intended to show the general persistence of economic humanism in Marx's discourse, and to demonstrate its particular effects on his conceptualization of the forms of economic property and ownership associated with land. Land, defined as a 'natural' object, is as such excluded from an economic sphere so designated by the production and circulation of commodities. The exchange relations governing the purchase and sale or rental of land fail to qualify as economic relations. They do not involve exchange of values and so belong to the world of 'appearance' whose face is 'deceptive'.

I have also argued that the assertion of the primacy of the categories of labour and value revives the status of the human subject in the discourse of *Capital*. This takes place mainly through a displacement of the structural categories, which in this case leads to the exclusion of the economic relations specifying the form of rent. The fact that capitalist rent consists of a portion of surplus value produced in the process of production is rendered irrelevant to its definition as a 'price' for the land-use. Marx, it was pointed out, envisages a paradox, arising from the presence of two mutually exclusive conceptions of property and ownership. But the paradox is resolved by subordinating the structural to the anthropological conception of property and ownership, which, in effect, results in the exclusion of exchange relations from his definition of the concept of capitalist rent. Conceptually, the exchange relations are replaced by their non-economic conditions of existence entailed in the notion of monopoly ownership. Hence the classical Marxist identification of economic with legal ownership, which is the basis for the denial of the economic role of the land-owning class in the process of production and appropriation of rent. In fact, the classical division of economic agents into labourers and non-labourers, a necessary outcome of the primacy of the categories of labour and value in Marx's discourse, seriously obscures not only the nature of the landlord's control over the land in the process of production, but also the very mechanism of the constitution of land as the means of production. The problematization of the role of the landlord in the process of production, of the nature of his control over land, necessarily leads to the discarding of economic humanism and philosophical anthropology in favour of structural categories in Marx's theory of capitalist ground rent. This is also true of the classical concept of feudal rent, whose theoretical prerequisites are intrinsically linked with the discursive primacy of the category of value in the conceptualization of the capitalist mode of production. In fact, the classical dichotomy of capitalism/pre-capitalism based on separation/non-separation cannot be sustained if the structural category of possession in separation is considered as the basis for the conceptualization of the processes of the formation and appropriation of economic property in land. This issue will be considered in some detail in the final section of this chapter.

It may therefore justifiably be argued, in contrast to the structuralist conception of Marx's theoretical development, that there are two distinct and competing conceptions of economic property and ownership present in the discourse of *Capital*: the anthropological and the structural, emanating respectively from the labour of the human subject (labour of transformation) on the one hand, and from the structure of the relations of production signified by the concept of possession in separation on the other. Structural Marxism, too, inherits from Marx this dual theoretical legacy. In fact, the Althusserian crusade against theoretical humanism, the 'practical ideology' of 'socialist humanism', in favour of the supposedly scientific and non-ideological character of Marx's post-1848 writings, meets its limitations in the structuralist adaptation and reworking of the basic concepts of historical materialism.[11] The general concept of the mode of production is the case in point. Balibar's reformulation of the concept in *Reading Capital*, considered in some detail in the previous chapter, argues for the primacy of relations over forces of production in the structure of the concept; a necessary theoretical provision for the structuralist political project of returning to Lenin, the designated exemplar of a genuine anti-humanist, anti-economist Marxism. Yet, as was shown, the assertion of the primacy of the labour of transformation by Balibar in effect reinstates the human subject as the source of economic property prior to the formation of the relations of production. The theoretical consequences of this position, in particular with respect to the conceptualization of the structure of pre-capitalist modes of production, have already been considered in some detail.

It should, however, be noted that the protagonists of structural Marxism were by no means unaware of the problems posed by the persistence of philosophical anthropology in the discourse of the 'mature Marx', in particular in *Capital*. Although the concept of the 'epistemological break' largely obscured the real extent of the 'deformation' of the structural categories of the relations of production in *Capital*, Althusser nonetheless does address the problem of the 'subject' in Marx's discourse, as his attempts to reconstruct the Marxist theories of history and ideology demonstrate. Althusser's concepts of the 'process without a subject' and 'interpellation', intended to abolish/explain the status of the human subject in the theories of history and ideology, signify a *de facto* admission of the persistence of philosophical anthropology in the discourse of the mature Marx. But conceptual means borrowed from Spinozist philosophy and Lacanian psychoanalysis (as he admits himself) fail to serve the intended purpose: to account for the obliteration and internalization of the subject within the structures of history and the social totality.

However, it is not my intention here to dwell on the underlying reasons for the failure of the structuralist theoretical project, but to emphasize its subsequent significance, in giving rise to radical critical trends which began to question the logical consistency of the major concepts of Marxist theory. The problematization of the classical Marxist concepts of the pre-capitalist relations of production, and the subsequent attempts to conceptualize feudal rent as an economic category, briefly indicated in previous chapters, should be seen within such a context. It is to the consideration of this issue that we shall now turn.

I have already referred to Hindess and Hirst's critique of the structuralist reconstruction of the Marxist theory of the modes of production on several occasions. The critique begins with a rejection of the general concept of the mode of production and, in a subsequent study, develops into a refutation of the concept of the mode of production in general. Hindess and Hirst's break with the discourse of *Reading Capital* signifies a process of gradual departure from structural causality and the rationalist epistemology in which it is grounded, initiated by a problematization of the concept of non-economic coercion. The gradual character of their break with the discourse of *Reading Capital* is significant, and should be emphasized particularly with regard to the conceptualization of feudal rent as an economic category. In fact, as will be shown in the following section, the developments and changes in the theoretical prerequisite of an economic concept of rent in the writings of Hindess and Hirst are clearly inseparably linked with their critique of and break with the discourse of *Reading Capital*.

In *Pre-Capitalist Modes of Production* (*PCMP* hereafter) Hindess and Hirst begin by problematizing the classical Marxist concept of non-economic coercion, focusing on the nature of control over land in the process of production. The concept, they maintain, involves a serious conflation of the relations of production with their non-economic conditions of existence; a fundamental error which completely obscures the economic role of the landlord in the process of production. The landlord's control is not derived from his effective possession of the land but from the politico-legal relations of ownership ascribed to him through his status in the hierarchy of political power. But while Hindess and Hirst thus reject the concept of non-economic coercion, they fail to identify or emphasize the intrinsic relationship between that concept and the primacy of the categories of labour and value in Marx's discourse. Consequently, in the discourse of *PCMP* we encounter a concept of feudal ground rent based on the separation of the direct producer from the land (*PCMP* pp.223–233), alongside a concept of capitalist ground rent defined in terms of the juridico-political relations of monopoly ownership of the land by the land-owning class, as the survival of the feudal past (ibid. pp.184–190). The underlying reason for this apparent paradox is the authors' uncritical approach to the mode of conceptualization of economic class relations in the discourse of *Capital*, which is also a characteristic feature of the discourse of *Reading Capital*. The concept of possession in separation, the proposed basis for an economic concept of feudal rent in *PCMP*, is taken in isolation from the effects of the category of value on the conceptualization of the forms of economic property and ownership in *Capital*. The economic concept of feudal rent outlined in *PCMP* remains distinctly at odds with the main body of its theoretical discourse, which is still largely structuralist, and is firmly grounded in the rationalist epistemology of *Reading Capital*. This point, important as it is, is almost invariably overlooked by critics of the theoretical position of *PCMP*.

In *Mode of Production and Social Formation* (hereafter *MPSF*) and subsequent works, notably *Marx's Capital and Capitalism Today*, by contrast, the theoretical arguments for an economic concept of rent are based on a sustained critique of structural causality and the rationalist epistemology of *Reading Capital*. In the discourse of *MPSF*, the critique of the concept of non-economic coercion is an integral part of the general theoretical position. Here the notion of non-separation, the foundation of the classical Marxist concept of pre-capitalist relations of production in general, is conceived as a necessary effect of the primacy of the category of value in the discourse of *Capital*, informing Marx's conceptualization of the structure of the capitalist mode of production. The problematization and rejection of the notion of non-economic coercion thus follows from the rejection of the category of value and the associated forms of economic class relations in Marxist theory. The concept of possession in separation in the discourse of *MPSF* presupposes forms of economic class relations which are not confined to the immediate process of production as such, that is, a process defined by the activity of the labour of transformation. The result is therefore the crucial inclusion of the exchange relations entailed in rent form and merchant's capital in the concept of the feudal relations of production. In the final section of this chapter, the implications for an economic concept of feudal rent of Hindess and Hirst's break with the discourse of *Reading Capital* will be considered in some detail, beginning with an examination of the concept of feudal rent in *PCMP*.

The main argument in *PCMP* is concerned with the discursive incoherency of the classical concepts of pre-capitalist modes of production, an incoherency resulting from the specificity of the relations of production characteristic of these modes. The concept of non-separation in classical Marxist discourse, it is maintained, is not theorized but asserted to highlight the specificity of the capitalist relations of production; it does not in itself entail the economic conditions which ensure the subsumption of the direct producer in the process of production. The result is a non-correspondence between the forces and relations of production: the structures of pre-capitalist modes are characterized by a disjunction between property relations and the unit of production, the former failing to subordinate the latter to their effects. Hence the necessity of non-economic, legal/political relations, so as to ensure the reproduction of the process of production as a process of exploitation. The discursive incoherency of the pre-capitalist modes, argue Hindess and Hirst, is thus rectified by incorporating the conditions of existence of the relations of production into the structure of the concept. In the case of the feudal mode, for example, relations of domination and subordination, the legal/political conditions of existence of the feudal relations of production, are an integral part of the definition of the concept. They are, more often than not, conceived as structural relations identical with feudal relations of production.

Marx's conceptualization of feudal rent in *Capital* (Vol.III, Chapter XLVII) is then taken as a case to illustrate this argument. Marx, according to Hindess and Hirst, provides for the economic subsumption of the direct producer through, first, feudal landed property, and second, the exchange relations entailed in the form of appropriation of rent. These elements, it is maintained, can provide the theoretical basis necessary for the construction of an economic concept of feudal rent. But Marx subverts this possibility by subordinating them to the effects of the notion of non-separation and the associated forms of property relations. Consequently, in Marx's conceptualization, feudal landed property is reduced to the effect of the relations of domination and subordination, and the form of appropriation of rent to the theoretical appendage of a non-economic mode of exploitation. Hindess and Hirst thus conclude:

> The pre-condition of subsumption of the direct-producer within the relations of production, which constitutes the process of production as a process of exploitation, is some form of separation of the direct-producer from the means of production. (*PCMP* p.229)

They thus argue for a concept of feudal rent involving the total or partial separation of the direct producer from the means of production. The emphasis, however, is on the separation from the land as the main means of production. The effective possession of land by the land-owning class is the essential condition for the existence of feudal rent.

The argument for an economic concept of feudal rent is thus further qualified in the context of a reconsideration of the role of the landlord in the process of production, which involves a corresponding reconsideration of the nature of control over land. The landlord's control over the land, Hindess and Hirst argue, cannot be sustained by the juridico-political relations of ownership alone; it requires a direct relationship between the landlord and the process of production sustained by two elements: first, rights of ownership over the land, which amounts to the capacity to exclude other economic agents from utilizing it in the process of production; and second, the form in which those rights of ownership over the land become economically effective, that is, the exchange relations entailed in the mode of appropriation of rent. The first element refers to the 'rights of exclusion' which result from positing the land, the object of ownership, in the process of production, while the second denotes the means of exercising control over the process of utilization of the land in the process of production. In this sense the possession of the land by the land-owning class is necessary but not sufficient for the existence of feudal rent. It provides the conditions for the extraction of rent but does not ensure its realization, which takes place through the exchange relations entailed in the mode of appropriation of rent; this may or may not involve recourse to the market for agricultural products (*PCMP* pp.234–5).

According to this argument, the land-owning class plays an active role in the process of production, through its control over the land as the necessary means of production. The elements which ensure this control are fundamentally obscured by asserting the non-separation of the direct producer from the land. They involve economic class relations similar to those entailed in the capitalist relations of production in *Capital*. The effective control of the land by the landlord, like the control of capital by the capitalist, presupposes its separation from the direct producers. The possession of and separation from the land therefore constitutes the structure of the production relations which, in turn, determine the boundaries of the unit of production and specify the mode of economic calculation operative within it. So conceived, feudal relations of production subordinate the labour process to their effects and specify the limit for the development of the forces of production within it. It follows that the correspondence between the forces and relations of production is a necessary consequence of the economic intervention in and control of the process of production by the land-owning class, consistent with its effective possession of the land as the primary means of production (ibid.).

For Hindess and Hirst, therefore, the separation of the direct producer from the means of production and the correlative economic role of the landlord in the process of production are essential theoretical prerequisites of an economic concept of feudal rent. The separation of the direct producer, his economic subsumption in the process of production, they emphasize, is not given. Rather, it requires the intervention of the landlord in the process of production and, as such, depends upon definite forms of economic policy and calculation on his part which continuously sustain and reproduce the structure of separation as a structure of exploitation. Economic subsumption is thus the object of the struggle between the landlord and the tenant/direct producer, centred on the relations of exploitation within and without the process of production. It is the primary form of class struggle in feudal social formation, and the continuity of this struggle ensures the effective possession characteristic of feudal landed property (ibid. pp.249–255).

The economic intervention of the landlord ensures the conditions for the continuous subsumption-separation of the direct producer. The landlord controls the size, the character and the reproduction of the unit of production by controlling the conditions of tenancy. He is thus capable of ensuring a correspondence between the reproduction of the means and conditions of production and the reproduction of the relations of exploitation, that is to say a coincidence between relations of tenancy and rent relations. In this sense, conclude Hindess and Hirst, feudal rent constitutes at once the form and the condition of existence of exploitation. It rests upon and sustains the continuous separation of the direct producers from the means of production (ibid. p.235).

However, Hindess and Hirst's conceptualization of the structure of the feudal mode of production in *PCMP* is not entirely consistent with the theoretical presupposition of their economic concept of rent. Here the boundaries of the feudal labour process, whether demesne or peasant holding, are defined by the productive functions of the 'independent' direct producers, which also specify the limits for the development of productive forces. They thus argue:

> The development of the forces of production in the FMP [feudal mode of production] is therefore limited to developing the productivity of the labour of the tenant within the *limits* set by independent peasant production. (ibid. p.246, emphasis in original)

It is clear that this conception of an independent peasant production specifying the development of the forces of production is inconsistent with the theoretical presuppositions of an economic concept of feudal rent, since, by definition, it excludes the forms of economic class relations entailed in the economic concept of rent. The fact that the notion of independent peasant production excludes economic class relations based on possession in separation from the land is clearly demonstrated by the associated conception of the forces of production. Hindess and Hirst's conception of the feudal forces of production here does not include the landlord, and his functions are considered irrelevant to the reproduction of the unit of production. Hence the persistence of the disjunction between the relations and unit of production characteristic of the classical Marxist concept of the feudal mode of production.

The theoretical inconsistencies of the discourse of *PCMP*, I would thus argue, primarily signify the persistence of the structural causality and the rationalist epistemology of *Reading Capital* in the discourse of *PCMP*. The discursive primacy of the category of labour which informs the general theoretical framework of *PCMP* undermines the attempt to appreciate fully the theoretical consequences of the rejection of the concept of non-separation. The inconsistencies entailed in the conceptualization of the structure of the feudal mode in *PCMP*, like the definition of the concept of capitalist ground rent already noted in this chapter, mark, above all, the confused nature of its critique of the discourse of *Reading Capital*. An appreciation of the theoretical consequences of the concept of possession in separation for the conceptualization of the structure of the feudal economic form, as is indicated in *MPSF* and subsequent works, presupposes the rejection of the discursive primacy of the categories of labour and value.

It should be noted here that these inconsistencies in the theoretical position of *PCMP* have been identified by a number of critics.[12] But these critics, with the notable exception of Martin, are not concerned with the theoretical implications of the rejection of the concept of non-separation. For the most part they address instead the consistency of the concepts of particular modes of production with the theoretical propositions which follow from the rejection of the general concept of the mode of production in the discourse of *PCMP*. Asad and Wolpe, for example, charge Hindess and Hirst with failing to retain the dominance of the relations over the forces of production in their conceptualization of the structure of the feudal mode of production. The specificity of the feudal labour process, argue these critics, is not derived from the corresponding relations of production, but is largely arbitrary, and as such it renders difficult, if not impossible, the concept of an articulated feudal structure (Asad and Wolpe 1976). Taylor, on the other hand, is mostly concerned with the concept of the Asiatic mode of production. The rejection of this concept, he claims, signifies a lapse into theoretical formalism—an 'all-purpose' charge seemingly referring to the mode in which the theoretical status and validity of the concepts of the modes of production in *PCMP* is investigated (Taylor 1975–6). The point here, however, is that the critics of the theoretical position of *PCMP* fail to appreciate the theoretical significance of its critique of the concept of non-separation. This significance is largely obscured by an inordinate concentration on its rejection of the general concept of the mode of production.

Martin's work, in this respect, is an exception. Pursuing a different line of argument, he focuses on the theorization of the structure of the feudal economic form in *PCMP*, and attributes its inconsistencies to an inadequate conception of the separation of the direct producers from the means of production. The case in point is the theorization of the feudal unit of production and the nature of the forces operative within it, already discussed in some detail in previous pages. Partial separation from the means of production—notably separation from the land, as emphasized in *PCMP*—is necessary but not sufficient to ensure the subsumption of the direct producers in the process of production (Martin 1986, p.14). Hindess and Hirst, maintains Martin, place 'inordinate emphasis upon land as a means of production', at the cost of neglecting 'to examine sufficiently the impact of the landlord's ownership and control of means of production other than land' (ibid.). Martin thus concludes:

feudal productive forces are structurally determined by the landlord's ownership and control of land and other means of production, and are distinctive to the FMP. The limits of these productive forces are defined by *the combination of the agents in the labour process*, as structured by the feudal relations of production, rather than by independent peasant production as Hindess and Hirst suggest. (ibid. pp.15–16, emphasis in original)

Following Hindess and Hirst, Martin argues that the continuous separation of the direct producer from the means of production is sustained by the extraction of rent sufficient to prevent the tenants from becoming autonomous producers. But this separation, according to Martin, should include all the means of production necessary for the functioning of the process of production. Thus a level of rent defined by the right of exclusion is necessary but insufficient to reproduce the feudal relations of production. It ensures only a *partial* separation from the land, which is not on its own sufficient to sustain the economic subsumption of the direct producers on a continuous basis. Martin, therefore, argues for *total* rather than *partial* separation. The direct producers should be separated from all the means of production if the reproduction of the feudal relations of production is to be ensured (ibid. p.16).

Martin is concerned here with separation from the 'ancillary' means of production which, he maintains, is necessary to ensure the level of rent required for the reproduction of the feudal relations of production—'ancillary' means referring to a variety of elements such as seed, draught animals, mills and working capital, all necessary for the reproduction of the feudal unit of production. But consideration of a separation from the ancillary means as such poses a number of problems for the conceptualization of the structure of the feudal relations of production. The first and most important issue is the question of ownership. Ownership of the ancillary means varies widely in different social formations. The landlord may not always be the sole owner of the ancillary means of production; indeed in most cases they are owned in part either by the direct producers, or by a third agent with no direct function in the immediate process of production—the merchant, the local money-lender, the mill-owner or the local holder of the draught animals. Secondly, the provision of the ancillary means to the process of production, especially seed and

draught animals, is generally subject tõ cultural relations, i.e. the rule
of tradition and of ancient customs, which vary widely not only from
one social formation to another but also within a social formation
from one locality to another. Given these conditions, the relevance of
the ancillary means to the structure of the feudal economic form is
conjunctural, depending on a variety of historical, cultural, geographic-
climatic and ideological conditions. Separation from the ancillary
means, important as it is, cannot therefore be considered as an
invariant in the definition of the structure of the feudal relations of
production.

Martin, however, seems to be aware of the problems which the
separation from the ancillary means poses for the conceptualization of
the feudal relations of exploitation. This separation, he suggests,
induces *non-rental* as opposed to *rental* forms of exploitation, resulting
from possession in separation from the land. To explain the
conditions of the ancillary separation and the associated mechanism
of exploitation, Martin introduces the concept of 'denial of possession'.

This concept of 'denial of possession' denotes a mode of separation
engendered by 'additional' political conditions: that is, additional
to the economic conditions which generate the separation of the
direct producer from the land. The mechanism of exploitation
entailed in the 'denial of possession' is non-rental and is sustained by
extra-economic coercion. Martin, nevertheless, insists that the
additional political conditions—hence the non-economic mechanism
of exploitation—in fact have economic foundations and rest on
explicit economic relations. He argues that the additional political
relations affecting ancillary separation constitute a 'secondary'
condition of existence, and as such are based on the 'right of
exclusion' which forms the basis for the primary separation of the
direct producer from the land. The 'denial of possession' is thus
effected through the right of exclusion, and the separation from the
ancillary means depends strictly on the separation from the primary
means (ibid. p.16).

Martin's argument here is reminiscent of the justifications of the
concept of the non-economic mode of exploitation in classical
Marxism; justifications which depend primarily on the classical thesis
of 'determination in the last instance by the economy'. The additional
political relations which induce ancillary separation are *simultaneously*
the conditions of existence and the effects of that primary separation

which, he admits, constitutes the structure of the feudal relations of production. Ancillary separation is not only associated with primary separation but is constituted by it. The non-rental forms of exploitation, the assumed secondary conditions of existence, are inconceivable without a continuous process of the rental form of exploitation. In fact the former presupposes the latter, without which it cannot exist as a mode of extraction of surplus from the direct producers. If, however, the persistence of the ancillary separation depends on the continuity of the primary separation, it would be more appropriate to define it as the effect rather than as the conditions of existence of feudal relations of production. In this sense, Martin's concept of the denial of possession as the secondary conditions of existence of feudal relations of production cannot be sustained.

Further, Martin's insistence on total rather than partial separation means that non-rental forms of exploitation should be conceived as an invariant in the structure of feudal relations of production. The structural conception of non-rental relations of exploitation leads to further problems if we bear in mind that these relations were generated by the additional political relations defined as the secondary conditions of existence of the feudal relations of production. Conceptually, this apparent paradox is accounted for by incorporating the additional political conditions into the structure of the concept of feudal rent, whereby the 'real' economic nature of the non-economic, political relations of exploitation is explained in terms of an essence and its phenomenal expressions. Martin's economic concept of rent, like the classical concept, signifies a self-contained structure, including both the feudal relations of production and their conditions of existence. Although Martin does not refer to a determination in the last instance by the economy, his essentialist explanation of the 'real' economic nature of non-economic relations of exploitation presupposes an element of that reductionism which is characteristic of the classical thesis.

There is no doubt that the separation of the direct producer from the ancillary means of production can significantly affect the level of ground rent. But ancillary separation as such cannot be conceived as an invariant of an economic concept of feudal rent. Further, the separation from the primary means of production, i.e. the land—the partial separation proposed in *PCMP*—suffices to ensure the reproduction of the feudal relations of production which, by definition, exclude any notion of an autonomous unit of production. For whatever the level of ground rent extracted from the direct producers, the reproduction of the unit of production and the pertinent forms of economic calculation will depend on the distribution of the land owned by the landlord. Separation from the ancillary means may well be a direct effect of this primary separation, and in certain conditions total rather than partial separation may be the dominant form. These conditions, however, are not in contradiction with an economic concept of rent based on partial separation. The political conditions which engender ancillary separation are indeed the conditions of existence of the feudal relations of production. But they should not be conceived as part of the definition of the concept of feudal ground rent. Their relevance to the structure of the feudal relations of production is conjunctural, depending on a variety of non-structural factors. In fact, Martin creates an insurmountable theoretical problem by assigning a structural status to feudal political relations. These relations by definition escape the forms of economic identity which Martin strives to assign to them, no matter how complex the medium of reduction in his analysis.

There are admittedly problems with Hindess and Hirst's theorization of the feudal economic structure in *PCMP*. But these problems do not concern the extent of separation from the means of production; rather they signify the continuing influence of the discourse of *Reading Capital* on the theoretical position of *PCMP*, as the authors have acknowledged in subsequent works. The rejection of the general concept of the mode of production in *PCMP* did not amount to the disappearance of structural causality and its epistemological foundation. Nor did the refutation of the non-economic concept of pre-capitalist relations of production lead to the refutation of the conceptions of forces and relations of production entailed in the discourse of *Reading Capital*. Hindess and Hirst's initial attempt to theorize feudal rent as an economic category clearly demonstrates the characteristic features of a structuralist reading of *Capital*. The discourse of *PCMP*, it was pointed out, falls short of uncovering the crucial link between the concept of non-separation and the primacy of the categories of labour and value in Marx's discourse; hence the authors' uncritical approach to the anthropological conceptions of economic property and ownership associated with the category of value, and the subsequent deformation of the categories of the relations of production in *Capital*—their proposed model for the construction of the concept of feudal rent as an economic category.

It is important here to consider Keith Tribe's contribution to the analysis and development of the Marxist theory of rent. Tribe, in his critique of Marx's theory of capitalist ground rent, focuses on the persistence of philosophical anthropology and its deformation of the categories of production relations in *Capital*. This critique is developed in the context of the conceptual framework of structural Marxism, and in fact, his early work (Tribe 1976) is largely informed by the theoretical position of *PCMP*; his later works show the influence of the critical theoretical currents within and without structural Marxism, with British post-structuralist thought remaining the main influence (Tribe 1977, 1978).

In his early encounter with Marx's theory of capitalist ground rent (Tribe 1976), Tribe acknowledges the theoretical difficulties that 'natural resources' pose for Marxist economic theory. Here he argues that the conditions of formation and appropriation of property entailed in Marx's analysis of capitalist relations of production in *Capital* should also be applied to the conceptualization of capitalist ground rent, since, according to Tribe, Marx's refusal to validate land as a commodity arises from the persistence of philosophical anthropology in the discourse of *Capital*. He further associates this with the privileged status of the category of labour in Marx's discourse, but does not elaborate on the theoretical possibilities of extending the argument to Marx's conceptualization of the pre-capitalist economic forms.

This neglect of pre-capitalist relations arises from the inordinate emphasis in his argument on the concept of the capitalist commodity as the main obstacle to the theorization of capitalist ground rent as an economic category: an argument elaborated in some detail in a further study of the conditions of formation and appropriation of capitalist rent (Tribe 1977). This study relates the inconsistencies of Marx's theory of rent to his labour theory of value, and argues for the rejection of that theory as a necessary condition for the conceptualization of rent as an economic category based on possession in separation from the land. Capitalist rent, argues Tribe, is inscribed within the distribution and circulation mechanisms of agrarian capitalism, and depends strictly on the continuity of capitalist production, which ensures the purchase and the sale as commodities of rights of ownership over the land. These rights are vested in particular categories of economic agents who, by virtue of their possession of land, appropriate ground rent. The emphasis on the

economic character of this exchange—rights of land-use in return for
a portion of surplus as rent—between landlord and capitalist is
essential, since it generates the elements constituting the structure of
agrarian capitalism, in which ground rent is the dominant economic
category and signifies the mode of appropriation of surplus (Tribe
1977).

The crux of Tribe's argument is the conception of rights as
commodities, as objects of exchange subject to the general rules of
economic exchange and circulation like any other commodity in the
market. This conception undermines the classical definition of rent as
the price paid for the right to use the land. It also entails a total
repudiation of the category of value and of the associated conception
of economic property and ownership. Tribe terms his. analysis the
'second revision' of the classical theory of rent, thus implying a
modification if not a refutation of the first revision: the theoretical
possibilities entailed in the discourse of *PCMP* which informed his
earlier reading and critique of the classical Marxist theory of rent.

Tribe's 'second revision', in effect, argues for the development of
these theoretical possibilities, much in line with the positions adopted
in *MPSF* and the subsequent works of Hindess and Hirst, in
particular *Marx's Capital and Capitalism Today*. The argument for the
'second revision' appeared in the same year as Hindess and Hirst's
auto-critique of *PCMP*, and it is thus not clear whether it was
informed by or simply anticipated the theoretical position of the auto-
critique; but this is not the concern of the present study. The point
here is that Tribe's position on pre-capitalist forms of rent is not
consistent with the theoretical prerequisites of his proposed second
revision. In fact, in so far as the conceptualization of the conditions of
formation and appropriation of economic property requisite for the
concept of feudal rent is concerned, Tribe's analysis falls behind
PCMP.

Tribe denies the possibility of constructing an economic concept of
feudal rent. For him, feudal rent is a form of revenue, subject to the
determinations of the political: an effect of the relations of lordship
and servitude entailed in the structure of the feudal relations of
production (Tribe 1977 p.86). But this is simply a reiteration of the
classical Marxist concept of feudal rent, which presupposes conceptions of economic property and ownership already repudiated by
Tribe as the main obstacles to the construction of an economic
concept of capitalist rent in *Capital*. In fact, Tribe adopts a

paradoxical position in this respect. He rejects the category of value and the conceptions of economic property and exchange relations it entails, while retaining the notion of non-separation as the foundation of economic property and production relations in the feudal economic form. In Tribe's reading of Marx, there seems to be no connection between the conceptualizations of the capitalist and pre-capitalist relations of production. The root of this apparent paradox in Tribe's theorization of the conditions of formation and appropriation of property should be sought in his analysis of the conditions of the formation of classical economic discourse; an analysis which, I shall argue, involves conceptions of capitalism and pre-capitalism defined by the separation and non-separation of the direct producer from the means of production. The transition from the latter to the former, conceived as the effect of the developing structure of commodity relations in eighteenth century England, is presented as the necessary condition for the formation of an economic discourse; that is, for the constitution of economics as an independent field of investigation with specified boundaries, distinct from other discourses and disciplines, especially politics. It will be shown that in Tribe's work the conditions of formation of this economic discourse and the emergence of capitalist ground rent are conceived as parallel processes with a uniform structure/history, namely the constitution of land as a commodity, subject to the rule of economic exchange in a market with specified legal boundaries (Tribe 1978 pp.24–34).

According to Tribe, the concept of rent is central to the formation of economic discourse in the eighteenth and nineteenth centuries. Rent, Tribe maintains, signifies a structure of social relations which 'simultaneously unites and divides land and labour in economic discourse' (ibid.). Rent, nevertheless, is not a uniform category, historically or theoretically. It presupposes different conditions of existence and realization in different economic forms, i.e. different forms of landed property and mechanisms of appropriation. In pre-capitalist economic forms, Tribe goes on, the notion of property basically refers to the right to revenue from the land as an economic object, and as such, it excludes reference to the economic object itself. Under feudalism land is an appendage of the relations of domination and subordination which define the form of feudal ownership in the first place. In the capitalist form, by contrast, the notion of property designates an economic object with the rights of appropriation and disposal specified in that object.

Tribe's detailed discussion of the diverse conceptions of landed property under feudalism and capitalism is intended to serve a double purpose. First, it suggests that rent as a structure of social relations does not have a unitary origin. The modern conception of property (economic object plus rights of ownership specified in it) is intrinsically related to the birth and development of the capitalist economic form, and to read this conception back into preceding social and economic orders seriously obscures their nature. This argument is mobilized to reject the possibility of constructing a history of rent.[13] Secondly, Tribe uses the argument about the diversification of the conception of landed property to substantiate his main thesis, which concerns the relevance of the category of capitalist rent to the formation of the economic discourse in eighteenth-century England (ibid.).

In Tribe's account, the diversification of the notion of property occurs basically during the eighteenth century, a period which also marks the formation of the economic discourse. This double process is discursively united by the notion of rent. During this period we witness the 'gravitation' of the economic discourse towards the land, and rent is conceived as a contractual relationship between 'free' economic agents. It signifies a payment for land-use whose level is determined by the price of the commodities produced on that land (ibid. p.27). This situation, Tribe further maintains, represents a radical departure from the hitherto prevalent conception of ground rent. Before this period, especially under feudalism, 'this precise formation in which land worked by labour bears a specific rent' did not apply and rent denoted a 'dislocation from the land and the gravitation of the referent of rent to labour' (ibid.). Its level, in this case, 'had little or nothing to do with the price of saleable agricultural produce, or even with the extent of land occupied'. It was 'unified not by the relation of landlord, tenant and land, but rather by the relation of landlord and tenant with land as an appendage'. Tribe thus concludes that 'feudal rent is in fact not a rent of land but is an expression of the subordination of feudal labour'; that is, an expression of the 'personal dependence' of the tenant on the landlord, which is 'conditional' in nature: 'it can only be effected via a territorial basis such that the possession and occupation of land is determined according to relations of superiority and subordination with which it is associated but of which it is not constitutive' (ibid. pp.24–30).

Tribe's definition, which is further substantiated in the context of his analysis of the structure of the feudal manor (ibid. pp.31–34), simply reiterates the primacy of the political in the conceptualization of the feudal relations of production. His retreat to the classical Marxist definition, and his departure from the theoretical premises of his second revision of the classical theory, above all signify the theoretical limitations of his analysis of the formation of the economic discourse. Despite his claim to the contrary, Tribe's analysis presupposes a relationship of correspondence between the economic discourse and the non-discursive conditions of its formation: conditions which underlie the diversification of property and the subsequent gravitation of the referent of rent from labour to land. These conditions are conceived in terms of the relationship of the labourer to the land. Hence the necessity of the notion of non-separation for his analysis of the formation of the economic discourse which centres on the concept of rent as a contractual relation among free economic agents.

Tribe's analysis of the conditions of formation of economic discourse, then, presupposes the classical dichotomy of capitalism/ pre-capitalism based on the separation/non-separation of the direct producers from the means of production. The point, however, is that the theoretical presuppositions of this 'revision' of Marx's theory of capitalist rent and his conceptualization of the conditions of formation of economic discourse are mutually exclusive: the former amounts to a rejection of the primacy of the categories of labour and value, while the latter presupposes it. His conception of feudal rent entails a conflation of the feudal relations of production with their non-economic conditions of existence. The relations of domination and subordination are central to his definition of the concept of feudal rent, a definition which excludes the crucial distinction between the process of formation and of appropriation of property, even though Tribe maintains that such a distinction is essential for the problematization of the status of the human subject and of the anthropological conceptions of economy and property (Tribe 1977 p.84).

Let us now return to a consideration of the theoretical prerequisites of an economic concept of feudal rent. As I have pointed out, Hindess and Hirst acknowledge the theoretical limitations of the discourse of *PCMP* in their subsequent works. The concept of non-separation is further scrutinized in the context of an overall reassessment of the discourse of *Capital* (Cutler et al. Vol.I 1977 pp.243–62). The critique of the concept of non-separation, in this context, is not an isolated moment but an integral part of a general critique of the discursive primacy of the category of labour in *Capital* and of its consequences for the conceptualization of property relations. The category of value and the associated conceptions of economic property and exchange, it is argued, at once presuppose and sustain a rigid distinction between capitalism and pre-capitalism based on their modes of exploitation: economic/separation, non-economic/non-separation. This argument—and above all, the concept of 'possession in separation'—has important implications for the theoretical requisites of an economic concept of feudal rent proposed in *PCMP*.

Before elaborating on the concept of possession in separation from the land, which is the outcome of a series of economic exchanges among the economic agents in the process of production, it is necessary here to say a few words about the notions of economic exchange, the economic agent and the process of production employed in this context. The rejection of the primacy of the category of labour in discourse means that human labour, i.e. the labour of transformation, no longer validates economic objects as objects of exchange. Nor does it define the character of economic agents as labourers and non-labourers. Both economic objects as objects of exchange and economic agents as bearers of exchange relations are constituted in the process of production as the process of exploitation, the boundaries of which are not defined by the labour of transformation, but by the relations governing the distribution of the means of production to the unit of production and the distribution of the product from the unit of production to the social formation at large. In this sense, however, economic agents and economic objects, as agents and objects of possession in separation, are not confined to the immediate process of production, i.e. the unit of production. They are located in the process of production which comprises spheres of distribution, production and exchange, and the circulation of products, and which is the focus of economic class relations. For example, according to this definition, exchange relations are to be conceived as an integral part of feudal relations of production, and the merchant's capital, when active in the completion of the process of production as such, as an economic agent, the bearer of feudal class relations.[14] The process of the production, extraction and realization of feudal rent may involve more than two categories of economic agents, depending on their contribution to the distribution of the means of production necessary for the functioning of the feudal unit of production; that is, depending on their possession in separation from that means of production.

In the feudal economic form, it was argued, possession in separation from the land, the primary possession, is sufficient to generate the level of ground rent necessary for the reproduction of the feudal economic-class relations. Possession in separation from the land as such involves the economic subsumption of the direct producer in the process of production as the foundation of feudal landed property. This conception of feudal landed property has further implications for the conceptualization of juridico-political relations of ownership in the feudal social formation. True, the juridico-political relations of private property-ownership are consequences of the mode of distribution of political power in feudal social formations. They are in fact constituted by it. These relations, nevertheless, should not be conceived as constitutive of the processes of the formation and appropriation of property in land, but rather as providing the non-economic conditions of existence of the process of formation of economic property in land—that is, in so far as they define the conditions of formation of the legal subject with the title to the land. The processes of the formation and appropriation of economic property, on the other hand, involve the economic subsumption of the direct producer in the process of production through the exchange relations entailed in the rent-form. While the economic relations involved in the processes of the formation and of appropriation of landed property are invariants of the definition of feudal rent as an economic category, the juridico-political relations of ownership, the conditions of constitution of the legal subject with the title to the land, are external to it. The juridico-political conditions of the specification of title to the land are not part of the definition of rent as an economic category. The production relations generated by possession in separation from the land suffice to subordinate the feudal labour process to their effects and to ensure the reproduction of feudal economic class relations.

Feudal landed property thus rests not on the legally-politically defined relations of lordship and servitude, but on the economic relations of the subsumption of the direct producer in the process of production. The relations of domination and subordination, legally defined or not, are not invariants of the conditions of formation of feudal landed property, but are associated with it. The association, however, is 'historical-conjunctural' and as such varies widely, in form and in content, depending on the exigencies of the political class struggle between the landlord and the peasants. Peasant dependency, in this sense, is not a logical extension of the mode of distribution of political power, but an outcome of the political class struggle between the two major classes in feudal social formations. The economic compulsion entailed in the separation of the direct producers from the land alone suffices to ensure the appropriation of surplus by their overlords.

The economic concept of rent, as such, thus presupposes a clear distinction between the processes of the formation and the appropriation of landed property. In other words, it presupposes a distinction between the process of the constitution of the subject with rights over the land, and the process of the transformation of legal rights to economic relations. The title to the land, legal property, is constituted politically and assigns to the holder the 'right of exclusion', that is, the right to exclude the direct producers from its use in the process of production: legal separation. It is the necessary legal-political condition of the economic process of the separation of the direct producer from the land, his subsumption to the relations of production as relations of exploitation: the real subsumption of the direct producer in the process of economic production. The landlord, by virtue of the rights entailed in his title to the land, possesses the capacity to control both the direct producer's access to the means of production, and the conditions necessary for the reproduction of the means of production. This, however, signifies only the landlord's potential powers, which can be realized through the exchange relations entailed in rent-form. The legal rights of ownership over land as rights of exclusion define the mode of extraction of surplus, i.e. the rent-form. They do not ensure the conditions necessary for the extraction of surplus in rent-form. This is ensured by means of the economic exchange relations entailed in the rent-form. In this sense, the concept of feudal ground rent signifies at once the form and the condition of existence of the relations of exploitation in the feudal economic form. It engenders the separation of the direct producer from the land, and reproduces that separation as the essential condition of its own existence.[15]

The economic concept of rent defined as such presupposes a notion of feudal landed property based on the economic subsumption of the direct producer in the process of production. This subsumption of the direct producer requires economic relations of possession in separation which cannot be derived from the right of exclusion entailed in the juridico-political relations of private property in land.[16] It is thus necessary to make a distinction between the processes of the formation and appropriation of economic property in land so as to avoid the conflation of feudal relations of production with their non-economic conditions of existence—a conflation which, as I have argued, leads to the identification of the economic subject with the human subject alone. It should however be added that, though the economic subsumption of the direct producer is the invariant of feudal landed property, the process of the formation of economic property varies widely from one social formation to another, owing mainly to the multiplicity of the non-economic relations pertaining to the process (a point already considered in the previous chapter). The variation in the conditions of the constitution of the legal title to the land expresses the variation in the modality of the distribution of political power in feudal social formations; while the variation in the form of the extraction of rent signifies the variation in the mode of articulation of the processes of labour and production and the relationship between them. However, the central point to recognise is that all feudal rent is based on landed property, structured by possession in separation from the land. The economic concept of feudal rent so defined has important consequences for the definition of the structure of the feudal economic form.

The Structure of the Feudal Economic Form

The structure of the feudal economic form denotes a combination of relations of production and labour processes. It is constituted by a series of exchange relations which arise from the possession in separation from the land under particular conditions, namely, the *absence* of *markets* with specified legal boundaries for the purchase and sale of *land* on the one hand and *labour power* on the other; that is, the *absence* of generalized commodity production in the structure of the economic form which defines the general conditions of the *economic* processes of the formation and appropriation of property in land in feudal social formations. The relations of production hold the position of dominance in the structure and are capable of subordinating the labour process to their effects, thus defining both the boundaries of the unit of production and the form and the level of development of the forces of production within it. The dominance of the relations of production and the associated mode of causality stem from the possession in separation from the land, which posits rent as the *mode* and *condition* of exploitation in the feudal economic form. Feudal rent is, as such, the direct consequence of the structure of the feudal economic form. The economic concept of rent, therefore, signifies the structure of the feudal economic form in its effects.

The above definition suggests that the conceptualization of the economic structure of Iranian feudalism should begin with a consideration of the theoretical presuppositions of the economic concept of rent outlined in this chapter; feudal landed property and the exchange relations entailed in the rent form. This will form the focus of the following chapters. However, before this, a brief explanation of the focus of analysis is required.

It should be noted that the emphasis on the structure of the feudal economic form, rather than its genesis or evolution, is not arbitrary. The contention is that the structure of the feudal economic form is the outcome of the articulation of elements with diverse histories, not reducible to a common origin. It follows that Iranian feudalism, as an economic form, has neither a unitary origin nor a uniform history which could be traced to the disintegration of a preceding mode of production. The distinction between the origin and structure of the feudal economic form should be particularly emphasized in the context of Iranian history, which, as I have shown, is dominated by the discourse of origins.

PART III

5. LANDED PROPERTY IN PRE-CAPITALIST IRAN

The analysis of the processes of the formation and appropriation of private property in land in pre-capitalist Iran centres on the concept of *iqta*: a form of land grant probably originating in the tenth century, which soon became widespread in the domains of the Eastern Caliphate including Iran.[1] The concept of *iqta*, along with the forms of landed property and the property relations which it signified, has long been at the heart of the controversy over the concept of Iranian feudalism, with opponents and exponents of the concept—as indicated in previous chapters—emphasizing respectively the 'bureaucratic' and the feudal character of *iqta*.

Definitions of *iqta* as a bureaucratic institution, common to all non-feudal characterizations of pre-Constitutional Iran, conceive it as the Iranian variant of a general Islamic form. The generality of the form and the specifically bureaucratic character of *iqta* are both deduced from their common Islamic origin. Islam, it is held, defines the nature of power as absolute and indivisible, thus excluding those forms of authority founded on the division and parcellization of sovereignty. The Islamic polity is accordingly organized around the delegation of authority and a vertical structure of domination and subordination which does not involve reciprocal forms of obligation, contractual or otherwise. It is the temporal manifestation of the universal Islamic dictum that power is sovereign.

It is the negative logic of this essentialist conception of the Islamic polity which informs the historicist conceptions of *iqta* as a bureaucratic institution. The absence of 'contractual relations', the alleged constitutive of feudal landed property in the West, disqualifies *iqta* as landed property. In its various forms, the Islamic *iqta* retains its original bureaucratic character, as 'fiscal licence' to revenue of the land legally owned by the state/sovereign. Conceptions of *iqta* as a

125

bureaucratic institution all presuppose the monopoly ownership of the agricultural land by the state/sovereign and taxation as the mechanism of the appropriation of the surplus product. Both these conditions are implicit in the notion of the common Islamic origin, the assumed constitutive of the Islamic polity as a universal form.

The Concept of *Iqta* as a Bureaucratic Institution

The concept of *iqta* as a bureaucratic institution is the microcosm of a concept of the Islamic state as a military institution, widely held by Western scholars, Marxist and non-Marxist; a concept denoting a monolithic structure, internally undifferentiated and essentially warrior in cast and rationale. The Islamic state, it is argued, is the product of military conquest, constituted by force, which defines the logic of its reproduction and development. The military conception of the state has, of course, older roots and wider application in historical writing, both traditional and modern.[2] It features variously in the studies of pre-capitalist political systems—the so-called empires of force and domination. However, in the context of the Islamic societies the application of the concept differs markedly from its wider usage in histories of pre-capitalist Europe. In the case of the former the concept is marked by subjectivism, deriving from the assumed universal Islamic origin of these societies. Arguments which attribute the monolithic structure and militaristic character of the Islamic state to the specificity of Islam are not new or rare; on the contrary, they are intrinsic to the cultural essentialism which has long informed the established canons of historical research on 'Islamic Society'. In fact, the more recent definitions and usage of the concept of the military state (in Islamic Studies) are merely a revival and reintroduction of the conventional definition into new contexts.

Anderson's discussion of the form and character of the Islamic state and the specificity of its development, in *Lineages of the Absolutist State*, is particularly instructive in this respect. Reviving the conventional definition of the Islamic state in the context of a 'Marxified Weberianism'[3] which is the hallmark of his comparative genealogy of Western and Eastern development, Anderson attempts a negative causal explanation of the genesis of capitalism in the 'Islamic social formations' in terms of the subjective will of the ruling classes of successive Islamic states. The Arab conquerors, Anderson maintains, disdained agriculture and productive activities of all sorts: 'medieval Arab economies . . . always prospered more in the sphere of exchange

than of production, trade than manufactures'. Their 'Turkic successors' on the other hand, did not share 'the traditional Arab esteem for
the merchant' and 'contempt for trade was a general hallmark of the
ruling class of the new states, whose commercial policy was at best
one of tolerance, and at worst one of discrimination against the
mercantile classes in the towns' (Anderson 1974b, p.516). The
subjective will of the Arab and Turkic ruling classes were thus
translated into policies carried out by centralized military states such
as that of the Mongols—the 'principal instrument of economic
exploitation of the ruling class' (ibid. p.520).

The centralized state remains the main force in the chain of this
negative causal explanation of the development of merchant fortunes
into proto-industrial capital in Islamic social formations (ibid. p.520).[4]
Anderson decribes the medieval Islamic state as:

> essentially warrior and plunderer in cast: founded on conquest
> . . . their whole rationale and structure was military. Civilian
> administration proper, as a functional sphere in its own right,
> never became dominant within the ruling class: a scribal
> bureaucracy did not develop much beyond the needs of tax-
> collection. The state machine was largely a consortium of
> professional soldiers, organized either in tightly centralized
> corps or a more diffuse form, in either case customarily
> supported by revenue-assignments from public lands. (ibid.
> p.505)

Anderson's definition of the Islamic state draws on the constituent
elements of conventional military conceptions of the state in ancient
empires. He considers military force and conquest as central to the
constitution of the state and the dynamics of its development, shaping
its political form and geographic boundaries. Military force, Anderson
contends, enables the state to function as a tributary structure
mediating between agrarian production in the countryside and the
network of surplus appropriation in the urban centres. The tributary
function, while enhancing the military character of the Islamic state,
prevents the emergence of economic class relations in agriculture.

The tripartite relationship and the tributary function of the military
state are reflected in the specific structure of the Islamic *iqta*. Arab
iqta, the precursor of the later Ottoman *timar* or Mongol *jagir*, was,
according to Anderson, an instrument of the fiscal policy of the

Islamic state, and reflected in microcosm the institutional organization of political power in Islamic societies. Arab *iqta* and the succeeding regional forms were:

> land grants to warriors, which took the form of fiscal licences distributed to absentee urban rentiers to squeeze small peasant cultivators. The Buyid, Saljuq and early Osmanli States exacted military services from the holders of these rents or their successor versions, but the natural tendency of the system was always to degenerate into parasitic tax-farming—the *iltizam* of the later Ottoman epoch. Even under rigorous central control, state monopoly of land filtered through commercialized rights of absentee exploitation constantly reproduced a general ambience of legal indetermination and precluded any positive bond between the profiteer and tiller of the soil. (1974b p.500)

The net result of this complex tripartite relationship was the absence of economic class relations in the countryside. The relationship between the direct producers and their overlords did not stem from the institution of private property in land but from political power, which ensured the *muqta*'s rights to surplus product. The *muqta* represented the state; he was state power personified. His *iqta* was his power base only in so far as it was an integral part of the state structure—that is, in so far as he performed the duties specified by the state; primarily the collection of the *kharaj*, the land tax, on which the military state depended for its existence.

Anderson's definition of *iqta*, which is inseparable from his conception of the Islamic state, thus entails a configuration of forces and relations, political and economic, intrinsic to the tributary structure which ensures the existence of the military state. According to Anderson, although the *iqta* carried the right to revenue, this was irrelevant to the process of the formation of revenue as such. In other words, the right to revenue constituted the very basis upon which the exploitation of the direct producer took place, but without actually contributing to the process of economic exploitation. It was irrelevant to the process of agrarian production, which was organized by the direct producers without intervention from outside sources. The source of this apparent paradox should be sought in the monopoly ownership of the land by the state, 'a traditional legal canon of Islamic political systems . . . from the Umayyad and Abbasid States down to Ottoman Turkey or Safavid Persia' (ibid. p.497).

The invocation of the state ownership of land, however, posits taxation as the relations of exploitation corresponding to the *iqta*, a proposition already rejected by Anderson himself in the context of his lengthy examination of the concept of the Asiatic mode of production and its more contemporary definitions (ibid. pp.484–549, esp. pp.490–1). Nevertheless what seems to justify the notion of taxes as social relations in the case of the Islamic societies is the alleged military character of the Islamic state; for, in the absence of any theoretical explanation, one is forced to conclude that the tributary relations associated with the Arab *iqta* and its Persian, Turkish and Indian variants were specific economic effects of military relations; and that military force determined the 'commercialized rights of absentee exploitation' through which the 'state monopoly of land' was economically effective (ibid. p.500). Such a conclusion is not unfounded in the light of Anderson's conception of the Islamic state, of which his notion of the *iqta* is a derivative.

Anderson's remarks on the character of the Islamic state are brief and general. They refer to a universal institutional form with regional variants: Arab, Persian, Turkish and Indian (Mongol). The regional variants all possess the structural characteristics of the universal Islamic form. They are monolithic structures of domination with an inner logic which is fundamentally military. The dynamics of military and logistic power—persistent mobilization, expansionism and pillage —determine the nature of state power and its institutional form. The Islamic state, Anderson contends, is institutionally and functionally military.

As mentioned above, Anderson's conception of the Islamic state, rendered schematically, entails the characteristic features of the conventional military theories of the state. These theories, though varied in form, rest on two general theoretical propositions: first, that the state is military force institutionalized; and secondly, that military and logistic power is the constitutive of the economy. But these propositions are fundamentally erroneous and misleading. The first rests on the assumption that the organizational structure of the state is coterminous with the military organization, while the second identifies social organization with the organization of the polity, hence treating the economy as a subordinate constituent of the state. In fact, the proposition which treats the economy as an adjunct of the polity presupposes the absence of civil society in general.[5]

Anderson's general remarks on the nature of the Islamic state, it was argued, clearly entail such propositions. That these propositions are in conflict with the basic principles of historical materialism needs no demonstration. Nevertheless it should be pointed out that Anderson's conception of the Islamic state is consistent with his 'Marxified Weberianism', and in particular with his definition of the concepts of pre-capitalist modes of production in terms of the discursive primacy of the superstructural elements. His assertion of the discursive primacy of the political in the structure of the feudal mode of production, it was argued, leads to the abolition of the economic as a distinct level of the structure; hence his identification of the concept of the mode of production with that of the social formation in the specific case of European feudalism. In the case of the so-called Islamic social formation this position amounts to the denial of the social in general. For Anderson not only identifies the organizational structure of the Islamic state with the organization of the military, but also treats the 'Islamic social formation' as the territorial basis of the state structured by military force and logistic power. This conception of the social formation, it should be noted, signifies the paramount influence of liberal political thought on Anderson's approach to Islamic history and society. The key issue in this respect is the assumed relationship between private property, free acquisition and the constitution of the civil society. The negative logic of this very same theme, we have seen, informs his genealogy of Eastern development.[6]

There is more to be said about his conception of the Islamic state. The structural attributes of the Islamic state in Anderson's discourse, i.e. land-ownership and militarism, presuppose contradictory conditions of existence. The monopoly ownership of the land by the Islamic state, we are told, presupposes a highly centralized organizational structure to ensure its exclusive rights to economic surplus. Militarism, on the other hand, requires a decentralized structure of command, finance and administration to ensure the logistics of the ceaseless quest for expansion and pillage. The crucial connection between land and military service central to the military function of the *iqta* clearly indicates the necessity of a decentralized structure.

The incoherence of Anderson's discourse becomes apparent if we consider the actual level of development of productive forces in the Middle Ages, and appreciate the implications for military technology and logistic power. For there is a logical inconsistency in the notion of a centralized military state in a pre-capitalist social formation. The functional logic of a centralized military state, cast territorially, presupposes specific economic conditions which are not given in Anderson's discourse; conditions associated with the capitalist mode of production, inconceivable in the Middle Ages. The concept of a centralized military state remains a logical impossibility unless conditions of generalized commodity production and a corresponding form of social division of labour are given in the discourse. In the absence of these conditions the connection between the land and the military refers precisely to the existence of a decentralized organization of domination and rule.

The paradox of the centralized military state underlies Anderson's conceptualization of the structure and the conditions of existence of the *iqta*. The *iqta*, Anderson argues, is an institution created by the sovereign state to perform two specific functions: first, to ensure the state's exclusive rights to economic surplus; and second, to facilitate the financial administration of the army in an expanding territorial empire. The functions attributed to the *iqta* entail two entirely different structural logics arising from land-ownership and militarism respectively, and hence different conditions of existence, in the form of centralized and decentralized organization respectively. The contradiction entailed in this conception of the *iqta* is an inversion of the paradox of the centralized military state, an inversion which here signifies the primacy of the political in Anderson's discourse. It is the consequence of the causal status assigned to the state and political relations in the discourse, and enables Anderson to overlook the incoherence of his concept of the *iqta* by reducing its economic and military functions to a single political function: 'fiscal licence to absentee exploitation'. What is excluded from this definition is the crucial connection between the land and military service, an exclusion which conceals the nature of the control entailed in the *iqta* as a form of land grant.

Anderson's definition of the *iqta*, as a fiscal licence to absentee exploitation, is a microcosm of his conception of the Islamic state, and rests on the assumptions that militarism is the structural logic of the Islamic state, and that the organization of the state and military organization are coterminous. It is assumed that the economy has no independent status, but is an adjunct of the centralized sovereign state, an integral part of it. But the persistence of this assumption and the subsequent reduction of economic relations and processes to the fiscal practices of the Arab, Persian and the Turkish states in

Anderson's definition amounts to the denial of the sphere of the social altogether. The absence of the social underlies the myth of the centralized sovereign states in the 'Orient'. The myth, we have seen, is an old one; but its modern recasting in Western historiography of Islamic society has its origin in the Enlightenment. Much historical writing on the nature and development of the *iqta* in pre-Constitutional Iran rests on the perpetual reassertion of this myth as historical reality. What stands between myth and reality, however, is the idea that despotism is sovereign.

The status of military power in the organizational structure of ancient states, and its role in the process of the constitution and institutionalization of state power, has long been the focus of attention in historical sociology and political economy. Marx, it is well known, did not deny military force a dominant status in the institutional form of the ancient state. Military force, he believed, can be the constitutive of the state and the supreme factor in the institutionalization of state power. But he refused to accord it determinancy in the structure of the social formation: in ancient states the military-political was dominant but not determinant. This mode of reasoning is consistent with the causal status assigned to the economic in his discourse. What denied the military-political determinancy in Marx's discourse was the category of productive labour; for the military-political, deemed unproductive, could not determine the structure of the mode of production. The apparent non-correspondence between the political form and the economic structure of ancient states was accounted for with reference to the determination of the economy in the last instance (*Capital* Vol.I. 1970, p.82). But the positive logic of this argument, we have seen, runs counter to the assertion that it was the absence of the economy which ensured the dominance of the military-political in the first instance.

Historical sociologies of the ancient state arguing for the determinancy of military power abound, old and new;[7] perhaps the most sophisticated statement of military determination in ancient history is to be found in the works of the English sociologist Michael Mann (Mann 1986, 1988). Although Mann openly favours military determinism, he is critical of military theories of the state. The conventional military theories of the state and their more contemporary definitions, he argues, are 'reductionist' and therefore theoretically erroneous. For the state is not institutionalized military force; nor is the organization of the state coterminous with the organization of the military (Mann 1988, p.18). The state, he contends, is an autonomous organization of power with diverse sources and multiple functions which cannot be reduced to the interests and functioning of a particular social force or institution, military-political or otherwise. The territorialized form of organization, the centralized character of power, and the multiplicity of functions assure the autonomy of the state *vis-à-vis* civil society (ibid. pp.13–15). Much of Mann's own analysis of the origins and autonomy of state power centres on the specificity and the development of the diverse functions of the state and their conditions of existence in ancient and modern times (ibid. pp.33–70).

Mann's argument for the determinancy of the military-political in pre-capitalist states is formulated in critical response to the Marxist theory of the modes of production. He has little, if any, disagreement with the concept of the capitalist mode of production. In modern industrial states, he argues, 'the economy determines' and the mode of production can 'explain' the specificity of the state and the political (ibid. pp.35, 70). In the pre-capitalist state, however, the relationship between the political and the economic is quite different: the mode of economic production is sustained by political coercion. This in effect means that the state is no longer distinct from the economy, but part of it. The 'explanans' and the 'explanandum' are parts of the same structure (ibid. pp.36–7).

The crux of the argument here is the nature of the relationship between state and mode of production, between the economic base and the political-legal superstructure in pre-capitalist social formations. Recognizing the discursive incoherence of the concepts of pre-capitalist modes of production, Mann refers to attempts by contemporary Marxists—Anderson, and Hindess and Hirst—to come to terms with this major theoretical problem:

> In opposite ways, therefore, these Marxian attempts to theorize the relationship between state and mode of production in pre-capitalist societies are in some difficulty. Either the two are merged [Anderson] or they are autonomous [Hindess and Hirst]. (ibid. p.39)

Mann concludes that 'this unsatisfactory state of affairs has something to do with the neglect, throughout most of twentieth-century sociology, of warfare between societies' (ibid. p.34).

'For a considerable stretch of human history', Mann argues, 'large-scale integration was dependent on military and not economic factors' (ibid. p.61). This meant that in ancient states 'military factors' reigned supreme in the organization of the state and economy. He thus concludes that 'one cannot explain either the political form of the ancient state or its economy without introducing distinctively social Darwinian and militaristic elements into one's theory' (ibid. p.68). The political 'form of the ancient state in large-scale societies', argues Mann, 'was "militant"'. The notion of 'militant' here is borrowed from Spencer, and designates a political form 'modelled on the organization of the standing-army—centralized, authoritarian and uniform' (ibid. p.64). The militant state, in Mann's reasoning, was a functional necessity dictated by the specificity of the existing economic relations and forces. More precisely, it 'was the only way disparate regions and peoples could be held together given the absence of economic interdependence' (ibid. p.64).

A few points should be made before considering Mann's analysis of the economy in ancient states. First, Mann's exposition of the political form of the ancient states evidently entails the characteristic features of the military theories of the state, which he has already rejected for their erroneous presuppositions (ibid. p.12). Second, his argument for the dominance of the military in the organization of the state, and for its political and military determination, is reminiscent of the Marxist argument for the necessity of extra-economic coercion in pre-capitalist economic forms. In both cases the dominance of the productive forces and its economic determinations stem from the absence of the economy. Mann, however, attempts to avoid the obvious pitfalls of the Marxist argument by assigning determinancy to the military-political.

The economic functionality of military power forms the basis of Mann's analysis of the relationship between the political and economic in ancient states. Military power, Mann argues, had a determining effect on the mode of economic production, at the level of both the forces and the relations of production. 'Three aspects of the militant state seem to have had marked effects on economic development: the heightening of stratification by conquest, the intensification of the labour process that authoritarian forms of labour control allow, and the provision of an infrastructure of order and uniformity' (ibid. p.64). Of these three Mann particularly emphasizes the processes of 'consolidation' and 'pacification' which followed military conquest. For these seemingly military-political processes enhanced the 'development of inter-regional economic exchange' and 'policies of uniformity', embodying 'formal rationality' (ibid. p.65). Military force generated a rational strategy of economic appropriation pursued by the militant state.[8] The rationality of the economic system in ancient states, Mann concludes, was military (ibid. p.67).

The economic functionality of military power constitutes the core of Mann's analysis of the ancient state. Marx, he argues, recognizes the dominance of the political-military in the structure of the ancient state but refuses to assign determinancy to it. The privileged causal status of the category of human labour in Marx's discourse denies military-political action its due place in the economic sphere. The result is the hierarchy of determinations which ensures the causal status of the economy by distinguishing the dominant from the determinant. This distinction can be sustained only in so far as military-political action is considered unproductive. Referring to Marx's oft-quoted remarks in *Capital* on status politics in the ancient world, Mann states:

> The ancient world, *pace* Marx, did 'live off politics' in one very crucial sense—that its material conditions of existence depended ultimately on structures determined by military-political considerations. In this respect there can be no clear distinction between supposedly 'dominant' and 'determinant' structures. (ibid. pp.67–8)

The economic functionality of military power thus obliterates the need for a hierarchy of determinations, and along with it the conceptual distinction between 'dominant' and 'determinant' structures, essential to the Marxist concepts of pre-capitalist modes of production. For the military-political, conceived as such, suffices to provide for both the conditions and the mechanism of economic appropriation. 'Concentrated coercion' is thus internal to the structure of the mode of production. It is in fact constitutive of the mode of production in ancient states in general.

This argument conveniently places Mann alongside Anderson, in that they both argue for the primacy of the political-military, and both subscribe to the same comparative historical-sociological method of investigation. Mann finds much empirical support for his analysis in Anderson's genealogies of Western and Eastern developments; while

Anderson hails the publication of Mann's *The Sources of Social Power* as another example of work in the grand tradition of comparative historical-sociological research.[9] There are nevertheless fundamental theoretical differences between the two authors. Mann, unlike Anderson, avoids politicizing the classical Marxist concept of the pre-capitalist modes of production unreservedly, for he realizes that a Marxist reading of Weber fails to rectify their discursive incoherence. Mann's solution clearly goes beyond Weberian multi-factoral causal accounts of the origins of antiquity and feudalism. The economic functionality of the military-political involves a displacement of the discursive primacy of the category of labour, which means that, unlike Anderson, Mann does recognize the cause underlying the incoherence of the Marxist concepts of the pre-capitalist modes of production.

Mann's critique of Marx's conception of military power and warfare in pre-capitalist social formations clearly involves a rejection of anthropological conceptions of property and economy. The causal status attributed to military power in the 'perpetual dialectic of movement between state and civil society' presupposes no less than the subordination of the category of labour to military political action. But Mann clearly subverts the radical consequences of his critique by linking the economic functionality of the political-military to a thesis about the specificity of the forces of production in ancient states.

In Mann's analytical scheme the primacy of the military-political is deduced not from the non-separation of the direct producer from the land, but from the specificity of the forces of production in ancient states.[10] It is the underdeveloped condition of the productive forces which accounts for the primacy of military relations in regulating the relationship between state and economy in ancient states. Mann highlights this argument by contrasting it with the capitalist state, in which the development of the productive forces in the wake of industrial revolution undermines the erstwhile dominance of the military-political; primacy (and determinancy) is thus assigned to the economic in the relationship between the state and civil society. The underdevelopment of the productive forces in ancient states precipitates state intervention in the economy; coercion is the most effective means of intensifying labour and enhancing productivity within pre-capitalist organizations of production. In Mann's analysis the relationship between the state and economy is established via the notion of compulsory cooperation, referring to an organization of production which is structured by coercion rather than economic exchange relations between the agents of production. Political-military coercion (concentrated coercion) enhances the productivity of labour in the organization of production, thus providing the state with economic resources to boost its despotic powers *vis-à-vis* civil society. Compulsory cooperation is the intersection of the dialectical relationship between the state and the economy. It ensures both the dominance of the military-political in the structure of the mode of production, and the autonomy of state power in relation to civil society (ibid. pp.20–2, 58–9).

So far, so good. Mann's argument for the economic functionality of military power/action linked with the specificity of the forces of production does indeed solve the problem entailed in the conceptualization of the relationship between the state and the mode of production in ancient states. But this solution, ingenious as it may seem, is only formal. Although the underdevelopment of the forces of production, emphasized by Mann, can account for the economic role of the military-political, it falls short of explaining the specificity of the relations of appropriation in ancient states. The concept of 'compulsory cooperation', intended to highlight the effects of the military-political on the economy, refers not to the organization of production, but to the organization of labour. These effects, variously listed by Mann, fail to explain the form and the conditions of existence of the tax-rent couple. The reproduction of the relations of appropriation, as he realizes, depends on the extent to which the direct producer is 'embedded in the economic exchange relations which characterize each mode' (ibid. p.38). The political-military can affect the *level* of exploitation in various ways, but it cannot change the basic form of the relations of appropriation. In his concluding remarks, Mann notes that his proposition that one cannot explain the ancient 'economy without introducing distinctively social Darwinian and militaristic elements into one's theory' is contentious and contestable. He writes:

Let us examine the economic effects [of the militaristic elements] a little more closely. It might be asked whether these effects are on the 'productive forces' or 'production relations'. I have emphasised the former: that is, the simple level of economic development. Yet substantial impact on relations can also be observed: heightening of stratification and of authoritarian modes of labour control. I am not sure that it is possible to be more *theoretically* rigorous about these effects. Now if one takes an extremely general view of a 'mode of production', *one could note that none of these changes affect the basic form of expropriation.* Tax/rent is the form at the beginning and the end of the imperial state, rent in the successor societies in Western Europe. (ibid. pp.68–9, my emphasis)

What, then, of the determinancy of the military-political? In what sense did the ancient world 'live off politics'?

Mann admits that he has no theoretical answers to these fundamental questions. Rather the proof of his argument lies mainly in the 'empirical terrain' where he finds 'support for Perry Anderson's position, that a "mode of production", to be used as an explanatory concept, has to include important non-economic elements, notably "militant ones"' (ibid. p.69). But can the inclusion of 'militant' elements in the concept of the mode generate the forms of exchange relations necessary for the reproduction of the unit of production? This question leads us to consider the condition of existence of tax-rent, the form of expropriation, according to Mann, 'at the beginning and the end of the imperial state' (ibid.). True, Mann's emphasis on the specificity of the forces of production in ancient states, linked with the Spencerian concept of 'compulsory cooperation', constitutes the military-political as the necessary economic condition of production; a necessary provision for tax-rent, if it is to be conceived as a form of relations of appropriation of surplus. But how is it possible for a state which is instrumental in the reproduction of the relations of production to exist?

This question leads us back to the starting point of Mann's analysis. For the inclusion of the militant elements in the structure of the mode of production necessarily obliterates the distinction between the 'explanans' and 'explanandum', the state and the mode of production. Mann's ingenious reconstruction of the concept of non-economic coercion involves forms of causality which are incompatible with his functionalist conception of the state. *'Necessity'* may well be 'the mother of state power' but it certainly has little to do with the mode and mechanism of the appropriation of surplus in society, ancient and modern. Similarly, *conquest* may well be important in establishing the *terms* of exchange to facilitate the expropriation of the conquered peoples and the existing subordinate classes, just as military power may be important in all modes involving significant territorial expansion. But neither the importance of conquest nor the backwardness of the productive force can account for the forms of exchange relations which the concept of tax-rent should involve if it is to subordinate the unit of production to effects.

The problem involved in conceptions of tax-rent as relations of appropriation, as was shown in Chapter 2, is not one of definition alone. It cannot be resolved by invoking the economic functionality of the state, however firmly it may be grounded in the specificity of the forces of production. Mann, I have argued, does not go beyond the discursive incoherence of the concept. From his point of view, the arbitrary nature of the relationship between the unit of production and the relations of appropriation of surplus signifies no more than a problem of definition, related to the manner in which it is initially posed and addressed. That the concept of tax-rent is also logically inconsistent does not present a problem, since he is not, in his own words, concerned with the 'correctness' of the Marxist theory of the modes of production (ibid. p.38). This omission, which signifies the dominance of empiricism and empiricist modes of proof in Mann's analysis, underlies his failure to come to terms with the consequences of his own critique of the classical Marxist concepts of the pre-capitalist modes of production.[11]

Mann's critique of Marx's conception of warfare in ancient states, it was pointed out, implies a displacement of the category of labour and the conceptions of economy and property associated with it. But Mann uses this point to attack economism and economic reduction-ism, to which he relates the discursive incoherence of the Marxist concepts of the pre-capitalist modes of production, and does not question its consequences for the Marxist concepts of pre-capitalist relations of production. Although the concept of non-separation is central to the confusion apparent in the Marxist conceptualization of the relationship between state and economy in pre-capitalist social formations, Mann, in an all-out battle to save his functionalist conception of the state and autonomous state power, omits this point in favour of the primacy of the productive forces. The invocation of this thesis, we have seen, helps to rectify the conceptual deficiencies of the state-economy relationship arising from the order of discourse, but at the expense of the logical consistency of his own analysis. This is most obviously demonstrated in his paradoxical approach to the discourse of *Pre-Capitalist Modes of Production*.

Mann is in agreement with Hindess and Hirst that non-economic coercion alone is not sufficient to ensure the reproduction of the pre-capitalist modes of production, and that concepts of pre-capitalist relations of production must necessarily involve forms of possession in separation from the means and conditions of production if they are to subordinate the unit of production to their effects. Indeed, he emphasizes in unambiguous terms the point that the economic exchange relations entailed in the forms of possession in separation define the character of the pre-capitalist modes of production (ibid. p.38). He nevertheless declines to endorse Hindess and Hirst's refutation of the classical concept of the Asiatic mode of production. Their argument that tax-rent cannot generate the economic exchange relations necessary for the reproduction of the unit of production is dismissed in favour of the empiricist argument which is the hallmark of Mann's approach to the theory of the modes of production. His critique of the authors rests on the misconception that they reject the concept of tax-rent solely on the basis of its discursive incoherence; an argument prompted by their view that tax-rent is merely a variant of feudal rent in general:

> Hindess and Hirst 'abolish' the Asiatic mode of production, because the tax-rent form of exploitation in Asia is merely a variant of feudal rent. They agree that an important difference remains between Asian and Western European feudal societies: the former had powerful states, the latter did not. They argue that the mode of production cannot explain this difference as it is identical in the two cases. (ibid. p.39)

The conception of tax-rent as a variant of feudal rent, Mann argues, has a further consequence, one which lies at the heart of Hirst and Hindess's failure to theorize the relationship between the state and the mode of production: that is, the failure to explain the 'economic effects' of state power 'which by any sociological standards must be regarded as important and worthy of explanation' (ibid. p.69). Hence Mann's thesis of the economic functionality of state power, already considered in some detail.

Mann's critique of Hindess and Hirst here is neither new nor radical, in substance or implication.[12] The rejection of the concept of the Asiatic mode of production, he assumes, is due to the discursive practice adopted by the authors which renders the concept of tax-rent incoherent. This, he further argues, can be rectified by reconceptualization of the role of coercion, functional and institutional, in the process of production. Hence the assertion that tax-rent constituted the main mode of appropriation of surplus in the ancient state, in the West as well as the East. This assertion, hitherto theoretically unsubstantiated, overlooks the fundamental reasons for the rejection of the concept of the Asiatic mode of production in *PCMP*; that is, the argument that the conditions of existence of the relations of production specified in the concept of this mode (i.e. the conditions of existence of the tax-rent couple) are secured without reference to the labour process; and that the insertion of the state in the concept of the mode, as an economic condition of production, cannot rectify the arbitrary nature of the connection between the relations and forces of production. This is because Mann does not realize that *PCMP*'s attempt to subvert the rationalist epistemology of *Reading Capital*, however rudimentary, implies a separation of the question of the order of discourse, of the internal relations between concepts, from the question of the forms of connections of the objects specified in that discourse. Nor does he realize that there is an intrinsic relationship between *PCMP*'s rejection of the concept of tax-rent and its proposed notion of pre-capitalist relations of production, based on the form of possession in separation from the means and conditions of production.

The omission of the conditions of existence of the concept of tax-rent is central to the paradox underlying Mann's conceptualization of military/political coercion as the relations of appropriation in ancient states. For the economic exchange relations attributed to the forms of distribution of product entailed in the concept of tax-rent presuppose the effective (total/partial) separation of the direct producer from the means of production. This, we have seen, excludes the possibility of forms of appropriation of product based on military/political coercion. The latter furnish the conditions of existence of the relations of appropriation alone; they cannot engender or be substituted for these relations in the process of production as a process of exploitation. Mann, however, does not realize that the admission of the separation of the direct producer from the means of production radically subverts the foundation of his dialectics of the state and civil society. True, the relationship between the state and civil society may well depend on the modality of the development of the economy and the economic field. The point, however, is that this economic field is not an adjunct of the political. The underdevelopment of the forces of production may well correlate with the underdevelopment of civil society, but this does not warrant the conception of economic exchange arising from political-military relations. The economic significance of the political-military structures in the ancient world, however undeniable, cannot justify Mann's thesis of the determinancy of war and military action in ancient states. Mann does not realize that the negation of the concept of the Asiatic mode of production in *PCMP* is intrinsically linked with its attempt to break with the rationalist epistemology of *Reading Capital*, which implies, above all, the separation of the question of the order of discourse, of internal relations between concepts from the question of the forms of connections of the objects specified in the discourse. Had he realized this point he would have noticed that the theorization of non-economic coercion beyond that which is given in the discourse of *PCMP* is a logical impossibility.

Let us now return to a consideration of the structure and conditions of existence of the *iqta* in pre-capitalist Iran. In the context of Iranian history the most systematic treatment of the *iqta* is to be found in the works of Anne Lambton (Lambton 1953, 1967, 1968, 1988). Lambton's authoritative studies of agrarian relations in pre-Constitutional Iran have long formed the frame of reference for historical and sociological research on the historical specificity and development of the *iqta*. References to her studies of agrarian relations and to her definition of the *iqta* are abundant, whether in refutation or approval.

Lambton's definition of the *iqta* owes much to the influential work of Cahen on the nature of *iqta* in medieval Islam, a debt which she acknowledges in her studies.[13] Following Cahen, Lambton locates her discussion of *iqta* in the context of the comparative genealogies of Western and Eastern developments, focusing on the mode of distribution of political power. In this sense her approach and her definition of *iqta* closely resemble Anderson's, considered in the previous section, and, like him, she traces the origin and development of the *iqta* to the historical specificity of the state in medieval Iran (Lambton 1967).[14]

The *iqta* in Lambton's discourse is a constituent element of the centralized military state, and reflects the specificity of its organizational structure. Although she refers to the military character of the pre-Constitutional state in Iran, her definition is markedly differen from the general conception of the military state discussed in the previous section. In her conception, the pre-Constitutional state is not an institutionalized military force, nor does it represent a monolithic structure of warfare and pillage; its military character arises rather from the dominance of the tribes and tribal relations in the social structure of political power. Although the consolidation of power in the wake of military conquest minimizes the significance of tribal relations and forces in the organization of the state, they continue to control the royal court and the command structure of the armed forces.

Lambton thus provides us with a quite different picture of the military state. The military state, she argues, is a product of conquest, founded by tribal forces who extend their domination over the sedentary population in towns and in the countryside. The outcome is a complex structure of domination and rule which does not follow a uniform dynamics of development and change. Although Lambton does not adhere to a specific conception of the state, her detailed commentary on the structure of the Saljuq state pertains to an arena of struggle between the military and civilian forces within the state apparatuses, represented by the Dargah and the Divan respectively (Lambton 1968, pp.203–283).

Lambton shows that political power is the focus of the struggle between the Dargah and the Divan; but she fails to specify the structural complexities of the intricate conflict within the Saljuq state. This failure should be attributed largely to her crude empiricism and her aversion to the use of theory in historical analysis. Lambton, more often than not, reduces history to a unilinear process, a sequence of events informed by a simple mechanical causality. The conflict between the Dargah and the Divan is perhaps illustrated most clearly in terms of the complexities of the tendency towards the militarization of the *iqta*, discussed in some detail by Lambton (1953, 1967, 1968). This tendency, it will be shown, is an outward expression of the struggle between the military and civilian forces for possession and control of the state lands, which was the main source of the military and the administrative *iqta* under the Saljuq rule. The rising ratio of the military to the administrative *iqta*, and the subsequent amalgamation of the two into a single unit, is an index of the development of the struggle and the increasing power of the military *muqtas*, who came to dominate the office of local and provincial governor under the great Saljuq kings. The militarization of the *iqta* consolidated the link between land and military service which had been obscured by the exigencies of the fiscal administration of the state.

Lambton pays little or no attention to the economic in her analysis of the conflict between civil and military forces within the Saljuq state. Nor does she attempt to explore the relationship between the conflict and the modality of the development of the *iqta*. The economic lies dormant in Lambton's interpretation of historical processes and practices, seldom invoked to aid the interpretation. There is no connection between the economic and political in her discourse. The connection, in so far as it underlies her interpretation of historical processes and practices, is arbitrary. Lambton's conception of the *iqta*, it will be shown, cannot be sustained if the economic foundation of the crucial relationship between the forms of political struggle and the modality of the development of the *iqta* is laid bare. A consideration of the economic process of production of land revenue, the focus of the political struggle within the state apparatus, will disclose not only the structural character of the struggle, but also the presence of another and no less important social force in the historical scene: that is, the undifferentiated mass of the Iranian peasantry, whose uncanny absence from Lambton's discourse lies at the heart of her definition of the *iqta* as a bureaucratic institution.

Let us now turn to Lambton's definition of the *iqta*, and assess its significance for her characterization of social relations in pre-Constitutional Iran. The *iqta*, as she defines it, is not a form of land-holding, but a 'bureaucratic' institution, devised by the state to serve a specific fiscal objective, namely, the maintenance of an expanding regular army required by the growing need for territorial centralism and the consolidation of power (Lambton 1967, pp.44–48). The assignment of the *iqta*, Lambton further contends, entailed a 'connection between military function and the possession of land' which persisted 'throughout' its history. The conditional possession entailed in the assignment of the *iqta*, nevertheless, was entirely different from that which was historically associated with the grant of the feudal fief, since in the case of the *iqta*, Lambton argues, possession of the land 'was not based on a feudal contract involving mutual fealty between sovereign and vassal' (ibid. pp.49–50). From this absence of contractual relations, she writes:

> stems a fundamental difference between the feudal institutions of Western Europe and the *iqta* system, namely, that whereas a

contractual relation was an essential characteristic of the
former, the element of contract never became a feature of the
iqta system. (ibid. p.44)

Seigneurial relations assume a pivotal role in Lambton's comparative
genealogies of Western and Eastern developments. Their absence in
Islamic society is an expression of the sovereign nature of power, the
origin of the negative causal relations which inform Lambton's
historicist account of the formation and development of the *iqta*. In
Islam, she argues, all authority is characteristically delegated, and thus
excludes the possibility of reciprocal/contractual relations of fealty
between the ruler and his subjects (ibid. p.44). The authority of the
Islamic rulers is absolute and indivisible, and defies practices which
are conducive to the parcellization of sovereignty. Political power
remains sovereign, despite the periodic emergence of decentralizing
tendencies within the polity which may seriously erode its foundation
and threaten stability:

> The source of all grants of *iqta* or *tuyul* and *soyurghal* was the
> absolute sovereignty of the Sultan or the Shah. They were
> entirely matters of grace and lacked any element of vassalage or
> contract, and the fact that when the central government relaxed
> control over the *iqta* system in Great Saljuq times and over
> *tuyuls* and *soyurghals* in Safavid and Qajar times, those who
> usurped power exercised this in an arbitrary fashion, was due
> not to the fact that these systems were feudal systems, but to the
> nature of the conception of power which prevailed in society.
> (ibid. p.50)

The sovereign nature of power in Islamic societies thus determines
the structural specificity of the *iqta* and the forms of land grant which
replaced it. They were all bureaucratic institutions characterized by
the absence of the reciprocal relations of fealty between sovereign and
vassal (ibid. pp.49–50).

Sovereignty, and the correlative absence of seigneurial relations,
thus inform the order of causality which specifies the structure of the
bureaucratic *iqta* in Lambton's discourse; and the status of seigneurial
relations is a negative determination of her conception of feudalism in
Western Europe. Seigneurial relations, constitutive of feudalism in
the West, arose out of a 'need for protection', Lambton maintains

(ibid. p.42). In fact, from her point of view, feudalism is institutional-ized protection operating through two institutions: *patrocinium* and *precarium*, involving persons and land respectively. The former signified the patron-client relationship arising from the need for protection. Roman *patrocinium*, states Lambton, was related to land and involved obligations of service and support. *Precarium*, on the other hand, denoted protection, which in Western Europe, gave rise to the commendation of lands: *patrocinium fundorum* (ibid. p.43).

Feudalism thus denotes the institutionalization of a subjective need for protection through contractual relations between patrons and clients. This involved a voluntary exchange of rights over persons and land in return for protection against extortion and invasion. The institutionalization of protection as such led to the emergence of a hierarchy of domination and subordination involving land, which subsequently became the basis of feudal landed property. The crux of Lambton's argument is that 'protection was not the dominant need in Islamic society, and that the need or needs which gave rise to the *iqta* system may be sought elsewhere' (ibid. p.43).

It should, however, be pointed out that Lambton admits the existence of institutionalized forms of patronage in early Islam, resembling *patrocinium* in Roman Law. The Islamic form, which emerged in the wake of territorial expansion and the conquest of non-Arab territories, governed the relationship between the Muslim Arabs and the non-Arab converts to Islam known as *mawali*, a term which implied a sense of social inferiority. Islamic patronage in this case was a means for the *mawali* to gain social status by being affiliated with one of the ruling Arab tribes. It did not, unlike the Roman *patrocinium*, involve reciprocal relations of service and protection; nor did it even involve land ownership. The Islamic form, Lambton maintains, was merely a relationship between two parties arising from the need for social status (ibid. pp.42–3). However, she refers to another form of patronage in early Islam known as *talji'a*, which, she argues, involved patronage, and resembled *patrocinium fundorum*, whereby the weak land-owner committed his estate to the protection of the strong to indemnify it. *Talji'a* often led to the ownership of protected land by the protector, though in some cases the protected retained the right to sell his estate or transmit it by inheritance (ibid. p.43). It thus, as Lambton admits, entailed the element of protection sanctioned by contractual relations between two parties, involving an exchange of rights of ownership over land for immunity from state extortion and outside invasion. But, unlike *precarium*, it failed to develop into a universal institution governing agrarian relations in Islamic society. This failure, she argues, was due to the heterogeneous and often arbitrary nature of the conditions governing the contractual relations between the two parties; in other words, *talji'a* failed because it was not institutionalized. It is interesting to note the shift of emphasis in Lambton's argument concerning the status of contractual relations in Islamic society. The failure and the eventual demise of *talji'a* here is not attributed to a universal Islamic origin, but to the prevailing juridico-political processes and practices of the time. In other words, Lambton implies that the prevailing conception of power was not in fact incompatible with contractual relations between patrons and their clients.

Lambton, then, attributes the origin and the structural specificity of the *iqta* to the sovereign and indivisible nature of political power in Islamic society. Sovereignty is essential to her definition of the *iqta* as a bureaucratic institution. But the concept of sovereignty requires conditions which are not produced in Lambton's historicist discourse, but assumed. The existence of a centralized state with monopoly ownership of the land is not theoretically or empirically constituted, it is simply given in the discourse. It is the assumed effects of the uniform origin which define the conditions of existence of the *iqta* as a specifically Islamic institution. But Lambton's account of the historical conditions of the formation and development of the *iqta* in fact entails political processes and practices which are incompatible with the theoretical requisites of a centralized sovereign power.

The Saljuq period features prominently in Lambton's writings on the historical specificity and development of the *iqta* in pre-Constitutional Iran. This period, in her account, sees the culmination of a trend towards the militarization of the state which began under the Buyids. The Saljuq state is marked by the eventual assimilation of the office and functions of the provincial governor into those of the military commander. This crucial development, Lambton maintains, manifests itself through a consolidation of the connection between military service and land revenue:

The dominant type of the *iqta* under the Buyids was the military *iqta*. These *iqtas* were controlled by the military diwan, the *Diwan al-Jaysh*, at the head of which was the *arid* or Muster Master. The military diwan was thus concerned not only, or even primarily, with military administration, but rather with the fiscal value (*ibra*) and characteristics of each *iqta* and the reallocation of *iqtas* as they fell vacant ... Under the great Saljuqs there took place an assimilation of the military *iqta* to the governorate or 'administrative' *iqta*. With this the careful estimate of the exact fiscal value of the *iqta* tended to be replaced by merely an approximate value; and the *iqta* to be defined not by fiscal value but by service, and for the *iqta* to become, by usurpation, a hereditary domain on which the *muqta* had governmental prerogatives. (ibid. p.46)

Lambton thus argues that under the Saljuqs the military and the administrative *iqta* were integrated to form a single unit, and the *iqta* system closely resembled European feudalism. The Saljuq *iqta*, like the feudal fief, was the site of the political and economic power of the *muqta-vali* as well as of his legal jurisdiction. The *muqta*, she contends, 'carried out all governmental functions with all costs defrayed locally'. He had legal jurisdiction over the inhabitants of all 'towns and fortresses in the province'. The *muqta* 'paid no taxes' to the central government but 'furnished a military contingent in the time of the war'. He could also, in most cases, make sub-assignments and constitute them into *iqtas* (ibid. p.46).

The most important feature of the *iqta* system under Saljuq rule was the crucial amalgamation of the political and the economic in the office of the *muqta*, expressed in the conditions of assignment as a reciprocal relationship between military service and the right to revenue. This fundamental change in the conditions of assignment, Lambton maintains, proved a lasting one. The reciprocal relationship between service and revenues remained a fixed feature of all forms of land grant down to the early twentieth century, when the practice of land assignment was abolished by the Constitutional government (ibid. p.46).

The transformation in the conditions of assignment, emphasized by Lambton, means that the Saljuq *iqta* was more than a bureaucratic institution. In fact the conditions attributed to it would seem to signify a private holding possessed by the *muqta* who, by virtue of his possession, controlled the process of production and appropriated the economic surplus in return for the service he rendered to the state. But Lambton quickly resorts to historical origin to subvert the positive logic of her analysis, invoking the notion of sovereignty to assert the purely formal character of the change in the conditions of assignment. The connection between land revenue and military service, Lambton suggests, did not affect the mode of distribution of political power. It implied a form of independence which 'did not in itself involve decentralization and relaxation of the authority of the central government. The grants of the *iqta* in all cases were simply delegations of authority and did not contain any implications of vassalage or permanent rights' (ibid. p.46).

It was argued earlier in this section that the centralized sovereign state, the alleged constitutive of the *iqta*, however, is not a historical construct. Rather it is the effect of the persistence of the 'Islamic origin' in Lambton's discourse, which by definition excludes forms of authorization involving autonomy and decentralization. Lambton's historicist discourse persistently defines the structure and the conditions of the existence of the *iqta* in terms of the specificity of the Islamic origins.

However, when she is less concerned with the ideological implications of the agrarian history of the pre-Constitutional era for contemporary Iranian politics, the uniform cultural origin is seldom invoked to aid historical interpretation, and we encounter quite a different conception of the Saljuq state.[15] For example, in her detailed discussion of the structure and organization of the Saljuq state, centralized power structure and indivisible sovereignty give way to a loose confederation of independent and semi-independent political-military units over which the sultan exercised nominal authority only. Lambton writes:

> The Saljuq had come to power with the support of the Ghuzz tribes, and their claim to the leadership of these tribes rested in the first instance on military prowess. Originally they were the hereditary leaders of a small group; gradually, as success attended their activities, the majority of the Ghuzz became associated with them. Their leadership, once established, was maintained by military might coupled with conciliation and consultation, though they *never* succeeded in establishing full control and unity over the Ghuzz. The outlying groups, although *nominally* acknowledging the overlordship of the sultan, acted *independently or semi-independently*. Politically the Saljuq empire was a loose *confederation* of semi-independent Kingdoms over which the sultan exercised *nominal authority*.

Saljuq princes were known as *maleks* in contradistinction to the paramount ruler, the sultan. Only for a brief period towards the end of Malik-Shah's reign was any degree of unity achieved. (Lambton 1968 pp.217–8, my emphasis)

But a political structure composed of 'independent and semi-independent kingdoms' which recognised the authority of the King only nominally and which never achieved any 'unity' within the designate territory of the empire is clearly far removed from the Islamic ideal of the centralized sovereign state asserted by the cultural origin. Sovereignty is an attribute of political power; the sovereign state must possess the monopoly of law-making and enforcement, and control the means and institutions of force and violence within its designated territory. The Saljuq state, Lambton's exposition clearly indicates, lacked the formal and structural conditions of sovereignty. The military strength of the Saljuq state consisted of the combined military strengths of its constituent entities, which converged upon the centre more than they diverged from it, due mainly to the centripetal dynamics of frontier politics in an expanding territorial empire. The administration of such a decentralized military force thus required a relationship between land revenue and military service to sustain a unity of command in military action within the inner and outer reaches of the state. In the higher echelons of the Saljuq command structure this relationship between land revenue and military service was firmly underpinned by tribal lineage: the main, though by no means the exclusive, site for the articulation of the political and the economic within the state.

Lambton's exposition of the structure of the Saljuq state has important implications for the concept of the *iqta*. The Saljuq state, it appears, was neither sovereign nor centralized enough to meet the requirements of the bureaucratic *iqta* as she conceives it. On the contrary, her exposition indicates quite clearly that the *iqta* owed its existence to the very absence of these conditions in the first place, and that the connection between land revenue and military service did not only reflect the supreme status of the military in the structure of power, but also the crucial position of the land as the site of political power. The *iqta*, like all forms of land assignment, provided for the particular articulation of the political and economic, essential to the logistics of a decentralized military power on which the survival of the Saljuq state depended.

Lambton would have little quarrel with the view that the Saljuq
state never achieved the measure of territorial centralism necessary
for the existence of a sovereign state; nor would she particularly
disagree with the view that the decentralized structure of the Saljuq
state owed much to the supreme position of the military in the
organization of state power. Nonetheless, she is reluctant to abandon
the claim that the Saljuq state, and the pre-Constitutional state in
general, was a sovereign power. In fact she continues to emphasize
the myth of sovereignty, both in *The Cambridge History of Iran* quoted
above, and in the rest of her writings on the agrarian and political
history of pre-Constitutional Iran. For Lambton identifies sovereignty
with the autocratic rule of the Shah/Sultan; that is, with the near-total
absence of juridico-political constraints on the exercise of power. She
explains this in relation to the Islamic *sharia*, admittedly the only
conceivable constraint on the exercise of absolute power in the
Middle Ages:

> The power of the sultan was in theory limited by the *shari'a*, to
> which he, like all Muslims, was subject. But the sanction of the
> *shari'a* in this case was simply moral, because no means was
> devised to enforce his subjection to it. (ibid. p.217)

The identification of sovereignty with autocracy, independence of
power with despotism, is central to Lambton's definition of the *iqta*. It
renders the fundamental question of the conditions of existence of
sovereignty irrelevant to the discourse. These conditions are already
given in Lambton's definition: a centralized apparatus of domination
and rule is entailed in the Islamic origin which, by definition, excludes
the parcellization of sovereignty, and hence a decentralized apparatus
of domination and rule.

Lambton traces the origin of the *iqta* to the fiscal crisis of the
Abbasid state in the middle of the tenth century. The Abbasid state,
she argues, faced a growing budgetary deficit, induced by the
combined effects of rising military and bureaucratic expenditure and
declining state revenue. Conventional devices such as tax-farming,
sale of office and crown lands, and confiscation of private fortunes
failed to remedy the deepening crisis. This precipitated the need for
an overall restructuring of the financial administration of the state.
The *iqta*, Lambton argues, was a direct response to that need, seizing
upon and transforming the military and administrative apparatus of

the state (Lambton 1967, pp.44–48). Subsequently the *iqta* became the principal instrument of the financial administration of the Abbasid state and of the states which emerged in the wake of the disintegration of the Caliphate in the eleventh century. These states, notably the Buyids and the Saljuqs, adopted and developed the *iqta*, and regularized its use in their expanding domains (ibid. pp.46–48).

This general scenario, which is also extended to the introduction and regularization of the *tuyuls* and *soyurghals* by the Safavids, conforms to a uniform causal logic governing the periodic rise and fall of the tribal states. The dynamics of this circular movement are said to be internal to the tribal structure of the state itself. Militarism and the expansionist thrust of the tribal state create a discrepancy between the territorial base and the social organization of state power. The military and civilian apparatuses of the state, welded together by lineage, are no longer capable of defending the changing frontiers of the state. Tribal confederacy thus gives way to a territorially centralized state, with a regular army and a scribal bureaucracy to enforce authority over the diverse ethnic and religious groups within its territory. This centralized state eventually falls victim to the upsurge of decentralizing forces and tendencies from within the state structure. The decentralizing forces and relations which, more often than not, correspond to tribal lineage undermine the territorial integrity of the state by gradually debasing its military and economic powers.[16]

My concern here is not with the validity of Lambton's interpretation of Iranian history, but with her account of the constitution and development of the *iqta* and the succeeding forms of land grant in pre-Constitutional Iran. Lambton's scenario, from this standpoint, is not wholly implausible. The quest for centralization of power by the state may well have been the principal cause of the introduction and the subsequent universalization of the '*iqta* system'. In fact, the causal relationship between the '*iqta* system' and the centralization of the state is clearly indicated by the notion of the fiscal crisis of the state and its recurrence in the early phases of the consolidation of power by successive dynastic states. However, what is important in this respect is Lambton's presentation of this causal relationship.

Lambton, it was seen, attributes the constitution of the *iqta* and the modality of its development to the voluntarist action of the sovereign state which is institutionally and functionally autonomous. This autonomy of state power underlies her interpretation of the historical conditions governing centralization and the ensuing fiscal crisis of the state in various periods. Lambton does not discuss the nature of the relationship between the state and the military; nor does she appraise the significance of the economic in the process of the centralization of the state in general and the reorganization of military forces and institutions in particular. The introduction of the standing army and the adoption of the *iqta* are both attributed to the rationality of the sovereign state. The state, Lambton maintains, replaces the tribal army by a professional standing army, deemed more efficient in defending the changing frontiers of the expanding empire. Similarly, the adoption and subsequent universalization of the *iqta* system by the Saljuq state is related to the cost-effectiveness of the practice and its superiority to alternative methods of financial administration such as tax-farming. Lambton attributes an element of rationality to the autonomous action of the sovereign state which forms the functional logic of the quest for centralization and the subsequent transformation in the organization of the military.

Marxist historians, as we have seen, do no better in this respect. Nomani, for example, will find little to dispute in Lambton's genealogy of the *iqta*. But unlike Lambton he believes that the decentralization of the Saljuq state and the subsequent autonomy of the military *muqta* transformed the structure of the *iqta* from a bureaucratic/fiscal apparatus of the state to a private holding. This disagreement, arising from two different conceptions of sovereignty, is not as fundamental as it may seem.

Lambton, it was pointed out, subscribes to an entirely juristic conception of sovereignty. Sovereignty in her view is not only absolute and indivisible but also transcendental, defying all social and institutional conditions of existence. The decentralization of the Saljuq state, however effective and widespread, does not invalidate the sovereignty of the Islamic state. For Nomani, by contrast, sovereignty is essentially an attribute of state power and as such presupposes institutional and legal conditions of existence, namely a centralized state capable of enforcing and defending its authority within its designated territory. The decentralization of the Saljuq state and the emergence of autonomous and semi-autonomous *iqta*-holders suffice to account for the transformation of the *iqta* from a state institution into a private holding. In both cases, however, the arguments are pitched on the political level, despite their seemingly opposed positions on the nature of the Saljuq *iqta*, and their different interpretation of the political conception of feudal landed property and rent.

Although Lambton and Nomani both consider seigneurial relations to be constitutive of the feudal landed property, they differ in their view of the real nature of these relations. Lambton, we have seen, holds an entirely juristic conception of seigneurial relations. Her normative argument about the necessity of legal contractual relations for the definition of feudalism is in line with her transcendental notion of sovereignty. Nomani, on the other hand, is less concerned with the legal contractual definition of seigneurial relations. From his point of view, seigneurial relations are essentially political in character, and the decentralization of the state suffices to ensure their existence. The relationship between the king and the *muqta* may not have been defined in legal-contractual terms, but this does not alter the essentially political character of the relationship; vassalage assumes different forms in different social formations. Even if the autonomy of the *muqta vis-à-vis* the sultan was not inscribed in the formal structure of domination and subordination, in practice it necessarily involved a serious erosion of sovereignty, and the subsequent parcellization of the state territory into independent and semi-independent units over which the sultan had only nominal authority (Chapter 3). So far, so good. But Nomani's argument, convincing though it may seem, is no more than an unfounded assertion. For, as we have already seen, juridical relations are essential to his political definition of the concept of feudal ground rent. They cannot be so easily excluded from the process of the formation and appropriation of feudal landed property. The conditional form of ownership associated with seigneurial relations defines the political mechanism of the appropriation of surplus, and as such is included in Nomani's definition of the concept.

The causal relationship between political form and property relations emphasized by Nomani's notion of seigneurial relations is the hallmark of his political definition of the feudal mode of production. This relationship, it was argued above, is a consequence of the conflation of the relations of production with their juridico-political conditions of existence. It rests on the exclusion of the economic exchange relations entailed in rent-form from the process of the formation and of appropriation of feudal landed property. This absence of the economic also holds true for Nomani's conception of sovereignty. In this case, too, the assumed causal relationship between the centralized state and the bureaucratic *iqta* rests on the exclusion of the economic exchange relations specified in the connection between land and military service. The nature of the connection is completely obscured by the postulate of the centralized sovereign state, which forms the starting point of Nomani's historical account of the adoption and universalization of the *iqta* by the Saljuq state.

Nomani, we have seen, deduces the bureaucratic (pre-feudal) character of the early Saljuq *iqta* from the institutional form of the political. In this sense his historical analysis bears remarkable resemblances to Lambton's historical scenario. In both cases the assumption is that the consolidation of power and the centralization of the state structure are identical processes, and that the former necessarily entails the latter. This assumption, as shown in Lambton's case, is unfounded. It cannot be sustained if the nature of the relationship between the economic and the military organization of the Saljuq state is problematized. For this relationship shows that the Saljuq state at the height of its power could not achieve more than a limited degree of political centralism which, at best, can be termed spatial centralism.[17] Hence the argument that the conception of the centralized sovereign state is not theorized but given in the discourse. It is a consequence of the conflation of sovereignty with the functional autonomy of the state; an error which is also present in Petrushevsky's notion of Eastern feudalism and in the various accounts of Asiatic despotism inspired by Marx's remarks.

The following section attempts a brief analysis of the structure and functioning of the Saljuq state. The aim of the analysis is not to uncover the complexities of the Saljuq state structure, but to specify the political and legal conditions of the existence of the *iqta*, beginning with a problematization of the nature of the relationship between the political and the military in the structure of the Saljuq state, and posing the following questions. First, why did the expansion and consolidation of the Saljuq state lead to a change in the organizational structure of the Saljuq army? And second, why did the financial administration of the new army require a connection between military service and land?

The Political-Legal Conditions of Existence of the *Iqta*[18]
The Saljuq state was constituted by military force. It was a product of military conquest, set up by a group of invading Turkoman tribes

which came to bear the common name of the Saljuqs; this common name was held to denote the common lineage of the confederate tribes, among which the Ghuzz was the leading force. The organization of the tribal confederacy with the Ghuzz in the centre underpinned the formal structure of political power in the Saljuq state. Tribal lineage remained the organizing principle of the confederal state, composed of a central government and a number of autonomous and semi-autonomous principalities. The central government was composed of the royal court and the military, political and legal institutions which were directly controlled by it, while the principalities were governed by the Saljuq Amirs, who had their own courts and military and civilian bureaucracies and held jurisdiction over their designated territory. The Saljuq Sultan was the leading member of the Ghuzz, the dominant tribe/clan within the tribal confederacy; the Saljuq Amirs (or *maleks*) were predominantly from the leading clans of the other prominent Turkoman tribes. The relationship between the Sultan and the Amirs was regulated by the prevailing principles of the 'Steppe tradition'. Consequently the Sultan's supreme political authority and the Amirs' allegiance to him both resulted from his supreme position within the tribal confederacy. The conception of the *Ilkhan* as the guardian of the tribal confederacy, and the forms of authorization that followed from this, remained the single most important regulator of the Saljuq polity and the underlying structure of domination and subordination.

Tribal lineage and military power were inseparably interwoven in the structure of the Saljuq state. The former defined the formal structure of political hierarchy, while the latter was the main cohesive force within the Saljuq state, specifying the nature of the reciprocal relations between the central government and the autonomous principalities. The political unity which underpinned the confederate organization of the state was essentially a military alliance. The confederate forces which constituted and sustained the state pursued a common strategic objective: to defend their territory against the invading external forces which threatened their survival. Since the confederate forces could not as a rule maintain sufficient military and logistic power to defend their territory individually, they gravitated towards the centre, which was the locus of the common strategic objective of the autonomous units within the confederate organization of the state.

The dynamic of the political-military (tribal) power in the formative period of the Saljuq state was thus centripetal: the exigencies of the common strategic objective drew the constituent units of the confederate state towards the centre. The military logic of this centralizing tendency also loomed large in the process of the institutionalization of political power, and the organizational structure of the Saljuq state bore its imprint. The office of the *amir-e hajeb* in the royal court and the prominence of the Dargah in the state structure signified the hegemonic status of the military-centralizing forces and tendencies in the institutional structure of the Saljuq state. The persistence of the common strategic objective alludes to a major historical characteristic of the Saljuq state. Always in possession of the external conditions of sovereignty, the state's ability to institute the requisite internal processes and practices was effectively hindered by prevailing economic relations and forces. In fact, the territorialization of the centralizing functions and institutions of the state depended primarily on the interaction between military and economic relations.

The crucial factor in this respect was land. The Saljuq *iqta* was the nodal intersection of the military and the economic, whose contradictory dynamics collided in the centre of the state apparatus. The tribal army, instrumental in the rise to power of the Saljuqs, was firmly grounded in pastoral production. It functioned as a mobile and largely self-sufficient economic unit with only a tenuous link to the land. This situation, however, changed rapidly when the Saljuqs extended their domination to Iran. The centripetal dynamic of the confederate political structure they created was now anchored in a sedentary agriculture whose characteristic backwardness necessarily forged a link between the army and the land. Tribal lineage, the organizing principle of the Saljuq polity, also governed the parcellization of the territory into administrative *iqtas*; but the crucial connection between military service and land revenue, which determined its character as a form of land grant, stemmed from the specificity of the forces and relations of production in agriculture. The administrative *iqta* of the early Saljuq period clearly reflected this articulation of lineage and economic relations which underpinned the military logic of the confederate state.

The rapid expansion of the Saljuq state, its transformation from a local power into an expansive empire, unleashed forces which could fundamentally transform its military-logistic capacity to territorialize its centralizing functions and institutions. The central government, the conquering centralized command, was now in possession of new resources. It was able to claim a higher degree of autonomy from the confederate forces which were instrumental in the creation of the state; to create an effective political unity within a centralized structure which would enhance rather than hinder the territorialization of the central political authority.

Military power, however, remained the most effective means in the quest for territorial centralism. The fundamental reason for the primacy of the military in the process of political centralization was again primarily economic. The specificity of pre-capitalist economic relations, in particular the underdevelopment of commodity relations, defined the position of the military as the most extensive integrative power available to the Saljuq central government. The introduction and subsequent expansion of a regular standing army by the central political command was a response to these conditions. Governmental authority, within the vast territory of the expanding imperial state composed of diverse ethnic and religious entities, was dependent on the ability to introduce and enforce rules centrally, without the customary reliance on the military power and cooperation of the confederate forces. This in effect meant the ability to muster and deploy military contingents when required.

The creation and subsequent expansion of a regular standing army considerably increased the autonomy of the Saljuq central political authority in the confederacy. This was enhanced by the social and ethnic compositions of the new army; the predominantly Turkish—slave and free—contingents enabled the central government to reduce the paramount significance of the tribal soldiery in the process of the integration of the state. Yet the degree of functional autonomy achieved by the introduction of the standing army was never sufficient to institute a centralized territorial state apparatus. The policy of territorialized centralism pursued by the Saljuq rulers met its institutional limitations in the economics of military power. The Saljuq regular forces, which were soon garrisoned throughout the empire, were essentially non-productive consumer units, depending for their upkeep entirely on the central government. The financial administration of such a force thus required that the central political authority have access to a large amount of economic surplus, a requirement which could not be satisfied by pastoral production and a sedentary agriculture based on peasant household labour. The production of economic surplus large enough to meet the logistics of military power demanded, above all, extensive agriculture, utilizing forced labour on a large scale. In the absence of this fundamental requirement, the Saljuq state opted for the universalization of the practice of land assignment. The upper ranks of the regular army were assigned land in *iqta* and were therefore entitled to its revenue. This land revenue, formed of rents extracted from peasants working the land, was then used to pay for the upkeep of the soldiery formally recruited by and operating under the command of the *muqta*. The military *iqta*, *iqta al-tamlik*, which was largely assigned out of state and crown lands, was not taxable. It signified a hereditary title to the revenue of a specified area of the state territory in return for the provision of soldiery and military service for the central government. The connection between service and land revenue, which was forged by the prevailing agrarian relations, formed the foundation of the logistics of military power under Saljuq rule.

This development had crucial institutional consequences for the functional autonomy of state power. For the link between military service and land revenue instituted a decentralized military organization, structurally tied to land and the productivity of peasant labour. The centrifugal dynamics of the economic organization of military power, created to enforce the functional autonomy of the state *vis-à-vis* its constituent parts, seriously militated against the centripetal process of territorialization of state power. In this sense the Saljuq *iqta* was the point of intersection of the political and the economic, the contradictory dynamics of which collided in the organizational structure of the Saljuq state. The conflict of interest between the Divan and the Dargah and the associated struggle for power between civilian and military groups within the state apparatuses signified the presence of these two counterposing structural tendencies in the Saljuq polity. These struggles, which often assumed ethnic and religious colouring, were fundamentally focused on land and land revenue, the primary source and instrument of the strategies of power and domination in pre-capitalist Iran. The structural contradiction of the Saljuq polity and the conflicting tendencies arising from it found temporary resolution in military expansionism.

Territorial expansion, access to new resources and the subsequent increase in the military-logistic power of the state significantly undermined the previously unchallenged status of tribal relations in the organizational structure of the Saljuq state. Tribal lineage, though it had retained its primacy in the higher echelons of the power structure within the royal court and the Dargah, was no longer the main determinant of the hierarchy of power. New forces had entered the apparatuses of the state, both civil and military, and the mode of distribution of power followed the structural exigencies of the politics of the centralization of the state. This displacement of tribal relations, important as it was, did not undermine the hegemonic status of military relations in the structure of the Saljuq state. Concentrated coercion remained the principal instrument of centralization of power available to the state. This, however, had little, if anything, to do with the arbitrary will of the Saljuq Sultan/state. On the contrary, the hegemonic status of military power in the structure of the Saljuq state and its pivotal role in the process of the centralization of power were both determined primarily by the specificity of the dominant economic relations. In fact it would scarcely be an exaggeration to argue that the dominant economic relations largely specified the limits of the institutional and functional autonomy of the state in the process of centralization.

The conditions of the constitution and universalization of *iqta* do not in themselves explain the processes of the formation and appropriation of landed property associated with it; rather, they serve to highlight its characteristic features as a form of landholding. Crucial in this respect, however, is the structural connection between military service and land revenue. This connection, forged by the articulation of the military and the economic in the organization of the Saljuq polity, clearly indicates that the status of *iqta* in the complex process of the territorialization of state power depended primarily on the productivity of agriculture—that is, on the conditions of the provision and articulation of land and labour in the process of agrarian production. These conditions are specified by the form of land tenure and the tenancy relations between peasants and the *muqta*. They suggest that the *muqta*'s right to land revenue was secured by his effective possession of the land necessary for the reproduction of the peasants living in his jurisdiction. Production and appropriation of land revenue arose from the structure of possession in separation which underpinned the *iqta* as a form of landed property. Although the connection between military service and land revenue does not refer to the precise character of the property relations involved in the processes of production and appropriation of revenue, it does refer to the exchange relations which underlie them; that is, the exchange of the right to land use for a portion of produce underlying the process of production as a process of exploitation. The exchange relations which form the structure of the processes of formation and appropriation of property in land stem from the forms of possession in separation, which defines the nature of the *iqta* as landholding.

It should, however, be noted once more that this explanation cannot account for the character of the property relations associated with *iqta* as a form of landholding. The determination of the precise character of these relations presupposes a direct reference to the distribution of the means of production to the unit of production, and the distribution of the product from the unit of production to society at large: relations defining the exchange of rights to land use for a portion of produce and those specifying the process of the realization of surplus product. The former refers to the forms of possession in separation specified in the forms and conditions of tenancy and the latter to the exchange relations entailed in rent form. In this sense the determination of the character of property relations entailed in *iqta* as a form of landholding presupposes direct reference to the following processes: firstly, to the form and conditions of the constitution of the *muqta* as a legal subject with rights of appropriation and disposal over the *iqta*; secondly, to the relations of distribution of land to the unit of production; thirdly, to the exchange relations involved in the actual mode of payment of surplus to the *muqta*. The first process clearly concerns the relationship between the Saljuq sultan and the *muqta*. The second refers to the form of possession in separation underlying share-cropping and fixed rent as the dominant forms of tenure in pre-capitalist Iran. The third process, however, denotes the extent to which exchange relations, goods and money, were involved in the process of appropriation and realization of the economic surplus produced by share-cropping and fixed rent-paying peasants.

6. POLITICAL AUTHORITY, SOVEREIGNTY AND PROPERTY OWNERSHIP IN MEDIEVAL POLITICAL DISCOURSE

In Chapter 5, I argued that the historicist–essentialist conceptions of landed property and ownership in pre-Constitutional Iran presuppose a direct and causal relationship between the institutional form of state power and the character of property relations in the sphere of agrarian production. The former, it is generally assumed, determines the character and the modality of the development of the latter. This assumption depends on the invocation of a historical origin in the discourse, whereby Islam is posited as the determinant of the mode of distribution of political power in the polity, and hence as the historical origin of the political and economic relations conventionally attributed to the *iqta* and the succeeding forms of land assignment. But analysis of the social and organizational structures of the Saljuq state showed that this Islamic origin had no relevance whatsoever to the conditions which specified the prevailing forms of distribution of power and the structure of domination and subordination in the polity. It was thus concluded that the notion of sovereignty underlying the historicist–essentialist definitions of the *iqta* as a bureaucratic institution is radically misconceived. Such definitions rest on the erroneous identification of sovereignty with autocratic rule. Although the pre-Constitutional state was undoubtedly autocratic, it lacked the essential economic, military and institutional conditions of sovereignty.

It was further argued that the absence of the conditions of existence of sovereignty in pre-Constitutional Iran had important consequences for the exercise and retention of autocratic power. The underdevelopment of economic forces and relations ensured the dominance of the military in the structure of the state, and determined the

162

organizational form of the armed forces. The autocratic state required a decentralized military structure largely maintained by means of land assignments and land revenue. Land assignments in pre-Constitutional Iran, *iqtas* and *tuyuls*, were responses to these requirements, which had their roots ultimately in the structural development of the Iranian social formation. They were the 'private possessions' of their holders, *muqtas* and *tuyuldars*, who exercised the rights of appropriation and use invested in them by their overlords. The rights of appropriation and use associated with land assignments in pre-Constitutional Iran, whatever their duration, were almost always 'private' and 'individual'.

However, the advocates of historicist–essentialist conceptions of landed property and ownership in pre-Constitutional Iran have never attempted to problematize the juridico-political and economic conditions of existence of land assignments. Rather, they have conventionally sought affirmation in medieval Islamic political discourse. The case in point, which this chapter examines at length, is the notion of the 'absolute ownership' of the king, a notion frequently invoked to support accounts of the origin and development of the *iqta* as a bureaucratic/fiscal institution.

The classical statement of the notion posits the reigning monarch as the sole owner of all agricultural land in unambiguous terms; taken literally, this amounts to saying that the king held absolute rights of ownership over the land which effectively excluded others from its possession and use. Current interpretations of the notion follow much the same line of reasoning.[1] They emphasize the absolute nature of the ownership rights invested in the person/position of the Sultan in a manner identical to those entailed in the modern capitalist conception of property ownership. For the characteristic exclusion of the assignees from the processes of the formation and appropriation of private property in land, by definition, implies that the ownership rights invested in the person/position of the king, as absolute ruler, sufficed to ensure the reproduction of agrarian production in pre-constitutional Iran. Contemporary interpretations of the notion of the king as absolute owner thus entail two interrelated presuppositions. First, it is assumed that the notion is an autonomous discursive construct amounting to a theory of ownership. Secondly, the theory of ownership is related to an autonomous agrarian economic form based on peasant labour in which rights to use the land are exchanged for a portion of surplus product/labour in the form of taxes and dues.

It will be argued in this chapter that current interpretations of the medieval notion of the king's absolute ownership are essentially misconceived and erroneous in their theoretical presuppositions. The notion, it will be shown, is not an autonomous discursive construct, but a derivative of the ancient Persian (Sassanian) concept of kingship which was intrinsic to the political ethics of 'secular' autocratic rule in medieval political discourse.[2] The historical conditions which precipitated the adoption of the Sassanian concept of kingship by the medieval writers also determined their recourse to the notion of the absolute ownership of the Sultan. These conditions, it will be further argued, were related directly to the exigencies of autocratic power and to the structures and processes of domination and legitimation in the independent 'secular' states which had emerged in the wake of the disintegration of the Caliphate in the early third/ninth century. They cannot be conceived as the juridico-political requirements of a particular structure of the relations of production. Furthermore, it will be argued that the ownership rights thus attributed to the king could not generate the relations and mechanisms necessary for the formation and appropriation of economic property in land. The theory of the absolute ownership of the king lacks a corresponding concept of relations of production other than that which is generated by the political relations of autocratic monarchy. It is an assertion rooted in the myth of the centralized sovereign state in pre-Constitutional Iran.

The idea that in medieval Iran the king was the sole owner of all agricultural land is not systematically stated in the political discourse of the period. Rather, it features as an assertion variously related to the problems of secular political authority, and to the structure of domination and subordination expounded in some detail in political treatises and administrative manuals written by medieval scholars and state functionaries. Contemporary statements of the notion often refer to Nizam ul-Mulk as the major protagonist of the idea of the absolute ownership.[3] An often-quoted passage from his *Siyasat Nameh* is taken to be the most systematic statement of the notion and the proof that the medieval *iqta* in its various forms did not constitute private property in land. In this passage Nizam ul-Mulk states:

> *[Muqtas]* who hold land in *iqta* must know that they have no authority over the peasants except to take from them—and that with courtesy—the due amount of revenue which has been

assigned to them to collect; and when they have taken that, the peasants are to have security for their persons, property, wives and children, and their goods and farms are to be inviolable; the assignees are to have no further claim upon them. If peasants want to come to the court to state their cases, they are not to be prevented from doing so; any assignee who does otherwise must be checked; his fief will be taken away from him and he will be reprimanded as a warning to others. They must know that the *mulk* [property, country, kingdom] and *raiyat* [subjects and peasants] belong to the Sultan [the ruling power] and the *muqtas* and *valis* are like *shihnehs* [prefects] over the peasants [on their *iqtas*], in the same relation to them as the king is to other peasants. In this way the peasants will be contented and the *muqta* will be secure from punishments and torment in the world to come. *(Siyasat Nameh* 1960, p.133)

This statement appears in a section of *Siyasat Nameh* dealing with the relationship between the Saljuq Sultan and his military *muqtas*. Here the hierarchy of command and obedience in the military organization of the Saljuq state is discussed directly in relation to land and land assignment. The author is quite emphatic that the organizational structure of the Saljuq state was firmly tied to land assignment which was in the economic possession and the legal jurisdiction of the assignee (ibid. pp.99–100). Similarities to a feudal fief, however, cease at this point, as the above quoted passage suggests that the assignees' rights to the land were strictly economic, confined to possession and exploitation without private property ownership. The assignee was the holder and not the owner of the land and the peasants living on it. The ownership rights remained the prerogative of the Sultan, the sole proprietor in an agrarian society characterized, above all, by the absence of private property in land.

Present-day advocates of the theory of absolute ownership assume that Nizam ul-Mulk's statement did in fact signify concrete economic conditions characteristic of the agrarian economy of Iran in the Middle Ages. But Lambton, despite her insistence on the allegedly bureaucratic character of the medieval *iqta*, is nonetheless sceptical about Nizam ul-Mulk's statement, suggesting that he may have adopted the theory to serve different aims:

it is possible that he [Nizam ul-Mulk] is extending the theory of the ruling Khan as the representative of the tribe to cover the position of the Sultan as the ruler of a territorial empire over which he held proprietary rights. Or perhaps he was attempting to invest the theory of the steppe with the content of the theory of absolute ownership which he derived from Sassanian tradition. Another possibility cannot be ruled out, namely, that in asserting the paramountcy of the Sultan he was attempting to protect the peasants from arbitrary exactions by the assignees. (Lambton 1953, p.61)

Lambton's argument suggests that political expediency rather than economic necessity was the main reason for Nizam ul-Mulk's assertion of the theory of absolute ownership. So far, so good. What is however left out in Lambton's account is the actual political reason compelling Nizam ul-Mulk to resort to the theory of absolute ownership; a question of utmost theoretical importance, which concerns not only the historical conditions of the formation of the discourse of *Siyasat Nameh* but also its conceptual structure.[4]

Nizam ul-Mulk, the author of *Siyar al-Muluk*—better known as *Siyasat Nameh*—was the Saljuq Prime Minister and administrator under Alp Arsalan and his successor Muhammad Malekshah. He claims to have written the text during the closing decades of the fifth/eleventh century; the date of completion is given as 485/1092, a few years before the author was assassinated (allegedly by his Ismaili adversaries). Nizam ul-Mulk indicates in the introduction that he wrote at the behest of his master, Sultan Muhammad Malekshah, who commissioned a treatise on the tradition and the conduct of kingship and the practical duties of the king. This claim, whatever its historical status, determines the formal organization of the text and the order of its discourse. *Siyasat Nameh* is written in the tradition of political treatises and administrative manuals commonly known as 'Mirrors for Princes'; in fact, along with the *Qabus Nameh* of Kai Kaous Ibn Iskandar (474/1082) and Ghazali's *Nasihat ul-Muluk* (499/1105), it is one of the three major 'Mirrors' of the medieval period.[5] These three texts, written contemporaneously, resemble one another not only in form and character, but also conceptually. The Sassanian concept of kingship and rule and its derivatives is their common conception and theoretical source, and this distinctive feature of the medieval 'Mirrors' reveals a direct relationship between their conditions of formation and the conceptual structure of their discourse.

The literary genre of 'Mirrors for Princes' appears in the wake of the Buyid seizure of Baghdad, the centre of power in the Islamic community, in the mid–fourth/tenth century. This event ended the institutional unity of the religious and political authorities, hitherto signified by the institution of the Caliphate—a universal institution of domination and rule with a divine claim to legitimacy arising from the prophetic tradition sanctioned by the sacred law.[6] The bifurcation of the structure of domination through an effective separation of the religious and political authorities also marked the onset of a gradual conceptual change in the discourse of authority, domination and legitimation. The result was a gradual separation of historic *imama* from the *sharia*, a process which culminated in the adoption of the concept of *saltana* and its assimilation in medieval political discourse by the end of the fifth/eleventh century.

The conceptual change in medieval political discourse and the political and ideological transformations which precipitated it were by no means uniform or universal.[7] But the emergence and subsequent consolidation of independent and semi-independent states in the domains of the Caliphate enhanced the assimilation of the concept of the *saltana* and its derivatives in medieval political discourse. It signified a particular relation between religion and politics, and a notion of legitimate domination and rule, appropriate to the new political and ideological conditions. This relationship, which is clearly expressed in the notion of the 'shadow of God on earth' (*zell ul Allah fi-al ardh*), the universal attribute of the institution of *saltana*, is similar to that which is entailed in the notion of *farreh-e izadi* (divine effulgence), the ethos of universal monarchy signified by the Sassanian concept of kingship.

The influence of the Sassanian tradition of government and administration on Islamic political discourse predates the Buyid conquest of Baghdad, and the presence of the Sassanian concept of kingship in the classical texts addressing the conditions of temporal authority and the administration of the state is widely registered by contemporary scholars.[8] Lambton refers to Abu Yusuf, who, in the introduction to his *Kitab ul-Kharaj*, acknowledges 'the prevailing cult of the Sassanian tradition' and protests against its increasing influence on the conduct of the government and the methods of administration (Lambton 1962, p.94). However, Ibn al-Muqaffa (executed c.142/ 759) is said to have pioneered this trend (Dawood 1965). In *Adab al-Kabir*, he used the Sassanian concept in support of his argument for the necessity of the centralization of the political and juridical processes and practices of the state, against his traditionalist opponents who successfully opposed the institutionalization and codification of the *sharia* (Schacht 1950, pp. 95–102).[9]

Ibn al-Muqaffa's attempt to revive the Sassanian tradition of government and administration was precipitated by an acute crisis, eroding the political and ideological cohesion of the institution of the Caliphate. His primary aim was to restore the authority and legitimacy of the Caliph, which was being seriously challenged by the decentralizing forces and tendencies released in the process of the transformation of the state from a tribal confederacy into an expanding territorial empire with complex institutional structures (Goitein 1949, 1966; Mottahedeh 1975, 1976). Ibn al-Muqaffa thus emphasized order and stability as the aims of the ideal government, which was from his point of view an autocracy headed by a monarch holding absolute power.

In Ibn al-Muqaffa's discourse, absolute power and order are mutually interdependent. Order is the object of political power, and the splendour and continuity of absolute power are ensured by order. Although the concept of order as the object and condition of existence of political power is unambiguously Sassanian, the identification of order with justice, a characteristic feature of the Persian theory of government, is absent from Ibn al-Muqaffa's discourse (Dawood 1965). In fact, he replaces the substantive concept of justice with a formal notion derived from Islamic discourse, denoting an ethical and religious quality attained by conformity with the principles of *sharia* (Dawood op.cit., Lambton 1970, p.422, 1981, pp.43–69). The substantive concept of justice, however, survived the classical period and is central to the medieval appropriation of the Sassanian discourse on government and authority.

For Ibn al-Muqaffa order is an effect of political power. It is attained and maintained by means of force and rigid control of the polity. Thus the discourse of the relationship between authority and order focuses, to a large extent, on military power, its organization, administration and composition. The historical context and the principal political objectives of Ibn al-Muqaffa's discourse suggest that he was fully aware of the dilemma created by the political and economic organization of the army in the expanding state (Dawood op.cit.). On the one hand, he realised that land assignment was becoming increasingly indispensable to the economic organization and financial administration of the army. On the other hand, he was aware that the direct institutional link between the system of land assignment and the hierarchical structure of command and obedience was a powerful decentralizing force undermining the vertical structure of autocratic rule. He thus seeks institutional provision to counteract or avert the decentralizing effects of the system of land assignment without severing the link between the political and the military, the foundation of order and stability. In this case, too, he resorts to the Sassanian tradition and ideal of autocratic kingship.

The Sassanian state was structured on a specific system of vassalage signified by the concept of *shahanshahi*. The vassals were suzerain monarchs, Shahs, with a local or provincial power base, who were appointed by, and owed allegiance to, the Sassanian king—the Shahanshah, the king of kings. The vassals' right to their land (kingdom, province, city, etc.) was a function of their status in the hierarchy of domination and subordination in the political-military structure of the state. The rights of possession and exploitation were duly invested in the status rather than the person of the vassal. However, the specific feature of the Sassanian *shahanshahi*, which set it apart from the Western forms of vassalage, concerned the status of the office of vassalage itself. The status of the vassal, and hence his right to the land and revenue in his territory, was not hereditary. In fact the Sassanian vassalage was unique in this respect; for it was the only status which, at least theoretically, had been excluded from the otherwise universal rule of hereditary transmission of status central to the substantive concept of justice in the Sassanian ideal of kingship. In other words, the structure of command and obedience in the organization of the Sassanian state was a negative affirmation of the notion of absolute ownership, which when asserted signified the specificity of the mode of distribution of political power rather than the juridical conditions of economic exploitation in the sphere of agrarian production. This point will be considered in more detail in the context of a discussion of the conceptual structure of *Siyasat Nameh*.

Ibn al-Muqaffa's writings proved a lasting influence on the development of the intellectual trend which revived the Sassanian tradition of government and administration in the Middle Ages. It provided the Sassanian conceptions of kingship, authority and legitimacy with an Islamic ancestry which facilitated their assimilation into the discourse of the medieval 'Mirrors'. Nevertheless, it took two centuries for the 'cult of Sassanian tradition' to be fully assimilated into Islamic political discourse.[10] The Buyid conquest of Baghdad and the subsequent eclipse of the Caliphate, in the mid-tenth century, largely undermined the powerful political and ideological barriers which had successfully deprived the revivalist intellectual trend of the requisite institutional support since Ibn al-Muqaffa pioneered it in the second/eighth century. The cult of Sassanian tradition found institutional support and political reasons for revival in the independent Buyid state established in the former domains of the Caliphate.

The rise to power of the Saljuqs was a turning point in this process which, as noted earlier, culminated in the assimilation of the concept of *saltana* into the discourse of government and authority in medieval Iran. Under the Saljuqs the problem of temporal political authority, its relationship with religion and its conditions of legitimacy and domination, was posed at two different but interrelated levels. First, at the level of the Islamic community, formally represented by the institution of the Caliphate, where the problems of authority and legitimacy concerned the relationship between the two institutions of Saltana and Caliphate. Second, at the level of the Saljuq polity in which the legitimacy of *saltana*—i.e, the Saljuq kingship—depended on the relationship between the king and the array of military and civilian forces with diverse ethnic origins (Turkish, Persian, Arab) and religious affiliations (Sunni, Shii including Ithna-Ashari, Ismaeli-Batini) which formed the hierarchy of political power in the empire. The relationship, as was noted earlier, was determined by the economics of military power, which linked the structure of political authority inextricably to land and land revenue. The *iqta* was the intersection of the political and economic in the vertical structure of authority expressed in terms of the reciprocal relationship between military service and land revenue. This in effect meant that the conditions and scope for the exercise of authority depended on the mutations in the crucial relationship between the political and economic; that is, on the stability of the form of conditional ownership/possession which characterized the *iqta*. Stability of the *iqta* system signified a condition of balance in the relationship between the political and economic. It was an expression of the legitimacy of the structure of command and obedience in the Saljuq state. The institutional form and practice of power in the Saljuq state had already identified legitimate domination with order and stability before the notion was deployed in the annals of government and administration.

The constitution and subsequent institutional development of the Saljuq state thus consolidated the political and ideological processes and practices which emerged in the wake of the Buyid conquest of Baghdad and the bifurcation of the structure of authority and legitimate domination. If the *sharia* and historic *imama* had already proved inadequate to suit the changing conditions of the Islamic state in the time of Ibn al-Muqaffa, they would hardly be relevant to the conditions of power and authority in the Saljuq state. The discourse of *Siyasat Nameh* shows that Nizam ul-Mulk was fully aware of this problem; as we shall see shortly, historic *imama* plays no role in his conception of ideal government. The *sharia*, too, is assigned a marginal role in the construction of the notions of authority and legitimate domination, which are essentially secular in character and pertain to specific institutional conditions and social relations. Nizam ul-Mulk also realises the fundamental discrepancies between the institutional conditions and relations of the ideal autocratic kingship and the institutional form and organizational structure of the Saljuq state. He repeatedly refers to the unstable conditions of authority embedded in the relationship between the Saljuq Sultan and the *muqtas*, and emphasizes the necessity of maintaining the supreme authority of the Sultan in the conflict of interests and struggles for power between the Turkish military caste and the Persian scribes and civil administrators. The text of *Siyasat Nameh* is inundated by remarks which show the author's acute awareness of the unstable nature of a temporal authority which rests on the land and land revenue. But his veiled reservations about the desirability of the *iqta* system are often counterbalanced by his overt admission of its necessity for the logistics of military power on which the very survival of the Saljuq state depends. His ambivalent attitude is matched by a growing concern at the increasing power of the Turkish military caste in the administration of the state and economy. Nizam ul-Mulk's insistence that the financial administration of the army is and should always remain the prerogative of the *Divan*, the civil government and administration, is an explicit admission of the pivotal position of the land and land revenue in the unstable structure of authority in the Saljuq state.

Nizam ul-Mulk was by no means alone in his critique of the decentralizing tendencies and the growing might of the Turkish military caste in the administration, which he attributed to the prevalence of the *iqta* system. In fact, he was in this respect representing a powerful tendency within officialdom of those who, like him, were aware of the importance of the *iqta* system in the institutional structure of the state but were opposed to the increasing power and influence of the *iqta*-holders and the adverse effects on the authority of the king and the central government.[11] The discourse of *Siyasat Nameh* clearly reflects this major concern with the nature and the conditions of existence of the supreme authority of the king in the Islamic polity. Nizam ul-Mulk, as we will see in the following section, directly links the problem of the 'secular' political authority and domination to the institutional form of political power in the Saljuq state. The latter, he is adamant, must serve to maintain and enhance the supreme authority of the sultan. His remarks concerning authority and rule are informed by the Sassanian concept of kingship which, as was noted, depicts a decentralized state structure, a system of domination and subordination based on land organized around the royal household.[12] The Sassanian system of 'vassalage' serves to sustain the supreme authority of the king who is posited as the absolute owner of the land in the kingdom. The notion of absolute ownership in the Sassanian discourse does not signify the institutional form of state power. Rather the mode of distribution of political power depicted by the *shahanshahi* system is incompatible with the juridico-political condition of existence of the notion of absolute ownership. The notion, it will be argued, is the 'negative' assertion of the forms of authorization entailed in the system of domination and subordination depicted in the Sassanian discourse. It is an assertion of the supreme authority of the king in a political system in which the structure of domination and subordination requires above all the division of the territory.

The problem of temporal authority and legitimate domination in Sassanian discourse is discussed in the context of the relationship between politics and religion, a relationship which the Sassanian concept of kingship postulates as intrinsic. Religion, it is stated, is the foundation of kingship, and kingship is the protector of religion. Texts attributed to the Sassanian period, notably *Ahd-e Ardashir* (The Testament or Covenant of Ardashir) and *Nameh-e Tansar* (The Letter of Tansar), expound this mutual relationship in similar terms.[13] *Ahd-e Ardashir* maintains that 'religion and politics are twin born. They are of the one womb'. (Dehkhoda, 1931, and Shushtari, 1970, esp pp.67–78). *Nameh-e Tansar* expresses this idea in similar terms:

For church and state were born of one womb, joined together and never to be sundered. Virtue and corruption, health and sickness are of the same nature for both. (Tansar, pp.33–4)

Religion and politics are the two pillars of right order, a notion signifying a state of harmony with the cosmic order on which the legitimacy of temporal authority ultimately depends. This is the ethos of universal kingship expressed in the notion of *farreh-e izadi* (divine effulgence), the attribute of the sun-king, the centre of the universe in Zoroastrian cosmology.[14]

Although the notion of *farreh-e izadi* assigns a divine character to the king, legitimate domination and rule which deserves obedience presupposes specific social and political conditions. For the state of harmony with cosmic order which signifies the divinity of kingship is not given, but created, maintained and enhanced by the exercise of authority in the service of justice. The two Sassanian texts cited above consider justice as an attribute of kingship. But justice, which creates harmony with the cosmic order and legitimizes temporal authority, is a substantive concept, referring to a social rather than juridical state or condition and synonymous with order and stability. A stable social order is stratified and hierarchical. It is divided into estates, the boundaries of which are specified by religion, and sustained and enforced by temporal authority. As Tansar explains:

Know that according to our religion, men are divided into four estates. This is set down in many places in holy books and established beyond controversy and interpretation, contradiction and speculation. They are known as the four estates and their head is the king. (ibid. pp.37–8)

In the *Ahd-e Ardashir* we encounter a similar though less detailed account of the ordered and stable society (Shushtari, op.cit., p.78). In both texts the four estates are identified as the clergy, the military, scribes and artisans (which includes craftsmen), and traders and landless peasants. At the head of these estates stands the king, who is charged with the task of maintaining justice by keeping subjects in their designated estates and preventing social mobility and disorder; for 'keeping men in their stations strengthens the foundation of the state and religion'. Tansar argues:

It is through these four estates that humanity will prosper as
long as it endures. Assuredly there shall be no passing from one
to another . . . when, however, men fell upon evil days under a
religion that did not hold fast the welfare of the world, the king
of kings, through his pure intelligence and surprising excel-
lence, caused these four estates which had fallen away to be
restored and brought back each to his own place and point of
departure. He kept each man in his own station and forbade any
to meddle with any calling other than that for which it had
pleased God to create him. (Tansar, pp. 38–9)

Minovi points out that the functional division of society into four
estates and the supreme position of the king at the apex of the social
hierarchy is also confirmed in *Pazand*, another Zoroastrian text
(Minovi and Rizvani, 1975). What is interesting in these texts,
however, is the conditions of legitimate rule. Although kingship is
divinely ordained, the legitimacy of authority and domination is
strikingly secular. It depends on maintaining and enhancing justice
and equity by keeping subjects in their designated estates and
preventing disorder. Justice is synonymous with good order, which is
the essential condition of legitimate domination. For without justice,
anarchy reigns and the relationship between religious and political
authority is undermined. The king thus uses manipulation, persuasion
and violence to restore good order. Where 'there is no kingship there
is no friendship, no counsel and no law and no good order', states
Tansar (p.40).

The notion of good order thus signifies a hierarchical society
structured by religion. In Sassanian discourse notions of good order
and good religion and justice are frequently juxtaposed. Consequently, good order and good religion appear identical and interchangeable notions. This point has long been acknowledged by
contemporary scholars. It informs the common argument that in
Zoroastrianism religion and social structure are coterminous. This
argument, which, in effect, emphasizes the substantive character of
the concept of justice in Sassanian discourse, should nevertheless be
qualified in the light of the preceding discussion.

The notion of good order in Sassanian/Zoroastrian discourse
entails the religious determination of the social. But the functioning of
religion in this respect depends strictly on the role played by the
political authority in maintaining and enhancing order and stability;

that is to say, in maintaining subjects in their designated estates. Political authority ensures order of rank and status by providing for and enforcing the hereditary transmission of rank and status within designated estates. The hereditary transmission of rank is held as a general religious-social principle which applies to all ranks but one. Sassanian texts state, in unambiguous terms, that *shahanshahi* is an exception to this general rule. Ardashir, the Shahanshah, addressing his subordinate shahs, states: 'we shall not make kingship hereditary as we have made other dignities' (ibid. p.34).

The notion of *shahanshahi* in this context denotes a system of vassalage in which the lesser king's access to a 'crown and realm' is a function of his status in the political hierarchy; that is, his relationship with the king-superior who 'sets the crown upon his head' and 'entrusts him with realm'. This is apparent in Tansar's response to Gusnusp, the King of Tabaristan, who asks his advice about declaring allegiance to Ardashir and submitting to the authority of the Sassanian king. Tansar states:

> As for your special case, my counsel to you is to take horse and come with crown and throne to the King's court. Know and understand that a crown is what he sets upon your head, and a realm is that which he entrusts to you: for you have heard how he has acted towards all who have received from him crown and realm. (ibid. p.34)

The exclusion of the system of vassalage from the prevailing hereditary transmission of rank and status is particularly significant, for it shows clearly that the religious determination of the social implied by the concept of justice has specific conditions of existence. More precisely it depends, above all, on the form and character of the existing political authority and institutions. Religious and social structure can be coterminous only when they are sustained by a strong autocratic kingship.

The strong emphasis on order, rank and submission to authority which characterizes Sassanian discourse is an assertion of the centrality of autocratic kingship to the organization of society. The ethos of universal monarchy requires specific institutional conditions capable of expressing forms of authorization which emanate from and sustain the absolute power of the autocrat; that is, a centralized state apparatus organized around the royal household and a structure of domination and subordination which excludes relations other than absolute and unconditional obedience. These institutional conditions are not given in Sassanian discourse, or at best they are present only partially. The *shahanshahi* regime which underlies the institutional structure of political power in Sassanian discourse is, on the contrary, a decentralized structure of domination and subordination based on reciprocal relations of fealty, similar to forms historically associated with Western feudalism. It can provide for despotic rule but falls short of sustaining the centralized structure of command and obedience necessary to ensure a sovereign monarchy's administration of a vast territorial empire. The institutional form of the state in pre-capitalist empires, as was argued in the previous section, was determined primarily by the economics of military power, as the single most important element of cohesion in the structure of domination. The latter, which was to a large extent a function of the level of the development of productive forces, necessarily required a decentralized structure of command and execution logistically supported by land assignments which might or might not be inheritable. In this sense the institutional form of political power given in Sassanian discourse, namely the system of vassalage entailed in the *shahanshahi* regime, corresponds with the exigencies of the administration of the imperial state.

This, in effect, means that the domain assigned to the lesser shah was not only the territorial basis of his authority or his jurisdiction, but also his private holding acquired by virtue of his position in the military organization of the state. The notion 'private' in this context should be qualified, as denoting a political-economic rather than formal-legal condition. The domain/holding was private in the sense that economic agents other than the holder had no access to it. The conditions of exclusion which defined the conditions of private access were political, while the process of access which defined the mode and mechanism of use—i.e. extraction of revenue—was economic in character. This distinction, which corresponds to the distinction already made between the conditions of formation and the process of appropriation of private property in land (see chapter 4), will be discussed in more detail in the following section.

So far so good, but what of the notion of the absolute ownership of land entailed in Sassanian discourse? This notion is deployed to assert the supreme authority of the king in the decentralized structure of domination and subordination which characterized the institutional form of political power in Sassanian Iran. In fact, references to absolute ownership feature in conjunction with calls for submission to authority, both precipitated by crises gripping the state in various stages of its existence, when their aim is to restore the authority of the king by enforcing the existing structure of domination and subordination. The restoration of the supreme authority of the king, therefore, is not a condition of centralized rule, which is required to ensure absolute ownership, but of the unity of a decentralized state structured by the logistics of military power, which is the object of authority and the means of the unity of the imperial state. The logistics of military power, it was argued, required parcellization of the territory among the military chiefs, the lesser kings and lords, who were also assigned the right to economic exploitation of the land in their domains. This was an essential condition for the structural cohesion of political authority and the unity of the state. The Sassanian state did not possess the internal conditions of sovereignty. The supreme authority of the king presupposed the persistence of a decentralized state structure which precisely excluded the economic and institutional conditions of absolute ownership. The assertion of the supreme authority of the king in terms of his absolute ownership of the land was a negative affirmation of the pivotal status of land in the organizational structure of the state. It did not concern the institutional form of political power, still less the economic relations which sustained it.

This argument is confirmed by the two Sassanian texts under consideration. Both are concerned with the reign of Ardashir (224–241 AD), the founder of the Sassanian dynasty, and reflect his attempts to consolidate state power and avert the internal opposition threatening the unity of the state. However, it is widely held that the *Letter of Tansar* was written at a later date, most likely in the reign of Khosrow Anushirvan (532–579), and draws on the prestige of the founder of the dynasty and his great *herbad,* Tansar, to buttress the reigning monarch's claim to legitimacy (Boyce op.cit. pp.15–16, and Christensen 1965, p.83ff). Christensen believes that the discourse of *Letter of Tansar,* with its strong emphasis on order, rank, tradition, and submission to the state, accords admirably with the reign of Khosrow, when 'the king was forced to restore order after the social and religious upheavals caused in the reign of his father by the Mazdakite movement' (Christensen op.cit. p.85). Whatever their respective dates, however, there are striking similarities between the two texts. The order and conceptual structure of their discourses are remarkably similar, giving the impression that they are responses to similar political and ideological conditions, even if written in different ages.

In the *Letter*, the chief *herbad* responds to questions put to him by Gusnusp, the King of Pariswar and Tabaristan, and a former vassal of the Parthian King Ardawan, whose state was overthrown by Ardashir. Gusnusp has declined allegiance to Ardashir and is reluctant to submit to his authority. Ardashir, he believes, has violated the principles of right religion and is not the true protector of the faith. His correspondence with Tansar expresses his reasons and reservations, and seeks his counsel on the matter. Tansar in response defends Ardashir's policy of centralization of religious processes and practices, and invites Gusnusp to declare allegiance and submit to the supreme authority of the king of kings. The central tenet of Tansar's argument, as we have already seen, is that the supreme authority of the king is an essential condition of the order and organizational unity of the state. Social order and political unity justify his claim to legitimacy and submission. The king is the owner of the realm and the crown, which he bestows on whoever submits to his supreme authority.

It is important to note that the ownership of the realm here is deduced from the necessity of authority to ensure the maintenance of social order and political unity in a decentralized state. Tansar's case for submission is not a negation of the authority of Gusnusp and the autonomy of his kingdom, but an affirmation of a form of authorization which depends on it. Boyce, in her introduction to the text, emphasizes the connection between authority, order and the territorial integrity of the state:

> This passage suggests that Tansar laboured, not only to establish a canon of scripture and religious orthodoxy, but also to promote concord in the land of Iran, which, in the light of his close link with Ardashir, could only mean that monarch's rule. It is precisely for this end that we see him striving in the *Letter*. He is writing to a co-religionist, he is not concerned to combat devil-worship, but to press Ardashir's claim as overlord and upholder of the faith, and to persuade Gusnusp not to stand out against him, nor to believe 'evil slandering' about him. (op.cit. p.7)

The crucial connection between authority and order, and the overriding concern with the territorial integrity of the state, also underlie the discourse of *Siyasat Nameh*. In this case, too, we encounter the substantive concept of justice denoting a hierarchical social order, in which political authority, filtered through ethnic-cultural relations, specifies the status of the subjects in the social structure. The political and social hierarchies coincide and the organizations of polity and society are identical. Although land occupies a pivotal position in the political hierarchy, property relations are presented as secondary effects of political authority, a quality attributed to the king alone. The Sassanian conception of kingship which informs Nizam ul-Mulk's approach to the questions of temporal rule and legitimate domination also specifies the status of the notion of absolute ownership in the discourse of *Siyasat Nameh*, to which we shall now turn.[15]

Siyasat Nameh constitutes a heterogeneous body of discourse, internally unified by a common objective. It seeks to define the nature of political authority and the conditions of legitimate domination within the established frameworks of command and obedience and norms of conduct in pursuit of order and stability. The concept of political authority entailed in the discourse of *Siyasat Nameh* is distinctly 'secular', in the sense that it is distinguished from religious authority, and religion plays little if any role in the author's depiction of the Saljuq polity as the institutional ensemble of the prevailing political relations and forces. The concept of authority is linked with a notion of legitimacy which presupposes specific social and economic conditions. The conditions of authority and legitimate rule, which are given in the discourse, are properties of a centralized autocratic kingship and a stratified social order. They are not derived from religious sources, i.e. the *sharia* or *sunna*, but rather from a tradition of kingship traced to the pre-history of Islam, notably Persian (Sassanian) history, and to a lesser extent Turkish mythology.

The conception of political authority and legitimacy entailed in the discourse of *Siyasat Nameh* sets it apart from the mainstream political discourse of medieval jurists and philosophers, in which the *sharia* and *sunna* define the source and the conditions of temporal authority and legitimate government, the frameworks of command and obedience and the norms of conduct in the Islamic community. In the discourse of the *Siyasat Nameh*, sacred law and prophetic tradition play a marginal role in defining the nature of authority and conditions of legitimate rule.[16] They are largely displaced by the political ethics of a divinely ordained kingship, reiterated through a sustained critique of weak and decentralized government and unruly social order. Autocratic kingship presiding over an orderly society signifies the ideal form of rule and government, and sets the standard for judging the existing state of affairs. In fact, the discourse of *Siyasat Nameh* operates in the gap between the real and the ideal, and as such, it generates general precepts which inform simple or complex ethical judgements in favour of authority and order. These ethical judgements, however, seek no notional or transcendental truth. Rather their truth is practical; the supreme value of order and stability. The omnipresent fear of chaos and anarchy always justifies the gravitation of the discourse towards authority.

In the discourse of *Siyasat Nameh* kingship is based on justice *(adala)* rather than right religion *(din)*. The concept of justice deployed by Nizam ul-Mulk is synonymous with order, i.e. the practical truth of the political ethics of autocratic kingship *(Siyasat Nameh* 1960, p.9). The synonymity of the two notions of justice and order in the discourse means that an authority which creates, maintains or enhances order and stability is by definition just and legitimate and must be obeyed. Obedience in this context is not a moral duty alone but also a social necessity, whose negative logic is explicitly expressed in the tyranny of anarchy and disorder: the tyranny resulting from the absence of effective authority (ibid. pp.9, 10, 12). The concept of authority is thus the antithesis of anarchy and disorder, and as such contains the conditions of legitimate domination. These conditions are largely given in the ethics of autocratic kingship. They are, for the most part, institutional and relational, embedded in the relationship between real or fictitious subjects as historical actors (ibid. pp.179, 186).

The conditions of legitimate domination also include religion. But the relationship between religion and temporal political authority in the discourse of *Siyasat Nameh* is rather complex. Though kingship is divinely ordained and religion is conceived as the foundation of the state, on a par with politics, the political ethics of autocratic kingship does not seek a transcendental truth, religious or otherwise. Religion serves to maintain just authority and order, on which it depends for its own survival. It is not the organizing principle of the polity, but an institution with specific conditions of existence, identical with the exigencies of order and stability. The legitimation function of religion, its role in the sustenance of just rule, depends on its capacity to conform with the conditions of order and stability.

The most important thing which a king needs is sound faith, because kingship and religion are like two brothers, whenever disturbance breaks out in the country, religion suffers too, heretics and evil-doers appear, and whenever religious affairs are in disorder, there is confusion in the country; evil-doers gain power and render the king impotent and despondent, heresy grows rife and rebels make themselves felt. (*Siyasat Nameh* 1960, p.60)

The legitimation function of religion thus depends on the existence of particular social conditions. These conditions are given in the concept of justice, the foundation and object of kingship. They are properties of a stratified social order in which the social hierarchy and the status of the subjects within it are specified by the temporal political authority. The king maintains justice by keeping subjects in their designated station, that is, by maintaining and enforcing the social hierarchy in which the socio-economic status of the subjects is defined by virtue of their relationship to the institution of kingship:

God has created the king to be the superior to all mankind and the inhabitants of the world are his inferiors; they derive their subsistence and rank from him ... He should know the measure and rank of everyone, and be constantly enquiring into their circumstances lest they deviate from the letter of his command or overstep the limits which are set for them. (ibid., p.186)

Justice is thus maintained by keeping subjects in their rightful place so that stability will prevail. 'If it was fitting that people should do whatever they wished', writes Nizam ul-Mulk, 'God most mighty and glorious would not have brought forth a king and placed him over them' (ibid. p.35). The king is 'chosen by God' to maintain order and enhance stability by ensuring that:

all things are restored to their proper order and each person's rank is fixed according to his deserts, with the result that affairs religious and worldly are well arranged and every man has work according to his capability. Nothing contrary to this is permitted by the king and all things great and small are regulated by the balance of justice and the sword of governance by the grace of Allah (be he exalted). (ibid. p.179)

The substantive notion of justice as such signifies a direct connection between religion and stability. Right religion is in conformity with stable social order, right order. This conformity, defining the conditions of legitimate domination, is sustained and enhanced by political authority. Authority which maintains order and security is by definition legitimate and merits obedience. Order is the necessity of compliance (ibid. pp.9–10).

The concept of justice in *Siyasat Nameh* alludes to a 'functional division' of society whereby the status of the subjects in the social hierarchy is specified by the political authority. The king is urged to maintain equilibrium by keeping subjects in their proper places within society. In this sense the concept of justice signifies the intersection of religion and politics. A functional division of society into specific occupational strata is necessary if religion is to remain the foundation of the state. In other words, the legitimation function of religion depends on the ability of the political authority to maintain and enforce the rules and conditions of social division among the subjects. Strong kingship and autocratic rule is a necessary condition of good religion, that which reflects and legitimizes the ordered society. Nizam ul-Mulk states clearly that ethnic origin and religious affiliation should be the principal, if not the sole, criterion in determining the status of subjects in the hierarchy of power in society. This statement, variously repeated in the text, is however qualified by an argument in favour of the hereditary transmission of status in order to maintain the ethnic-religious structure of the social hierarchy. In this sense, the concept of justice in Nizam ul-Mulk's discourse signifies a caste society, in which socio-economic relations are functions of the articulation of ethnic-religious with political re-lations. Turks and Persians, Sunnis and Shiis, Christians, Jews and Zoroastrians stand in a specific order in relation to the king which also specifies their status in the society. It should, however, be noted that Nizam ul-Mulk's argument for the maintenance of the caste system does not stem from practical or ethical considerations of efficiency and meritocracy, but rather from its relevance to order and stability.[18] Autocratic kingship and the caste system are two pillars of right order (ibid. pp.139–40, 148–9, 159–60, 171–3).

In *Siyasat Nameh*, just as in Sassanian discourse, landholding is excluded from the hereditary transmission of rank and status, thus implying that it is irrelevant to the social organization of order. But the exclusion of land-ownership and property relations from the organization of social order means that society and polity are identical entities. Assertions to this effect, which underlie the notion of absolute ownership in Nizam ul-Mulk and in current historical writing, completely obscure the institutional form of political power in the Saljuq State.

The discourse of *Siyasat Nameh*, which posits order and unity as the fundamental means and objectives of legitimate rule, also specifies the institutional form of authority, i.e. the organizational structure of the Saljuq state, though only in general terms. Nizam ul-Mulk's comments on the institutional forms of authority are imbued with ethical precepts which link absolute authority to the welfare of the subjects. This relationship is stated in negative terms. The absence or weakness of authority is the affirmation of oppression. It enables the army to 'over-exploit' and oppress the 'people':

> When the army has power over the country to strike, to fetter, to imprison, to usurp, to extort, to dismiss and to impose taxes, then what difference is there between the king and them? For these things have ever been the king's prerogative, not the business of the army; armies have never been allowed to exercise such power and authority. In all ages the golden crown, the golden stirrup, the throne and the coinage have belonged by right to the king alone. *(Siyasat Nameh p.187)*

Oppression which is not exercised by the king is a negative quality. It leads to discord and promotes disorder, thus undermining the natural (i.e. hierarchical) organization of society, which is in conformity with the spirit of justice and good religion (ibid. p.139). Oppression exercised by the king, by contrast, is a positive quality; it enhances authority, which is the natural constitution of the ordered and prosperous society.

The ethical precepts which define the quality of oppression are properties of the substantive concept of justice. The need for order and unity which links royal authority and popular welfare is also the 'temporal' logic of the king's divine right to 'the golden crown, the golden stirrup, the throne and the coinage'. The mode of legitimation of authority is reminiscent of the relationship between religion and political authority in the Sassanian concept of kingship. The efficacy of the king's right to rule depends on his authority to claim and secure submission, and his authority presupposes institutional conditions which are synonymous with the exigencies of order and stability. In fact Nizam ul-Mulk invokes the Sassanian tradition; referring to Buzurjmihr-e Bakhtgan's advice to Nushirvan the Just, he states: 'The country belongs to the king and the king has given the country, and not the people of the country, to the army' (ibid. p.187). This statement entails two propositions concerning the form and character of the king's rights to the country. The first proposition posits the king as the absolute owner, with the right of disposal over the land in his kingdom. The second proposition suggests that the military were lesser tenants of the king and held land from him as he divided the country among them.

The above statement, important as it is, leaves out a number of crucial factors which have direct bearing on the form and character of the ownership rights attributed to the king. Firstly, the statement is silent on the conditions which impel the absolute owner to dispose of the land and divide it among the command structure of the soldiery. Secondly, it omits any consideration of the conditions which governed the disposal of the land. Nizam ul-Mulk attributed the division of the country among the soldiery, i.e. the practice of land assignment, to the need to ensure the maintenance of order and the territorial integrity of the state:

> Furthermore, the kingdom is kept in order by its tax-collectors and army officers . . . For countries are held by men and men by gold. (ibid. pp.165, 170)

Statements of this kind are abundant in *Siyasat Nameh*. While they clearly assert the centrality of military power to the maintenance of order—and hence of authority—they do not explain why the army had to be sustained by means of land assignment. We encounter the same problem in the works of the modern historians of pre-capitalist Iran, who are equally silent about the historical conditions which precipitated the practice of land assignment. For example, as we have seen, Lambton attributes the introduction and universalization of the *iqta* to the financial administration of the army which, according to her, 'decided the general principles of the military organization and administration which were to persist in Persia in a more or less modified form down to the Constitutional Revolution' (Lambton 1953, p.57). In fact, as in much contemporary historical writing, the system of land assignment is seen simply as a method of financial administration, and its introduction is attributed to the arbitrary will of the medieval rulers and their administrators. Such subjectivist views of the conditions of formation of the *iqta* are closely associated with contemporary statements of the notion of absolute ownership, which unequivocally deduce the character of ownership rights from the absolute and indivisible authority of the despotic ruler, exercised through a centralized apparatus of domination and rule.

The conditions of formation of the *iqta* and its place in the organizational structure of the Saljuq state have already been discussed in some detail in the preceding chapter, where it was argued that the medieval *iqta* and the succeeding forms of land assignment were structural conditions of political order, partial sovereignty and territoriality of the state in pre-capitalist Iran. They were forms of dependent landholding, constituted by the articulation of the political and economic relations which had ensured the primacy of the military in the social and economic organization of the state. The property relations associated with the *iqta* and the succeeding forms of land assignment were expressions of the mode of articulation of political and economic relations, which, as previously argued, was determined by the level of development of economic relations and forces in pre-capitalist Iran. The underdeveloped state of commodity relations in agriculture specified the position of the military as the most effective means of securing order, stability and unity of power in an expansive territorial state with a highly heterogeneous ethnic and religious population. The ability of the state to muster, organize and exercize military power, on the other hand, depended primarily on the level of development of productive forces in the agrarian economy of pre-capitalist Iran. The articulation of the political and the economic expressed in the logistics of military power determined the character of the *iqta* as a form of dependent landholding, and specified the nature of the conditional rights of ownership associated with it. The parcellization of territory among the soldiery in return for military service, which inextricably linked political power with landholding, was a structural requirement for the order and unity of the state.

The discourse of *Siyasat Nameh,* as argued above, entails a concept of order as the object and the condition of existence of good government. The Sultan, whose authority is sanctioned by the divine will, is assigned the task of maintaining the order and stability which are the essential conditions of his legitimate rule. *Siyasat Nameh* further maintains that order and stability are ensured by military power, which in turn was sustained by the practice of land assignment. Much of the discussion of the crucial connection between authority and order focuses on the relationship between the Sultan and his *muqtas,* thus affirming the structural link between land and military power. In the discourse of *Siyasat Nameh,* the Saljuq *iqta* features as the point of intersection of authority and order, the nexus of the dialectics of the political and economic in the logistics of power.

The conditions of assignment, the structural link between revenue and military service, reveal at once the conditional form and the private character of the rights associated with the *iqta.* The discourse of *Siyasat Nameh* reiterates that the king's right to the land is an attribute of his authority as the sovereign personified. The sovereignty of the crown is expressed through the central government's monopoly control over coinage, taxation and foreign policy, which are, in effect, expressions of the economic cohesion, political unity and territorial integrity of the state; and the ability to institute and maintain monopoly control over the monetary, fiscal and foreign policy of the state depends primarily on the government's capacity to muster and exercize military force territorially. The structural exigencies of this process underlie the practice of land assignment, forging the link between land and military power which remains the basis of authority and the condition of domination. In other words, the exchange of rights over the land for military service, and the subsequent parcellization of the territory, are the conditions of existence of 'partial' sovereignty signified by the state's universal territorial 'rights' to administer the coinage, levy taxes and conduct foreign relations. The authority of the institution of kingship was an expression of this partial sovereignty, personified by the crown.

That the practice of land assignment was the condition of the authority and partial sovereignty of the state is clearly indicated by Nizam ul-Mulk's discussion of the politics of the restoration of order following incidents of insubordination and rebellion by the *vali-muqta.* In such events, historical and contemporary, the restoration of the authority of the central government, more often than not, involves an invocation of the supreme rights of the Sultan to the land, followed by the reconquest of the *velayat-iqta* in question. The re–establishment of the authority of the central government, however, did not alter the status of the *velayat* as land assignment; it merely restored its former financial and military links with the central government. In this respect, the restoration of the status of the rebellious *velayat* as *iqta* was both the object of the reconquest and the condition of the partial territoriality of authority. The causal relationship between political authority and ownership rights was always filtered through the connection between land assignment and military service, and the division of the territory was tantamount to the parcellization of sovereignty. The structural conditions of Saljuq society determined not only the institutional form, but also, and more importantly, the efficacy and the range of political power.

The structural logic of the *iqta*, the reasons compelling the Sultan to dispose of land acquired by conquest or bequest, should be sought in the level of development of economic forces and relations. The underdevelopment of commodity relations, which deprived the state of the most extensive and effective integrative mechanism, was also responsible for the positioning of the military in the widening gulf between the spatial character of state power and the territorial basis of the state. The articulation of the economic and the political as such determined the form and the character of the property relations associated with the *iqta*. It constituted and sustained the link between land and military service, and reproduced the corresponding sep-aration of the rights of ownership from the object of ownership which remained the hallmark of agrarian property in pre-capitalist Iran.

Nizam ul-Mulk indicates clearly that the Saljuq Sultan disposed of the bulk of agricultural land in his kingdom and assigned it to military magnates and political notables as *iqtas*. The *muqtas* functioned as the Sultan's lesser tenants, who held land from him in return for their provision of specific services, military and administrative. The *muqtas'* rights to the land assigned to them by the Sultan were expressions of the positions which they held in the hierarchy of domination and subordination within the Saljuq polity. The political/military positions held by the *muqtas*, however, were to a large extent functions of their ethnic and tribal origins, which specified the subject's access to political power. In this sense the *muqtas'* rights to the land were constituted by the articulation of the political and ethnic relations which also determined the typology of the *iqta*, hence the form and derivation of the rights and services associated with each type. According to *Siyasat Nameh*, the *iqta al-tamlik* (the administrative *iqta*) which generally amounted to a provincial governorate, was as a rule assigned to the Saljuq Amirs, the leading members of the ruling tribe, who formed the command structure of the tribal army maintained in the provinces (ibid. p.102). The Saljuq Amirs, however, had to take possession of their *iqtas* by force. This practice, a common feature of the system of land assignment in pre-capitalist Iran, highlights not only the conditions of the *muqta*'s access to the land, but also the very nature and extent of the Sultan's control over it. It shows that the possession of military force by the *muqta*, which defined the conditions of his access to the land, was also an essential condition of the territoriality of the Sultan's authority, and hence of his partial control over the land. The Sultan's partial control (expressed in terms of the ability of the central government to impose and maintain a uniform coinage, fiscal and foreign policy) in fact involved a negation of the absolute ownership rights attributed to him. The conditions which governed the disposition of the land by the Sultan simultan-eously constituted the Saljuq Amir as a *muqta*, as a legal subject with rights over the land. The economic control of the *muqta* over the *iqta*, which involved direct exploitation of the peasants to provide for the upkeep of his army as well as payment of taxes to the central government, was a necessary condition of the partial control and territoriality of the Sultan's authority.

Siyasat Nameh shows clearly that the hierarchy of domination and subordination in the Saljuq polity was closely linked with landholding, and that the assignment of the *iqta* as a universal practice essentially involved an exchange of rights for military service. The documents of authorization of the *iqta* pertaining to the Saljuq period further specify the nature of these exchange relations (Lambton 1953, pp.60, 70), indicating that the administrative *iqta* was considered as the property *(melk)* of its holder, who was addressed as owner *(mālek)* The relationship of the holder to his property was one of ownership *(malekiyat)*. Yet the term *malekiyat* in this context refers to a set of rights bestowed on the position of the *muqta* as provincial governors by the king, which concerned not the land itself but its produce (usufruct).

This point is made clearly in a diploma of governorship from the Sanjar era, in which the Saljuq ruler assigns the governorship of a province to Malek Masoud, a Saljuq Amir, to hold it as his *iqta*. The diploma is specifically clear on a number of important points. Firstly, it indicates that the Saljuq *muqta*/governor's right to the *iqta* is a right to the revenue and produce of the land, not the land itself, which he holds as an officer of the crown, on behalf of the King. Secondly, the *muqta* is assigned the right to create sub-assignments and grant military *iqtas* to his soldiery. Thirdly, it shows that the revenue of the land which accrued to the administrative *muqta*/provincial governor consisted of land rent, and was fundamentally different from the state taxes, extracted by the state or by the provincial government on behalf of the state (ibid. pp.70, 170–1). The grant of the administrative *iqta* followed the tribal (i.e. steppe) rules, which regulated the relationship between the Saljuq King, the Ilkhan, and the members of the ruling tribe/clan and sub-tribes/clans in the very centre of the Saljuq confederacy. It was, therefore, excluded from the sphere of the *sharia* and the Islamic laws of inheritance. In so far as the land relations were concerned:

> the Islamic law-books represented the ideal and not the actual practice. Conformity with the legal theory was abandoned in practice at an early stage—if it ever existed—and once abandoned there was little check on arbitrary action, and the system which grew up in many respects bore little resemblance to the exposition of the jurists. (Lambton 1953, p.53)

The administrative *iqta* and the rights of ownership associated with it were usually transmitted undivided to the legitimate heir of the holder, who thus became the new *muqta*/governor with the king's consent.

The military *iqta*, on the other hand, was granted to the standing army in return for services rendered to the Saljuq Sultan, under whose direct command it remained. The standing army, as noted earlier, was composed of non-tribal (non-Saljuq) soldiery, mostly Turkish slaves and freed men, who entered the Sultan's service as professional soldiers, men of the sword. Nizam ul-Mulk states that the standing army under Malekshah numbered 400,000 men who were maintained financially by the grant of *iqta* or by drafts on revenue *(Siyasat Nameh* p.144). This point is also made by Hafiz Abru, who maintains that the payment of the standing army and professional soldiery was largely by *iqta*.[19] Nizam ul-Mulk further indicates that the holders of the military *iqtas* were of non-Turkish (non-Saljuq) origin, raised as pages in the royal court to occupy positions as regional or provincial military commanders at the Sultan's behest (ibid. p.102). The military *muqtas* did not possess their own private armies before their appointment. Nizam ul-Mulk states clearly that access to military power and resources and the right to land revenue were both direct consequences of the *muqta's* position in the hierarchy of political-military power which underpinned the Saljuq power structure.

The military, like the administrative, *iqta* signified rights to the revenue of the land specified in the document of assignment. The land theoretically remained part of the crown/state lands, while the *muqta* held exclusive rights to its revenue. These rights were inheritable and were usually transmitted to his heir and successor, who occupied his position in the military-political hierarchy. In this case, too, the transmission of rights was excluded from the sphere of the *sharia* and the Islamic laws of inheritance, which, in effect, prevented the sub-division of the *iqta*. In other words, political relations governing the conditions of assignment of *iqta*—both military and administrative—instituted juridical processes which closely resembled the right of primogeniture historically associated with Western feudalism, in form and outcome. The *muqta* treated the *iqta* as his domestic jurisdiction. He was legally empowered to administer justice and make sub-assignments to his soldiery, who held land from him in the hierarchy of domination and subordination which sustained the regional/provincial military power structure.

Siyasat Nameh also refers to a third type of land assignment, the personal *iqta*, assigned to the Saljuq Amirs and prominent *ulama*. The personal *iqta* was generally viewed as a gift from the Sultan to provide for the livelihood of the assignee—often a personal favourite—and as such carried no financial, military or bureaucratic obligation. The personal *iqta*, too, signified a private holding and was therefore inheritable. But the transmission of the rights associated with the personal *iqta* was governed by the *sharia* and the Islamic laws of inheritance, which set it apart from the military *iqta*. This type of *iqta* was not universal or even widespread, and its presence did not contravene the general conditions governing the distribution and possession of the *iqta* in the Saljuq era. The development of the *iqta* under the Saljuqs 'decided the main lines along which the system [of land assignment] was to develop, and this system lasted in its essentials through the Middle Ages down to the twentieth century' (Lambton op.cit. 1953, p.53).

The separation of rights from the object of ownership was the characteristic feature of property relations associated with *iqta* and the succeeding forms of land assignment in pre-capitalist Iran. Induced and sustained by the mode of articulation of the economic and the political, this separation further obscured the actual process of formation and appropriation of economic property in land. It underlies the commonplace conception that the relations which specified the link between political/military hierarchy and landholding also defined the mode and mechanism of the appropriation of economic surplus, and that juridico-political relations of domination and subordination alone were sufficient to ensure the relationship between military-administrative service and land revenue which underpinned the structure of the *iqta* and its variants. The logistics of military power which specified the mode of articulation of the political and the economic undoubtedly defined the conditions of the formation of landed property in *iqta*, specifically the conditions of the constitution of the *muqta* as a legal subject with specific rights over the land specified as his *iqta*.

However, the form of the rights over the land, and hence the conditions of the *muqta*'s access to it, varied in the case of both the administrative and the military *iqta*. The conditions of formation of the rights, which also defined the conditions of the constitution of the *muqta* as a legal subject, cannot explain the conditions and process of the realization of the rights over the land specified as *iqta*. This process, which involves the transformation of legal to economic property, was constituted (determined) by relations governing the surrender of the land by the *muqta* to the peasants for use. This point is of prime significance in the determination of the nature of the property relations associated with the *iqta*; for it suggests that the character of the *iqta* as landed property cannot be deduced from juridico-political conditions of assignment. Rather it also requires a consideration of the following factors:

(i) forms and conditions of the distribution of the land to the unit of production

(ii) forms and conditions of the articulation of the land and labour in the process of production

(iii) forms and conditions of the distribution of the product from the unit of production to the social formation at large.

A consideration of the above factors, in turn, involves an analysis of the structural processes and practices underlying agrarian production in pre-capitalist Iran, specifically:

(i) forms of land tenure and the conditions of tenancy
(ii) forms and conditions of the subsumption of labour in the process of production
(iii) forms and conditions of the involvement of the unit of production in economic exchange relations

The remaining section of this study will thus be chiefly devoted to an analysis of the processes of the formation and appropriation of economic property in land in pre-capitalist Iran: the analysis of the forms and conditions of tenancy and the processes of production, appropriation and distribution of surplus labour-product.

7. THE ORGANIZATION OF AGRARIAN PRODUCTION IN PRE-CAPITALIST IRAN

Agrarian production in pre-capitalist Iran was organized in different forms, each signifying a specific combination of labour process and relations of production. The structure of the combination, i.e. the organization of production, was determined by the relations and conditions governing the distribution of the land by the landlords to the peasants. These conditions, which were formally expressed by the terms and conditions of tenancy, specified the peasants' rights to use the landlords' land in return for a portion of the product. The exchange of rights to land use for a portion of the product formed the structure of the relations of production as relations of exploitation. The exchange relations generally stipulated in a contract between landlord and peasant specified the form and boundaries of the unit of production and the technical division of labour within it. Share-cropping and fixed rent were the two forms of organization of production which historically prevailed in pre-capitalist Iran.

Share-cropping

Share-cropping was the dominant mode of appropriation of surplus product in agriculture in pre-capitalist Iran. The dominance of share-cropping relations in the Iranian countryside, from the Sassanian to the Pahlavi era, is variously recorded by contemporary scholars.[1] Official statistics released in 1960 on the eve of land reform suggest that in 54 per cent of all cultivable land in Iran, agrarian production was based on share-cropping (Behnam and Rasekh 1963, p.38).[2] It was widely practised in most agricultural regions, with a higher concentration in grain-producing areas such as Azarbayjan, Khorasan and Kurdistan.[3]

The bulk of historical evidence concerning share-cropping relations in pre-capitalist Iran is related to the post-Safavid era, primarily the nineteenth and twentieth centuries.[4] But this period can essentially be taken to exemplify the historical specificity of share-cropping relations in pre-capitalist Iran in general. Contemporary historical research is unanimous that the general form and the fundamental structural characteristics of share-cropping relations remained unchanged in the course of their complex and prolonged development in pre-capitalist Iran.[5]

Historically, share-cropping peasants in pre-capitalist Iran did not own agricultural land; the land they worked was owned by the land-owning class, who granted them the right to use it in return for a portion of its produce. This exchange of rights to land use in return for a portion of the product was stipulated in a contract between the share-croppers and their overlords. The contract was usually verbal, less often written, and its duration mostly unspecified, subject to the landlord's whim. The share-cropper's tenure was, for the most part, insecure. His rights to the land were not guaranteed even in the course of a production cycle, much less permanently.

This exchange of right to land use for a portion of product between the landlord and the peasant was the starting point and the foundation of the process of production as process of exploitation. The fact that the exchange involved a specific time period meant that the transfer of rights over the land was 'partial' and 'contractual'. Although the landlord, as legal subject, held exclusive rights over the land, his ability to alienate those rights in an act of exchange, i.e. to treat them as rights over a commodity, depended on specific economic and juridical conditions; namely, generalized commodity production and a market with specified legal boundaries for the purchase and sale of land. In the absence of these conditions the contractual rights remained partial. Their efficacy depended on the non-economic coercion entailed in the juridico-political conditions of tenancy.

The peasant's tenure, the *nasaq*, signified individual rights to the land, even when it was effective through his membership of the production team, the *boneh*. The peasant's *nasaq* was regulated by local custom and tradition, which formed the foundation of the share-cropping contract in general. The wide variations in tradition and customary law, and hence in the form of the share-cropping contract in the Iranian countryside, meant in effect that there was no general mechanism of determination of share-cropping relations; the level of rent varied widely not only from one province to another but also within each province, where usually a wide range of rental relations was practised. But despite the wide variations in terms, the share-cropping contract displayed a remarkable structural uniformity throughout the country, as is evident in the work of numerous writers commenting on the state of Iranian agriculture in the late nineteenth and early twentieth centuries (Mostowfi 1942 vol.III, pp.182, 279, 283, 284).[6]

Along with local tradition and customary law, religion played a role, though a less important one, in regulating share-cropping relations. Share-cropping was widely practised prior to the Arab conquest, and the Arab conquerors, as the new landlords, did not attempt to change the existing agrarian relations, but rather to modify them according to Islamic precepts. The early Islamic attempts to modify the structure of share-cropping relations, however, were unsuccessful, due mainly to the lack of an established point of reference; the Quran does not address landholding and agrarian relations in any detail, nor does the term *muzara'eh* (share-cropping) feature in its discourse. Nonetheless, the persistence of share-cropping relations in the post-Classical period impelled the Islamic jurists, both Sunni and Shii, to come to terms with it. The rules and regulations concerning the terms and conditions of *muzara'eh* thus feature prominently in the heterogeneous body of discourse forming the bulk of the Islamic *sharia*, Sunni and Shii.[7]

The Islamic jurists are in general agreement as to the definition, status and principles of share-cropping relations in Islamic law.[8] Share-cropping is considered as a contract (*aqd*) in land-use between two parties in return for a specified portion of produce; *muzara'eh* is contractual in that it involves an exchange of the right to land use for a portion of the produce of the land. The *muzara'eh*, the owner of the land, provides the *amel*, the share-cropper, with a piece of land to cultivate for a specified time on condition that the latter can cultivate it and divide the proceeds in accordance with the rules laid down by the *sharia*. The *sharia* on the whole argues for the division of the produce on the basis of the provision of the means of production, a legacy of the pre-Islamic period (Khosravi, op.cit. p.70), and the main means of production considered are land, water, seed, labour and draught animals.[9]

Although there is thus general agreement, share-cropping relations have undergone numerous revisions and modifications within Islamic jurisprudence, and Muslim jurists, Sunni and Shii alike, have frequently attempted to codify them, but unsuccessfully. Customary law (*urf*) and tradition remained the main regulators of share-cropping relations in Iran up to the eve of land reform in 1962. Although the Civil Code of 1936 assigned a larger role to the Islamic, and in particular the Shii, *sharia* in regulating agrarian relations, in practice they still remain subordinate to local custom and tradition.[10]

The Division of Product in Share-Cropping

It is difficult to present a uniform and accurate view of the division of product in share-cropping in the late nineteenth and early twentieth centuries. The principles on which the crop was divided varied widely from one locality to another, and within each locality, according to the type of crop, the soil and the methods of cultivation and irrigation. This is clearly reflected in the scanty historical evidence which informs contemporary scholarship on agrarian relations in pre-capitalist Iran.[11] But the main picture that emerges, although one of wide variation in form, is generally based on a universal principle; this principle, which divides the product according to the provision of the means of production, has its origin in pre-Islamic Iran.[12] Generally speaking, the peasant provided, apart from labour (mainly his own and that of his household, occasionally that of others), a portion of the means of production, draught animals and sometimes seed. The landlord, apart from the land, which he usually owned, provided another portion: usually water and seed, and money capital when required. The product was then divided between the landlord and the peasant or production team in definite proportions. Major Stack, who visited Iran in the second half of the nineteenth century, wrote of the principle of crop division:

> These [irrigated] lands are annually distributed among the plough-owning cultivators. They are measured out in strips, and then these strips are assigned to the cultivators by lot, or by mutual agreement ... The cultivator who takes wet lands pays two-thirds of the crop, i.e. one share for the land and one share for the water, and retains one-third as his own share. His status may be that of a tenant holding under an *arbab*, or of a tenant of the state, or he may be a kind of under-proprietor ... They [the cultivators] pay two-thirds of the crop, or its equivalent in money, as happens to suit the *arbab*; and they receive some assistance from him in the matter of seed. (Stack 1882, pp.253–4)

Fraser, visiting Iran in the early nineteenth century, states that in the neighbourhood of Nayshabur, in the north-eastern province of Khorasan, the landlord took two-thirds of the crop and was responsible for the payment to the state of all financial dues (Fraser 1833, p.390). In Azarbayjan, he further records, the landlord's share of the produce of the land which he owned or held by virtue of some grant or by lease (e.g. *khaleseh* or *waqf* lands) amounted to one-third of the yearly produce in the case of the *daym* (unirrigated) lands; while in the case of irrigated land he received an extra portion if he was responsible for providing the water (ibid. p.208). However, when the proprietor furnished seed and cattle he received two-thirds or more of the produce, and met the claims of the central government (ibid. p.209). Fraser states that the landlord usually rented out the natural water for irrigation, by measurement of the surface area before sowing, or by that of the crop where standing when ripe (ibid. p.209). The general principles of the division of product seem to have persisted over time, a continuity registered by Black, visiting Iran a century after Fraser:

> In practice therefore, the landlord gets 2/5 of the crop for supplying land and water as these are almost never separated. He may get an additional 2/5 for supplying seed and equipment, although these are almost always supplied by the peasant. The peasant always gets 1/5 for performing the labour ... In the case of dry land cultivation, daim lands, the landlord customarily receives 1/5 of the returns or so many kilos per juft. (Black 1948, p.426)

Historically, as mentioned above in relation to *sharia*, share-cropping agreements included five means of production: land, water, draught animals, seed and labour. Theoretically each factor of production was allotted a share of the produce. In practice, however, the produce was seldom divided on this basis. The landlord usually deducted from the gross product seed required for the next harvest before it was divided on the basis of the provision of the means of production; thus, in practice, it was the 'net product', i.e. the gross product minus the seed required for the next harvest, which was divided between the landlord and the share-croppers. This, in effect, meant that share-croppers lent to the landlord a portion of their share of the produce in the form of working capital to renew the cycle of production, free of interest charges. Chardin, visiting Iran in the seventeenth century, observes that the landlord generally took one-quarter to a half of the produce according to the situation of the land, but usually after seed for the next harvest had been deducted. This arrangement, Chardin indicates, prevailed both in land held in private ownership and in Crown lands (Chardin 1988). Stack confirms the prevalence of such practices in the nineteenth century:

> The distribution of produce, as explained by the ryots [subor-dinate peasants], is this: [the lord] takes one-tenth for himself and one-tenth for seed-corn; of the remaining four fifths, one half is [the lord's] on account of the cow and the balance is divided in the usual ration of one share for the land and one for the water, leaving one share as the ryot's own, or two fifteenths. (Stack op.cit., p.258)

Evidence further points to the persistence of the practice up to the eve of land reform, when pre-capitalist relations were finally undermined by state legislation. Lambton, writing about the division of the crop in the 1940s, observes:

> In many areas of the country seed is provided by the landowner. Where this is the case, and the harvest is divided into five shares, one share is set aside for the seed; in other cases an equivalent amount is deducted for the landowner (or lease) from the total harvest, i.e. before it is divided between the peasant and the landowner according to their allotted shares. (Lambton op.cit. 1953, p.308)

The persistence of the practice clearly indicates that the common view that the division of the crop was based on the provision of the main means of production is largely unfounded; for the landlords, who exercised near-total power on their estates and controlled the process of production, often divided the produce at their own discretion (Issawi 1971, pp.222–3). The share-cropper's position was further weakened by payment of a number of other dues, levied on him by the landlord. These dues, payable in kind, were deducted from the share-cropper's portion, and in fact his actual share could be estimated only after all dues and obligations had been taken into consideration. Lambton extensively documents such non-rental dues in various regions, stating that they were a traditional feature of agrarian relations in the Iranian countryside (Lambton op.cit. 1953, Chapter XVIII). According to her, an inverse ratio could be observed between the size of non-rental peasant obligations and the amount of produce that fell to his share: 'In those areas where the peasant receives a larger share of the crop under the share-cropping agreement he has to pay heavier dues under other heads, while in those areas where his share is smaller the extra levies made on him are fewer' (ibid. pp.308–9).

Characterization of the Organization of Production under Share-Cropping

This brief exposition of the conditions of the provision of and access to the means of production shows clearly that the organization of production under share-cropping was structured by forms of *partial* possession in separation. The share-cropper's partial possession of the means of production provided a basis for the landlord's 'economic' intervention in the process of production. But the landlord's near-total control of the process of production indicated that the five main means of production did not carry equal weight. The share-cropper's perpetual separation from land and water, reproduced by rental and non-rental forms of exploitation, was the source of the landlord's disproportionate power and capacity to control the processes of production and distribution. However, the landlord's income, the available surplus product, came not only from the monopoly possession of land and water, but also, in the majority of cases, included an excess above the rent: usually the interest on capital advanced in the form of the means and conditions of production. Nor did the share-cropper gain his share of the net produce in return for the provision of labour alone. His share, too, included an element of interest on capital: usually draught animals or seed, and sometimes working capital.

The conditions of partial possession in separation from the means of production, a structural feature of share-cropping relations, present a major problem with respect to the characterization of the organization of production. If the mechanism for the extraction of surplus is taken as the criterion then the organization of production can be characterized as pre-capitalist. But, on the other hand, the conditions of tenure in general indicate clearly that the right to surplus product required legal relations which were essentially capitalist in character.

The difficulties apparent in characterizing share-cropping relations have been a persistent feature of economic theory since the early nineteenth century. The classical economists, who approached the issue in a systematic manner, considered share-cropping as a mechanism which facilitates the transfer of surplus product in agriculture. It was conceived as a rental relationship quite distinct from pre-capitalist and capitalist rent relations, though containing certain elements of both forms. This view led the classical political economists, and later Marx, to characterize share-cropping as a *transitional* phenomenon. Such an approach places share-cropping within a wide spectrum of rent relations, on the two poles of which stand pre-capitalist and capitalist forms of rent, characterized by their respective forms of property relations. It signifies a wide range of contractual relations involving a greater or lesser degree of possession of the means of production by the direct producer.

The classical political economists, then, stress the transitional character of share-cropping relations. More precisely, share-cropping contractual relations are located within a general classification of land tenure arrangements ordered by the notion of 'efficiency'. The notion of efficiency in this context implies incentive to investment, and involves a relationship between productivity and forms of appropriation of labour. Share-cropping represents an advance on forms of direct appropriation of labour, but, from the standpoint of capitalist agriculture, it is an inferior form of rental contract. Share-cropping is a disincentive to capitalist relations in agriculture.[13]

Adam Smith, exemplifying this mode of analysis, approaches share-cropping within a comparative framework, examining the relatively 'backward' French and Italian agricultures and the more advanced English farming. According to Smith, share-cropping as practised in France and Italy, though superior to feudal rent characterized by labour villeinage, has nonetheless an inhibiting effect on the development of the productive process:

> It could never, however, be in the interest [of the metayers] to lay out, in the further improvement of the land, any part of the little stock which they might have saved from their own share of the produce, because the lord, who laid out nothing, was to get one-half of whatever it produced. The tithe, which is but a

tenth of produce, is found to be a great hindrance to improvement. A tax, therefore, which amounted to one-half, must be an effectual bar to it. (Smith 1937, p.366)

Smith's conceptions of productivity and efficiency were both derived from his analysis of the capitalist economic form, which led to the argument that share-cropping was an intermediate and transitional form of rental contract. Share-croppers, Smith believed, would be succeeded, though by a 'very slow degree', by farmers 'who cultivated the land with their own stock, paying a rent certain to the landlord' (ibid. p.368). The end result of this evolutionary process is capitalist agriculture, the epitome of economic productivity and efficiency.

Although Smith did not attempt an economic analysis of the share-cropping system, his general remarks, and in particular his emphasis on the relationship between the mode of appropriation of labour and the efficiency of the unit of production, remained a lasting influence on classical economic thought. Classical economists after Smith continued to view share-cropping from a capitalist perspective, using economic categories specific to the analysis of capitalist agriculture. Jones, following Smith's line of argument, his evolutionary framework and his notion of efficiency, argues in much the same fashion:

If the relation between the metayer and the proprietor has some advantages when compared with ... the serf ... it has some very serious inconveniences peculiar to itself. The divided interest which exists in the cultivation of produce, mars almost every attempt at improvement. (Jones 1831, p.102)

John Stuart Mill is another case in point.[14] His commentary on share-cropping emphasizes the share-cropper's unwillingness to improve, i.e. his disincentive to investment in land:[15]

The metayer has less motive to exertion than the peasant proprietor, since only half the fruits of his industry, instead of the whole, are his own ... so long as the increase of hands increases the gross produce, which is almost always the case, the landlord, who receives half the produce, is an immediate gainer, the inconvenience falling only on the labourer. (Mill 1909 Vol. II, pp.365–66)

Mill concludes that 'improvements must be made with the capital of the landlord', but 'custom is a serious hindrance to improvement' (ibid. p.367). The emphasis on custom and tradition as sources of economic 'inefficiency' brings Mill closer to the neo-classical economists.

The notions of custom and tradition in neo-classical economics refer to economic conditions where the postulate of wealth or utility (profit) does not apply. More precisely, they denote the absence of modern market relations, competition and an average rate of profit, elements necessary for the application of the principles of capitalist economic calculation to the unit of production. As such, the notions of custom and tradition are tantamount to the concept of 'inefficiency' which is central to neo-classical writing on share-cropping. Here, too, inefficiency implies 'disincentive to investment', but chiefly in relation to resource allocation, i.e. capital and labour inputs,[16] albeit within a capitalist economic form. Share-cropping is shown, through partial equilibrium analysis, to provide less than optimal levels of output and rent.[17] Thus Marshall comments:

> When the cultivator has to give his landlord half of the return to each dose of capital and labour that he applies to the land, it will not be in his interest to apply any doses the total return to which is less than twice enough to reward him. If, then, he is free to cultivate far less intensively than on the English plan [fixed rent], he will apply only so much capital and labour as will give him returns more than twice enough to repay himself: so that his landlord will get a smaller share even of those returns than he would have on the plan of a fixed payment. (Marshall 1920, pp.535–6)

Later neo-classical writings on share-tenancy, however, attempt to modify the negative view of the early theorists. It is thus argued that under share-cropping, yields and rents can be as much as those achieved under fixed-rent forms of agricultural production. The argument, which is informed by the 'general equilibrium analysis', suggests that where the constraints of private property in land operate in the context of labour market imperfections, share-cropping can be no less 'efficient' than owner-occupation and fixed-rent leases.[18] In this case, too, the analytical model presupposes an order of classification retrospectively informed by the specificity of capitalist agriculture.[19] Cheung, in his analysis of neo-classical writing on share-cropping, indicates this point clearly:

> It should be noted that Marshall, like Smith, Jones and Mill before him, attempted to 'rank' various land tenure arrangements according to some notion of economic efficiency. They did not tackle the issue by identifying a specific set of property rights and constraints subject to which several forms of land tenure arrangements may imply the same resource use. In their discussion of share-tenancy, the freely alienable rights implicit in their analysis suggest that the constraint of private property rights was assumed. (Cheung op.cit., p.49)

The general evolutionary schema deployed by the classical and neo-classical economists to explain the character of share-cropping relations is essentially ahistorical. For the teleology of the evolution of land tenure in Western Europe is informed by a notion of efficiency which is characteristic of an economic form based on free wage-labour. The persistence of this notion, in effect, posits capitalist agriculture as the point of reference for the analysis of share-cropping relations, at the expense of the prevailing non-capitalist property relations, which are either ignored or excluded from the analysis. These relations thus have little, if any, impact on the conceptualization of the mode of appropriation of surplus, and still less of the organization of production, which is conceived as an autonomous economic base capable of self-reproduction in isolation from the wider structure of the economy.

Marx inherits this evolutionary perspective on share-cropping from the classical political economists. He, too, argues that share-cropping represents a transitional mode of appropriation, intermediate between those specific to feudalism and capitalism:

> As a transitory form from the original form of rent to capitalist rent, we may consider the metayer system, or share-cropping, under which the manager (farmer) furnishes labour (his own or another's), and also a portion of working capital, and the landlord furnishes, aside from land, another portion of working capital (e.g. cattle), and the product is divided between tenant and landlord in definite proportions which vary from country to country. On the one hand, the farmer here lacks sufficient

capital required for complete capitalist management. On the other hand, the share here appropriated by the landlord does not bear the pure form of rent. It may actually include interest on the capital advanced by him and an excess rent. It may also absorb practically the entire surplus-labour of the farmer, or leave him a greater or smaller portion of this surplus-labour. But, essentially, rent no longer appears here as the normal form of surplus-value in general. On the one hand the sharecropper, whether he employs his own or another's labour, is to lay claim to a portion of the product not in his capacity as labourer, but as possesser of part of the instruments of labour, as his own capitalist. On the other hand, the landlord claims his share not exclusively on the basis of his landownership, but also as lender of capital. (*Capital*, Vol. III 1971, p.803)

This long and often-quoted passage from *Capital* sums up Marx's views on the character of share-cropping relations as a mode of appropriation of surplus-product. The capitalist perspective and the technicist conception of efficiency, characteristic features of the classical political economists' commentaries on share-cropping, are clearly absent from his analysis. In fact Marx's analysis of share-cropping is based on the forms of possession in separation that it involves as an organization of agrarian production and as a mechanism of appropriation and distribution of product. The pre-capitalist forms of property and property relations hold a pivotal position in the discussion of the conditions of partial possession in separation which he uses to characterize share-cropping relations. Thus, his characterization of share-cropping as a 'transitory form', though implying a teleology of the modes of appropriation of surplus, is derived from the structure of the property relations associated with it: an articulated structure of pre-capitalist and capitalist forms of property underlying the process of production and distribution.

Furthermore, Marx's characterization of share-cropping as a 'transitory form' is based on the assumption that partial possession in separation is an unstable structure of the relations of production, which cannot ensure the subsumption of the labourer without the dominance of extra-economic coercion in the relations of exploitation. Marx also assumes that this dominance is essentially incompatible with the progressive involvement of the unit of production in commodity exchange relations. The first assumption clearly attributes the presence of extra-economic relations of exploitation in share-cropping to the non-separation of the labourer from the land, and the second argues for its disintegration in the face of the development of commodity relations.

The mechanistic logic of Marx's assumptions is informed by the paradox apparent in his characterization of pre-capitalist relations of production in general: a structure of property relations in which ownership and possession are separated and held by different economic agents, already encountered in Marx's conceptualization of the feudal relations of production. The concept of non-separation of the labourer from the land is central to Marx's conceptualization of the forms of partial possession in separation characteristic of share-cropping; the notion of partial separation refers to the means of production other than the land. This point may seem rather curious, given the contractual character of share-cropping to which Marx clearly refers, and which governs the distribution of the land to the unit of production. But it is the primacy of the category of the labour of transformation in Marx's conceptualization of the processes of formation and appropriation of economic property which leads him to assert the non-separation of the share-cropper from the land. Hence the assumed dominance of non-economic coercion in the articulated structure of exploitation deemed necessary for the reproduction of the condition of partial possession in separation in share-cropping.

The reproduction of partial possession in separation specific to share-cropping relations clearly involves non-economic forms of coercion. But, contrary to Marx's assumption, the presence of non-economic coercion in the structure of exploitation arises from the separation of the labourers from the land as the main means of production. The landlord's effective possession of the land is not only the source of the rental relations of exploitation, but also generates and sustains the forms of non-economic compulsion which are entailed in the conditions of tenancy. The forms of non-economic coercion associated with share-cropping rest on the effective possession of the land by the landlord, and help to reproduce the conditions of the continuous separation of the share-cropper from it. They are, in effect, secondary conditions of exploitation, and support the dominance of rental relations when the labourer is in possession of the means of production other than land and water, i.e. labour, draught animals and, at times, seed or the working capital. The non-economic relations of exploitation as such ensure the reproduction of the conditions of partial possession in separation, by creating a non-correspondence between the unit of production and the unit of tenancy, whereby the peasant household would remain dependent on the landlord for its reproduction. The form and the conditions of this non-correspondence in share-cropping in pre-capitalist Iran will be discussed in some detail in the following pages.

The forms of agrarian production based on share-cropping relations thus presuppose the effective possession of the land by the landlord. The share-cropper's effective separation from the land is the essential condition of the extra-economic coercive relations which ensure his subsumption in the process of production. These relations, which are inscribed in the conditions of tenancy, counteract the economic effects of the share-cropper's possession of the means of production, other than land and water, on the organization and process of production, thus reducing his share below that which is stipulated in the share-cropping contract. The reproduction of the conditions of non-correspondence between the unit of production and the unit of tenancy as such ensures the stability of share-cropping relations. Commodity relations can effectively undermine the stability of share-cropping, precipitating a transition to capitalism as indicated by Marx; but their effects on the process of production and distribution are diverse and depend on a variety of conditions, chiefly in the form and conditions of tenure. Marx, however, ignores the conditions which specify the mode and outcome of the involvement of the share-cropping unit of production in commodity relations. He holds an essentially unilinear view of the process of commodity production and exchange, the mechanistic logic of which arises from the assumption that the share-cropper is in possession of the land. Marx further derives both the dominance of extra-economic coercion in the relations of exploitation and its essential incompatibility with commodity exchange relations from this main assumption.

Marx's theoretical remarks on the character of share-cropping are also informed by his analysis of the 'English case'. In his study of the primitive accumulation of capital in England, Marx considers the effect of commodity relations on the organization of production under share-cropping (*Capital* Vol I. 1970, p.742). In this context, clearly the conditions of tenancy do not preclude the direct involvement of the share-cropper in commodity exchange relations, thus leading to the rapid disintegration of the conditions of partial possession in separation. Marx thus generalizes what is in fact a particular historical case, to emphasize the essentially proto-capitalist character of share-cropping (Cutler op.cit. 1975). Like the views expressed by the classical political economists, Marx's general theoretical remarks on share-cropping relations tend to reassert the teleology of the modes of appropriation of surplus, although without resorting to the technicist concept of efficiency. The mechanistic logic of this teleology informs the bulk of Marxist writing on the form and character of share-cropping relations in Iran. For example, Soudagar argues:

> owing to the particular mechanism of the share-cropping system, i.e., the participation of the peasant and the landlord in the division of the produce, it is susceptible to change in the face of the development of capitalism and disintegrates rapidly ... Share-cropping, which is based on a natural economy, cannot resist the pressure exerted upon it by market relations. It breaks down as a result of the penetration of commodity relations. (Soudagar, op.cit. p.140, my translation)

Evidently a conception of share-cropping as a system of agrarian production based on a natural economy overlooks not only the condition of tenancy, but also the structure of property relations which sustains the processes of production and distribution. Soudagar's mechanistic account of the dissolution of share-cropping relations and their transformation into capitalism logically follows from such omissions.

The transitional character of share-cropping, I have argued, depends on the extent to which partial possession in separation can ensure the subsumption of the labourer in the process of production; that is, the extent to which the relations of production can subordinate the unit of production to their effects, and ensure the production and distribution of the product. It should be added here that under share-cropping the relations of production largely coincide with the conditions of tenancy stipulated in the contract between the lord and the peasant. In fact it is not unreasonable to say that the conditions of tenancy signify the relations of production in their effects. It follows that the form of partial possession in separation characteristic of share-cropping relations can subordinate the unit of production to its effects and ensure its reproduction in so far as the conditions of tenancy remain in force; that is, in so far as they can enforce the sharecroppers' separation from the land and reproduce the crucial non-correspondence between the units of tenancy and production. It was also argued that the conditions of tenancy specify the mode and outcome of the involvement of the unit of production in commodity relations. This point should be qualified.

The conditions of division of produce stipulated in the share-cropping contract determine both the size of the marketable surplus accruing to the economic agents and their overall relationship with the commodity market in general.[20] For example, if the peasant's share of produce is too small to leave him with a surplus sufficient to engage in market exchange relations, then the landlord will be the only agent capable of establishing contact with the commodity market. In such a case, the progressive involvement of the unit of production in exchange relations is unlikely to affect the mode of the economic calculation and alter the conditions of the provision of the means of production, especially land, water and labour, to it. This is because, despite the involvement of the landlord in market relations, the peasant household will remain the main source of labour input to the unit of production. Hence the persistent absence of the category of wages in the economic calculation of the unit of production. In fact, as will be shown in the case of pre-capitalist Iran, the landlord's almost exclusive access to the commodity market can lead to the consolidation of the conditions of tenancy, and the forms of non-economic coercion which sustain the structure of partial possession in separation specific to share-cropping. The involvement of the unit of production in commodity production for the market therefore signifies a conjuncture, the modality and the development of which depend on the character of the prevailing relations of production.

Let us now return to consider the Iranian case. In Iran, traditionally the land was leased out for no shorter a period than a full production cycle. The net harvest was then shared between tenant and landowner on some legally stipulated basis, conventionally termed the *aqd-e muzara'eh*, or the share-cropping contract. The system and conditions of tenancy were usually enormously complex, varying widely from one locality to another and from case to case within a locality, according to the following conditions:

  (i) whether the tenant supplied any working or fixed capital, or whether the entire amount was supplied by the landlord
  (ii) whether the tenant had some land of his own or worked entirely on landlord's land

(iii) how secure the tenancy rights were in practice.

The conditions of tenancy in Iran were at best precarious, and the peasants' rights to the landlord's land, *haq-e nasaq*, were insecure, since, generally speaking, the share-cropper's tenure was limited to a single production cycle—i.e., a period extending from twelve to eighteen months.[21] Stack suggests that, although peasants suffered insecurity of tenure, in practice their rights to use the landlord's land were secure so long as they paid their rents and met their other non-rental obligations (Stack op. cit. pp.279–280). Contemporary observers, however, do not share Stack's view. Lambton and Soudagar both refer to the practice of the *nasaq bandi-ye zamin*, the periodic redistribution of peasants' plots, enforced by the landlords to prevent continuity of rights and permanency of tenure. Soudagar indicates that while the Iranian peasant often spent his whole life in a single village, the land he cultivated varied in size and quality from year to year, owing to the annual or periodic redistribution of land (Soudagar op.cit. pp.156–7).

The practice of the *nasaq bandi* was ancient and universal, but the criteria for the redistribution of agricultural land among the share-croppers were various. The *boneh*, the production team, was the common basis for the redistribution of the land, but the manner in which it was constituted differed substantially from one area to another. In some areas the *boneh* was based on the rotation of the water supply or the number of shares into which the water was divided. In other areas, the *jofi*, i.e. the amount of land ploughed by a pair of oxen, formed the basis of its organization. Although the distribution of forms of the *boneh* did not follow a specific economic logic or a particular geographical pattern, the *jofi* remained the common basis of the *boneh* in most provinces. Production teams assumed different names in different localities; Stack provides a detailed account of the various types and functions of production teams in Khorasan and Fars provinces, where they were called *sahra*,[22] and performed similar functions so far as the redistribution of agricultural land among the peasants was concerned (Stack op.cit. 1988).

The practice of the *nasaq bandi-ye zamin* had a twofold aim. First, it prevented the tenant from acquiring *haq-e risheh*, literally meaning the right to take root; that is, the right to permanent tenancy, in local tradition. Second, it helped the landlord to keep the size of the unit of tenancy below that normally required for the reproduction of the means and conditions of production; that is, below the size which would enable the peasant to meet his rental obligations and provide for the upkeep of his household.

Insecure tenancy remained a characteristic feature of agrarian relations in Iran up until the 1962 land reform, when pre-capitalist relations in agriculture were formally abolished. Compounded with economic relations of exploitation, insecure tenancy acted as a powerful lever enhancing the landlord's control of the processes of production and distribution, and enabling him to extract a larger share of produce than had been allotted to him by the share-cropping contract. Insecure tenancy pushed up the level of the rent extracted from the share-cropping peasants. Generally speaking, the over-exploitation of the peasantry, commonly practised in the Iranian countryside, was directly related to the form and conditions of the land tenure. The persistence of this relationship in modern times has been variously registered by contemporary writers (Lambton 1953, pp. 297–304).

It is widely noted that the peasants seldom contributed anything but their labour to the production process. In fact the chronic lack of working capital, necessary to renew the cycle of production, on the part of the share-cropping peasants was another factor contributing to their over-exploitation by the landlords. Thus Fateh comments:[23]

> With regard to working capital much can be said to discredit the system now practised in Persia. In short, the peasants generally do not possess any liquid capital and are exploited either by usurious moneylenders or by their landlords, who advance them money for the purchase of animals, implements, etc., at a very high rate of interest and recover the advances at harvest time. In fact, what the peasant receives at harvest time is only factor five i.e., labour entitling him to one-fifth of the total produce. (Fateh 1926, p.15)

The chronic lack of working capital on the part of the peasant was the main cause of the accumulated debt which perpetually consumed a substantial part of his already meagre share of the net produce. The repayment of the debts and the interest they carried usually followed the harvest, before the net produce was divided between the peasant and the landlord. In some cases the peasant's share of the crop sufficed to pay off his debts to the landlord; in others it fell short of the outstanding amount. The result was the perpetual indebtedness of the share-cropper, which inescapably tied him to the land and the landlord. Frequently the share-cropper could only repay a fraction of the outstanding debt, so the indebtedness accumulated over time and the interest charges on the accumulated debt rose steadily until his position became hopeless: he could survive the year only by borrowing for consumption. Consumption loans were regular and universal phenomena in the Iranian countryside in the nineteenth century, and persisted into modern times (Lambton 1953, pp.80–83). The consumption loan represented an advance given to the peasant to tide him over hard times. The price of the subsistence crops fluctuated sharply in the local village market; usually the lowest prices were reached immediately after the harvest, and the peak prices prevailed some time before the harvest. The practice was for the advance to be given in kind during the winter, when prices were high, and for the repayment to be demanded in summer in cash, or in the equivalent amount of grain at current prices, which were then at their lowest. Consequently, the amount of grain required to repay the debt was considerably greater than the amount originally given as an advance. This repayment of consumption loans in kind calculated at current market prices in practice often implied an exorbitant rate of interest, and the peasant once forced by poverty to take an advance was likely to be kept in a state of perpetual indebtedness. Contemporary research suggests that at the turn of the century consumption loans attracted rates of interest at least as high as 30 to 40 per cent (Hershlag 1964, p.149). Djamalzadeh states that in the early decades of the present century, interest rates on consumption loans reached the level of 40 per cent (Djamalzadeh 1935, pp. 341–2).

There were other factors which contributed to the persistently high interest rates associated with consumption loans. First of all the lender was almost always the landlord; this near-universal phenomenon further increased the landlord's already substantial control over the process of production and distribution (Issawi, op.cit. 1971, pp.223–5; Djamalzadeh, op.cit. 1935, pp.341–2; Lambton, op.cit. 1953, pp.245–330). Secondly, the existence of a large number of landless labourers in the countryside, ready to take over the share-cropper's plot and comply with the landlord's demand for high rents, made the share-cropper's position indefensible; he was forced to agree to the landlord's demands for higher rents and rates of interest in order to secure his tenancy rights. Given these conditions, the need for sheer physical reproduction of labour was the only limit to high rents and interest rates charged by the landlord, and this for reasons of expediency. It was not in the long term interest of the landlord to reduce the share-cropper below a certain level of poverty and indebtedness, to the point where the steady supply of labour to the unit of production might be seriously impaired.

The over-exploitation of the share-cropping peasants, in effect draining their resources, had further consequences for the reproduction of the unit of production. It often left them with little or no money-capital to cover the cost of the reproduction of the means of production. Commentators on the state of Iranian agriculture prior to land reform maintain that the share-cropping peasants were in constant need of money-capital to replace livestock, agricultural implements and seed, and to cover other production expenses (Lambton op.cit. 1953; Soudagar, op.cit. 1979). Fateh, for example, notes that the replacement of livestock, the purchase and repair of implements of production, and other current expenses were often more costly than the purchase of the seed for renewing the cycle of production (Fateh, op.cit. p.14). In the case of 'production loans', however, the landlord was the main, though by no means the sole, lender of the money-capital. Local money-lenders in the nearby urban centres, or richer peasants in the village such as the headman, shopkeeper and pedlar and the like, often furnished the share-cropping peasant with money-capital to renew the production cycle. But whatever the source of the production loan the result was always the same as in the case of the consumption loans: spiralling debt. Since the peasant did not have sufficient marketable surplus to cover his financial obligations, the loan was usually secured against his share of the crop in the next harvest. This meant that the peasant acquired the loan in money but repaid in kind, a practice the disadvantages of which, especially with regard to the seasonal fluctuation of the prices in local markets, have already been discussed in some detail. Usury remained a characteristic feature of agrarian relations and rural life prior to the land reform. It was a direct product of the form and conditions of tenure and signified their particular effects on the structure of the relations of production. Loans, in particular consumption loans, were in fact an integral part of the working capital required to renew the cycle of production.[24] The landlord's possession of this portion of the working capital, and the share-cropper's correlative separation from it, was the source of usury as a mechanism of exploitation in agriculture. The reproduction and persistence of usury as a mode of appropriation of surplus therefore required that the balance of the subsistence crops accruing to the share-cropping peasant should necessarily fall short of his consumption requirements; hence his constant need for consumption loans.

Usury as a mode of appropriation of surplus product was an effect of the form of land tenure historically associated with the dominant relations of production in agriculture in pre-capitalist Iran. Its operation alongside ground rent largely offset the effects of the capitalist contractual relations entailed in share-cropping on the organization of production. For, as was seen, usury seriously restricted the peasants' recourse to the commodity market, leaving them with little, if any, marketable surplus to engage in exchange relations. Furthermore, although the repayment of loans, both consumption and money-capital, required calculation at current market prices for subsistence crops as well as money, the method of repayment in kind required no engagement with the commodity market. The compound structure of exploitation, i.e. the prevalence of rents amounting to a half to two thirds of the net produce and interest rates of 25 to 40 per cent, ensured perpetual non-correspondence between the unit of tenancy and the unit of production, and hence the perpetual subsumption of the share-cropper in the process of production.

The existing evidence suggests that production for subsistence rather than exchange remained the main object of the share-cropping unit of production up to the early decades of the present century:

> rates of rent payments varied sharply, and ranged between 10 and 80 per cent of the crop. However, in all cases, the share of the peasant did not usually exceed the amount required to provide his family with the minimum means of subsistence. (Houman, 1954, Vol I. pp.320–1)

The unit of production was mainly organized on the basis of peasant household labour, and exchange with other production units in the village seldom took place in any significant and continuous manner (Lambton 1953, p.379). In those cases in which the *boneh* provided the labour, the total labour input to the unit of production may have included more than household labour. But in either case the calculation of the labour input required no reference to the commodity market and exchange relations. The price of labour did not feature in the economic calculation of the unit of production. There is, therefore, sufficient grounds to argue that under share-cropping conditions the object of reproduction of subsistence in the unit of production was achieved without reference to the domination of commodity exchange relations. The mode of economic calculation operating in the unit of production was predominantly pre-capitalist.

The combined structure of exploitation, high rents and high interest rates defined the essentially pre-capitalist character of the form of partial possession in separation on which the share-cropping unit of production in pre-constitutional Iran was based. The economic class relations associated with share-cropping seriously hindered the development of productive forces in agriculture. Low productivity of labour and technological backwardness were the hallmarks of Iranian agriculture before the land reform. Black, commenting on the state of the Iranian agriculture in the early decades of the present century, indicates:

> Agricultural productivity in Iran is low by almost any measure —per acre, per man, per animal unit, per village . . . Agricultural techniques have changed but little during the past centuries, and today much of the produce is obtained by means that would have been familiar to slaves of 2,500 years ago . . . As production often only slightly exceeds the needs of the peasant producers, and as marketing systems are badly developed because of poor communication and means of transportation, low crop production often results in local famines and severe shortages. (Black, op.cit. pp.436–7)

The landowners had a vested interest in depressing productivity and hindering the development of the productive forces, for increased productivity and technological development could boost production and seriously undermine the conditions of existence of partial possession in separation in two ways. First, an increase in the peasant's share of the produce would free him from the need for consumption loans, hence undermining the foundation of usury which enabled the landlord to subsume the peasant and control the process of production under the conditions of partial possession in separation. Second, such an increase could leave him with surplus over and above subsistence to engage in commodity exchange in the local market; a process which could subordinate the unit of production to the effects of commodity relations, change the calculation of labour input, and provide the necessary basis for the social differentiation of the mass of the share-cropping peasants.

Fixed rent

Along with share-cropping, fixed rents were fairly common in the Iranian countryside, though the extent to which this form of appropriation of surplus product was practised is not quite known to us. The existing evidence assigns a secondary position to fixed rents compared with share-cropping, which remained the dominant mode of appropriation of surplus before the land reform. This is partly due to the specificity of fixed rent, which made it a less 'desirable' mode of exploitation for the Iranian land-owning class (Lambton 1953, p.319): a point which will shortly be considered in some detail. The practice of leasing out agricultural land in return for a fixed rent during and since the nineteenth century has been noted by several commentators. Stack, for example, indicated that fixed rents regulated the relationship between the landlords and the peasants working on the dry lands. Thus he writes:

> Perhaps the general rule is that the dry lands are *divani* [state lands] even where the wet lands are *arbabi* [private lands]. But in either case the cultivation of dry lands seems to be subject to the payment of a fixed proportion of produce by the cultivator whether he holds them under the state or under a private proprietor ... He [the cultivator] is not assisted by the state or the *arbab* [the landlord], if any, with advantages of seed, but makes the venture entirely on his own responsibility. (Stack op.cit. pp.251–2)

Lambton in the 1950s refers to fixed rents *(muqasameh, masahat, muqata'eh)* as the second form of relationship of appropriation existing in the countryside:

> The second type of relationship, where the peasant pays a fixed rent in cash or in kind or both, according to the area of land (or the amount of water) which he holds, is not found in many areas. (Lambton 1953, p.319)

Stack and Lambton seem to suggest that the prevalence of fixed rental relations depended on the climatic conditions, that is on the type of soil and the amount of water available to the cultivators. Contemporary commentators, on the other hand, indicate that it was directly related to the type of crop produced, i.e., rice production in the paddy belt on the Caspian sea and in parts of Isfahan province (Ono op.cit. p.458). According to Demin, however, the practice of the fixed rental relations did not conform to a specific pattern, climatic or otherwise, and they 'were fairly widely used in the Iranian village . . . for the cultivation of one crop or another' (Demin 1967, pp.44–50, cited in Issawi, op.cit. p.224).

Fixed rent in Iran, as elsewhere, was a payment by the peasant for the right to use the landlord's land. The exchange of the right to land use for a portion of the produce formed the structure of the fixed rent, which arose from the monopoly possession of the agricultural land by the land-owning class. Fixed rent assumed different forms according to the manner in which this exchange was effected in practice. Payments in kind or in money (or a combination of both) were regularly practised in different localities, though on the whole payments in kind prevailed in pre-capitalist Iran. Whatever the form of payment, fixed rent where it was practised defined both the mode of appropriation of surplus and the organization of production. As in the case of share-cropping, this was due to the fact that units of production and of tenancy coincided with one another. The existence of fixed rent depended strictly on the complete possession in separation of the means and conditions of production by the landlord. This was the prerequisite for the economic subsumption of the direct producer in the process of production, regardless of the form that rental relations took in practice.

The three different forms of fixed rent, variants of the same structure of production relations, nevertheless presupposed different conditions of realization, which significantly affected the organization of production. Rent in kind, for example, required no recourse to the commodity market and exchange relations: the direct producer simply paid the fixed amount in produce to the landlord or his representatives. The organization of production required little direct supervision by the landlord, nor did it imply legal dependency of the direct producer on him; the juridico-political conditions of existence of rent in kind often excluded forms of legal dependency of the peasant on his overlord, and the Iranian case was no exception.[25] The payment of fixed rents in money, on the other hand, presupposed a direct engagement of the direct producer with the commodity market. The involvement of the peasant in exchange relations, however limited, could affect the calculation of the unit of production. For, though he continued to produce mainly for subsistence, a portion had to be converted into commodities, which in effect meant producing it as commodities for sale in the market. Monetary expenditure, little as it may have been, thus informed the peasant's calculation of the cost of production. The character of the organization of production under money rent depended largely on the ratio of the monetary to the non-monetary portion of production, which provided for the reproduction of both the means of production and the household labour.[26]

However, payment of fixed rent in money was never significant in pre-capitalist Iran. It seems that the sharp seasonal fluctuations of the prices for agricultural goods in local markets made it an unattractive option for the landowners, who were accustomed to the economic advantages of payments in kind. The evidence suggests that the peasants, by contrast, preferred the fixed rent regime to the share-cropping system, and often demanded a change in the organization of production from share-cropping to the payment of fixed rents in kind as a means of countering over-exploitation and economic hardship (Lambton 1953, pp.111–13; Keddie 1960, pp.30–1). The logic of the peasants' demand, too, was unmistakably economic. Fixed rents, when paid by means other than labour service, resulted in a higher degree of elasticity of surplus in the unit of production; for, in contrast to share-cropping and labour rent, in this case the peasant did not have to share the increase in output with the landlord. This gave him an incentive to increase the output of the plot without fear of losing the extra produce to the landlord and his representatives at harvest time. It is generally agreed that peasants paying fixed rents were on the whole better off than the mass of share-croppers, since they could increase their income by increasing the productivity of the unit of production (Lambton ibid.; Keddie ibid.). This may explain the relative prosperity of the peasants in the provinces of Gilan, Isfahan and Yazd, where traditionally fixed rent prevailed, and the main crop, usually rice, made the imposition of share-cropping difficult.

The specificity of the form of land tenure under fixed rent has been the source of theoretical confusion, in particular over the precise character of the organization of production associated with it. The functional autonomy of the direct producer in the process of production and the elasticity of the economic surplus have led a number of writers to identify the organization of production with the enterprise of peasant producer as an autonomous and self-contained unit of production. Banaji's study, 'The Peasantry in the Feudal Mode of Production', is an example of this approach:

> The first of these [structure of the unit of production], defined by the preponderance of payments other than labour-rent, posited a higher elasticity of surplus in the sector of peasant production, and a distribution of arable between peasant holdings and demesne so heavily biased towards the former that it conferred on the totality of these holdings the determinate forms and functions of a sector of small peasant production. Here the rate of feudal exploitation of the peasantry was not immediately evident in, or deducible from, the ratio of the two arable (where demesne existed at all). Thus the preponderance of payments in cash or kind posited an autonomous small peasant production. (Banaji 1970, p.303)

Theoretically, Banaji's characterization of the feudal unit of production under fixed rent entails two presuppositions, derived from Marx and Chayanov respectively. The first is the general supposition that the direct producer is not separated from the means of production, and that this is the source of his functional autonomy in the process of production. The second supposition concerns the nature of the labour input to the unit of production: the labour of the peasant household, it is believed, is the basis of the autonomy of the unit of production, hence its alleged resemblance to small peasant production. What, however, links these two presuppositions together in Banaji's work is the exclusion from his analysis of the conditions of the formation and appropriation of feudal landed property; a theoretical omission, moreover, which underlies the identification of the feudal relations of production with the non-economic coercive relations of domination and subordination in both Marx and Chayanov. The non-economic conception of pre-capitalist relations of production and its theoretical presupposition, i.e. the non-separation of the direct producer from the land, are central to Chayanov's typology of 'pure economic forms', in which the autonomy of the peasant unit of production is asserted, an assertion taken for granted by Banaji.

Chayanov's discussion of non-capitalist economic systems is secondary to his main object of investigation: the construction of a 'general theory of peasant economy'. His aim is, in fact, to emphasize the specificity of the peasant economy as an autonomous and essentially non-capitalist economic form. Chayanov establishes a typology of pure economic forms on the basis of two criteria: the absence of commodity relations in the structure of the unit of production, and the predominance of non-economic coercion as the mechanism of appropriation of surplus. These conditions are used to define five pure non-capitalist economic forms which are then differentiated by their specific non-economic mode of exploitation. Chayanov's typology of non-capitalist economic forms includes, apart from communism, the family labour farm, the quit-rent farm, and the feudal peasant economy.[27] All these share a common 'internal private economic structure' constituted by the 'family labour unit', which balances the production and the consumption of the peasant household by striking an equilibrium 'between the amount of the family's drudgery and the degree of its demand satisfaction' (Chayanov 1966, p.17). The equilibrium is achieved by the 'subjective' evaluation of the on-farm process, 'informed' by the absence of the traditional categories used to analyze the process of production under capitalism.[28] The concept of the labour-consumer balance which signifies the state of equilibrium is the main regulator of economic activity within the unit of production (ibid. p.42), achieved by adjusting the labour effort of the family to its consumption needs. The degree of labour effort in Chayanov's discourse refers to the quantity of labour which the peasant household, the working adults and the children, can supply to the unit of production.

The labour-consumer balance is specific to the family labour farm which, according to Chayanov, is the internal economic structure of the non-capitalist economic forms. However, the subjective evaluation of the on-farm economic process rests on conditions which also ensure the autonomy of the unit of production *vis-à-vis* the wider structure of the pre-capitalist economy. The chief condition, repeatedly stressed by Chayanov, is the absence (or minimal presence) of commodity production for exchange in local or distant markets. This amounts not only to the 'indivisibility' of the family labour product/ income, but also to the economic autonomy of the unit of production. Chayanov nonetheless admits that commodities do exist in pre-capitalist economic forms; in fact, they are a familiar feature of the slave, quit-rent, serf and feudal landlord economies; but their presence does not undermine the indivisibility of the family labour product. This is because commodity production remains 'external' to the internal economic structure of these economic forms, and the labour-consumer balance continues to regulate their production units.

Chayanov's argument concerning the externality of commodity relations is based on the assumption that in pre-capitalist economic forms the unit of production exhibits the fundamental features of a 'natural economy', i.e. self-sufficiency and production for use. This assumption is crucial in maintaining the conceptual indivisibility of the single labour income, enabling him to argue that, despite the presence of commodity relations in the economy, the subjective evaluation of the on-farm process remains essentially valid (Little-john 1977, p.122). Chayanov's conceptualization of the feudal economic system is a case in point. He effectively divides the economy into two distinct economic sectors, peasant and landlord, dominated by production for use and production for exchange, respectively. The peasant sector is regulated by the labour-consumer balance, and monetary relations do not enter into the calculation of the unit of production. The landlord economic sector, on the other hand, is dominated by monetary gain, which guides the landlords' production for the market. The two sectors of the feudal economy therefore have different objects and different systems of economic categories which are not reducible to one another (Littlejohn ibid., p.123). The symbiosis of the peasant and landlord economies is effected by two sets of relations: rental and commodity relations. Rental relations are extra-economic, arising from the juridico-political relations of landed property ownership which are essentially non-capitalist, and remain so in so far as the land is not commercial-ized. Commodity relations, though economic in character, originate in the landlord sector, and do not affect the functioning of the peasant sector. The labour-consumer balance holds even when feudal commodities are sold in the market, owing mainly to the absence of the category of wage-labour.

The absence of this category is the main condition of the subjective evaluation of the on-farm process. The concept of labour-consumer balance, in asserting the autonomy of the unit of production, thus assigns a non-structural status to the relations of production. Thus, according to Chayanov, land rent in both a quit-rent serf economy and in feudalism is an adjunct of the landlord economy, with no basis in the peasant economic sector. So far as the latter is concerned, rent represents a non-economic (i.e. political) deduction from the family labour product, to be met by adjusting the rate of labour drudgery. Thus to the extent that the household remains the sole source of the provision of labour to the unit of production, rent does not feature in the cost of production (Chayanov 1966, p.17). The feudal lord, who may realize his rent as commodities on distant markets, does not regard the labour of the household as a production cost affecting their price:

> In this [feudal-serf] system price formation for those products collected by the feudal lord in the form of payment in kind and realised on distant markets is specially interesting. Obviously, the cost-of-production element cannot play any part in this, unless one regards as a prime cost the upkeep of a (non-economic) coercive apparatus to collect tribute and suppress rebellion. (Chayanov ibid. p.21)

Chayanov clearly notes that the realization of the feudal rent may require recourse to the commodity market. He further indicates that the exchange relations involved in the process of realization are part of the definition of the concept of feudal rent. In fact, he argues that, given the particular exchange and monetary orientation of the feudal system:

> the rent going to the feudal lord on the strength of his feudal tenure is dependent not only on the amount of payment in kind but also on the market situation for selling the products received. Fluctuation in the market situation can, in spite of a constant amount of payment in kind, favourably or unfavourably influence the rent and, thus, the price of the tenure. (ibid. p.21)

Assuming that there is a market with specified legal boundaries for the purchase and sale of the land, Chayanov here is speaking about the controversial category of 'absolute rent', which by definition, implies a high degree of commoditization of agriculture, and the domination and control of the state by the land-owning class.[29] Chayanov nonetheless maintains that neither the increasing intervention of commodity relations in the process of the realization of feudal rent, nor the subsequent change in the market price of the land, influences the economic calculations of the unit of production. The labour-consumer balance remains the chief regulator of the economic activity of 'the basic stratum of primary producers—the tributary peasants—[which] continues to be a completely natural economy and pays tributes to the feudal lord in kind'; accordingly, the only possible economic activity of a feudal lord must be confined to certain measures of an 'economic and political kind which seem appropriate to him for increasing his tenants' prosperity and, thus, their ability to pay taxes' (ibid. p.21). Chayanov's subjectivism, the discursive primacy given to the subjective perception of the economic actor in relation to the objective conditions, leaves no room for the determination of the wider structure of the economy, local, regional or national.

Littlejohn, in an intelligent review of *The Theory of Peasant Economy* referred to above, discusses the problems entailed in Chayanov's conceptualization of rent and commodity relations in pre-capitalist economic forms. From Littlejohn's point of view, these problems arise from Chayanov's subjectivism, and the consequent marginalization of the 'objective' economic factors in the analysis of the relationship between household production and the wider structure of the economy. He rightly points out that the division of the feudal economy into two distinct sectors (i.e., an autonomous peasant and a landlord sector), each with its own specific object, mode of calculation and determination, creates a tension in Chayanov's theory, between on the one hand the subjective evaluation of the on-farm process and the concept of the labour-consumer balance, and on the other hand the objective monetary determinations of the landlord economy. Chayanov, however, overrides this tension by asserting the autonomy of the peasant economy, at the cost of reducing commodity relations to mere external 'residues' and rental relations to non-economic 'constraints' necessary to maintain the landlords' regime. Commodity and rental relations are both conceived as properties of the landlord economy, 'whose determination is not reducible to the constitutive action of economic subjects' (Littlejohn 1977, p.125). The total marginalization of the structural determination, concludes Littlejohn, enables Chayanov to argue that neither change in the conditions of formation nor fluctuation in the level of feudal rent affects the economic autonomy of the peasant unit of production.

Banaji's argument concerning the autonomy of the small peasant producer paying fixed rent in cash or kind is essentially informed by a similar logic (Banaji op.cit. p.303). In his case, the autonomy of the peasant unit of production is asserted by the identification of feudal rent with non-economic coercion, which, as we have seen in Chapter 4 of this study, effectively excludes the economic exchange relations underlying the processes of the formation and appropriation of private property in land. A consideration of the exchange relations involved in rent-form would undermine those theoretical approaches which divide the feudal economic system into two distinct sectors, dominated by two different modes of calculation, indicating that commodity production should be regarded as an 'integral' part of the economy.

Marx's analysis of rent-form in *Capital* (Vol.III Chapter XLVII) is instructive in this respect. Here Marx argues that the elasticity of the surplus product is primarily a function of the level of rent (Vol.III 1971, pp.796–8). If the rent is low, enough surplus will remain for the direct producer to engage in commodity exchange in the market. The relationship with the market means that the price of agricultural commodities will affect both the amount of land to be cultivated (the unit of tenancy) and the composition of the product. On the other hand, high rents will absorb almost the entire surplus product over and above the necessary cost of production which, in pre-capitalist economies, includes the subsistence of the peasant household (ibid. p.805). Marx further indicates that when high rents encroach on production costs, in order to obtain access to the conditions of production (i.e. land and water) the peasants will be forced to underfeed their household and their draught animals. High rents seriously imperil the reproduction of the unit of production, reducing the direct producer below the subsistence level and forcing him to borrow for the reproduction of household and the means of production (ibid. p.796). Marx's analysis clearly indicates that changes in the level and conditions of existence of rent are effective on and influence the reproduction of the unit of production. Fixed rent, in its various forms, structures the peasant unit of production and specifies its boundaries. The household of a fixed rent-paying peasant is not an autonomous economic unit.

To return to the case of pre-capitalist Iran, the evidence suggests that high rents absorbed about half, and at times two-thirds, of the total produce (Stack op.cit. p.280). The main reason for the prevailing high rents, it seems, was insecure tenancy, resulting chiefly from the concentration of the agricultural land in the hands of a small number of large proprietors. Large land-ownership *(bozorg maleki)* a prominent feature of agrarian relations in Iran before 1962, created landlessness and hunger for land in the countryside.[30] The landless labourers, the *khosh neshinan* (*khosh neshin* singular), constituted a very high proportion of the rural population, permanently struggling for their livelihood.[31] The absence of alternative job opportunities in urban centres compelled them to work for low wages, usually paid in kind, which barely met their subsistence. The permanent availability of a vast pool of surplus labour not only kept the level of wages in agriculture down but also affected the conditions of both tenancy and production. Insecure tenancy and high rents were the direct result of these conditions, which prevailed in varying degrees in different parts of the country. Peasants had little choice but to pay high starvation rents in order to secure their access to the landlord's land. The need to obtain bare subsistence was the main condition for the exploitation of the peasant household in the Iranian countryside, the economic logic of which manifested itself in the permanent hunger of the peasants for land.

However, high rents were not the only means available to the landlords to control the reproduction of the peasant household; in addition, they determined the size of the plot and the conditions of tenancy. The efficacy of this method, widely practised in pre-capitalist Iran, was a result of the economic specificity of the household as a unit of production: the unit of production had a limited source for the supply of the labour, restricted mainly to the working members of the household. The productivity of the unit of production was therefore primarily an expression of the size of the plot. The periodic or annual *redistribution* of the land among the tenants, practised almost universally, furnished the landlords with another means to control the reproduction of the unit of production. The landlord's control of the economic life of the peasant was almost complete if we also consider the conditions of access to water and pasture. These conditions, which varied widely from one locality to another, essentially resulted from the peasant's separation from the land, and entailed additional dues and obligations, in kind and in labour. The combined effect of these conditions was a growing disparity between the reproduction of the *unit of production* and the reproduction of the *unit of tenancy* which furnished the necessary ground for the landlords' intervention in the process of production. The landlords were able effectively to prevent the development of units of production large enough both to provide for the reproduction of the units of tenancy and to leave the tenants with surplus to engage in exchange among themselves. The landlords' intervention reinforced the conditions of the continuous separation of the peasants from the land, thus perpetuating the conditions of exploitation. High rents and the periodic redistribution of the land were major obstacles to the development of commodity relations among the mass of the fixed rent-paying peasants. Their persistence indicated the predominance of the pre-capitalist form of calculation in the unit of production.

High rents and the periodic redistribution of the land had less dramatic effects on the reproduction of those peasant households which paid fixed rents in money, rather than in kind; for the payment of rent in money by definition required the exchange of all or part of the surplus product as commodity in the market. The price of agricultural commodities in local markets therefore affected the calculation of the peasant household. The recourse to the commodity market, a necessary condition for the realization of money rent, necessarily weakened the conditions of the landlord's control over the peasant household. However, in the particular case of Iran these remarks have a very limited application, and should not be generalized; it is widely agreed that money rent was insignificant in pre-capitalist Iran, and the direct producers paying this type of rent constituted only a small proportion of the peasantry.[32]

Labour Rent

Labour rent did not play a significant role in the organization of agrarian production in pre-capitalist Iran. It usually functioned as a supplementary form of exploitation of peasant labour, alongside the major modes, chiefly share-cropping and, to a lesser extent, rent in kind. In its supplementary function, labour rent did not determine the reproduction of the unit of production. As usual, it assumed different forms in different localities; prevailing cultural relations (custom and tradition) and geographical conditions were significant factors in determining the form and the level of labour rent in each locality. Labour rent was customarily paid in terms of working days expended on specified tasks, such as the construction and repair of underground irrigation canals (*qanat*), the maintenance of buildings and roads, the cultivation of the landlord's demesne or the provision of fuel for his household, and so on.[33] Labour service (*bigari*) was the most common form of labour rent in pre-capitalist Iran. It consisted of a number of working days during which the peasant had to perform specified services for the landlord. The extent and the type of service was usually specified in the rent contract, share-cropping or fixed rent, whereby the peasant was obliged to give to the landlord, in addition to a share of the produce, free labour for a specified number of days. Lambton states:

> The most onerous of the personal servitudes is probably labour service, or *bigari*. The performance of such service or the provision of so many men for labour service was a normal obligation upon those who held land in Safavid and Qajar times and probably in earlier times also. (Lambton 1953, p.330)

Lambton suggests that labour service was originally 'regarded as a service to be rendered to the ruler by those who held land grants or who owned land', but in practice, she maintains, 'it was presumably performed by those who actually tilled the soil' (ibid). In more recent times the general practice was to levy the labour service not on the individual peasant but on the production team, usually so many days of labour service per plough-land or per share of water. Local and provincial variations mostly resulted from the manner in which the production team was organized. In certain areas, however, the labour service could be converted to payments in kind or in money, or in a combination of both (Lambton ibid. pp.330–6).

The predominance of labour rent in agriculture is historically associated with demesne production, in which the arable land is divided into the peasant's plot, producing for household subsistence, and the landlord's demesne, producing usually for exchange in the market. This is because the existence of labour rent as a mode of exploitation presupposes the division of the direct producer's labour into necessary and surplus labour time, which generally coincides with or fluctuates around the division of the arable land into household and landlord's plots. The specificity of the organization of production under labour rent, especially the general market orientation of landlord production, required the active supervision and control of the processes of labour and production by the landlord. This, however, was not the case in pre-capitalist Iran; the evidence suggests that demesne production was a very marginal form, bearing out the point that labour rent was not a major mode of exploitation.[34] It supplemented the dominant mode of exploitation and further enhanced the landlord's control over the process of labour and production in agriculture in general.

CONCLUSION:
THE CONCEPT OF IRANIAN
FEUDALISM

Was pre-capitalist Iran a feudal society, or did it exhibit the characteristic features of an Asiatic social formation? This essay argues that Iranian history is a discursive construct and that enquiry into its character requires theoretical forms of analysis, demonstration and proof. The conceptual definitions of pre-capitalist Iran are forms of historical knowledge. They are grounded in specific epistemologies which determine specific forms of the conceptualization of the relationship between theoretical concepts and the real concrete entailed in them. The problematization of the epistemological basis of these definitions renders them untenable in their own terms.

A rejection of the epistemological forms of historical knowledge thus informs the core of the argument underlying the concept of Iranian feudalism developed in the course of the essay. This concept, briefly defined below, is not identical with the historical phenomenon it signifies, for two main reasons. First, the constituent elements of Iranian feudalism and the forms of the connection between them in discourse are specified in terms of the economic, political, legal and ideological conditions of their existence; but the specific forms in which these conditions were historically given (namely, the economic, political, legal and ideological apparatuses of the feudal state in Iran) are not included in the concept. Second, the concept does not entail a definition of the dynamics of Iranian feudalism, which would need to address the determination of the economic and political forces operating within and outside the feudal state apparatuses and the specific forms and conditions of struggle among them. It cannot therefore give an account of the process and the modality of the development of Iranian feudalism from the early medieval to the Constitutional period. Thus, although it draws on the economic and political histories of pre-capitalist Iran, the concept of Iranian

227

feudalism defined in this section is still a theoretical construct, abstract and general, which does not exist in chronological time.

Iranian feudalism, conceived as such, signifies a social form composed of an economic structure and a specific set of political, legal, military and ideological processes and practices. The relationship between the two is conceived in terms of the conditions of existence, a form of mutual dependence in which each secures the conditions of existence of the other in the course of their combined but by no means uniform or homogeneous development. The economic structure of Iranian feudalism is a combination of the relations of production and labour processes constituted by a series of exchange relations, arising from the possession of and separation from the land under particular conditions; namely, the absence of markets with specific legal boundaries for the purchase and sale of the land on the one hand, and labour power on the other. The distribution of land and labour therefore requires no reference to the commodity market. The mere exchange of rights to land use for a portion of the produce between the possessing and non-possessing agents suffices to ensure agrarian production.

Feudal ground rent is the mode and the condition of existence of feudal exploitation, resulting from and reproducing the possession of and separation from the land. The perpetual separation of the direct producer from the land is the essential condition of the formation and appropriation of landed property under feudalism; feudal landed property rests on the subsumption of the labourer to the land in the process of production. This definition of feudal ground rent affirms the primacy of the relations of production in the economic structure of feudalism, suggesting that they are capable of subordinating the labour process to their effects, and thus defining the forms and boundaries of the organization of production.

The feudal economic structure so defined is not specifically Iranian, but an invariant of feudalism in general; the economic structure of Iranian feudalism itself bears the imprint of the specific demographic and geographic conditions of Iran. Aridity and the relative scarcity of water, along with the abundance of landless peasants and agricultural labourers in the countryside, both affected, though in different ways, the organization of production and the conditions of the appropriation of the economic surplus. Aridity influenced the conditions of distribution of water to the unit of production, increasing its value as a means of production in some areas quite drastically, placing it on a par with the land. The abundance of labour, on the other hand, resulted primarily in insecure tenancy and higher levels of rent, affecting the conditions of appropriation of surplus. The net economic result of these two non-economic factors was the consolidation of the landlord's control over the processes of production and appropriation, defining the mode and the condition of involvement of the unit of production in commodity relations. These adverse geographic and demographic conditions reinforced the subsumption of labour, acting as a powerful non-economic means to tie the direct producers to the land. They may well have been the main reason for the conspicuous absence of legally defined forms of peasant bondage in Iranian feudalism.

The political, legal and ideological processes which ensured the existence of the economic structure of Iranian feudalism, on the other hand, were specific to the Iranian social formation. They were intrinsic to the feudal state, provided in its political, military and ideological apparatuses, and varied widely in form and efficacy from one period to another, the variation defining the modality of the existence of the feudal economic structure. The political and legal conditions of existence of the economic structure were consequences of the domination of the feudal state apparatuses by the land-owning class, in particular their domination and control of the military apparatus of the state. Cultural relations, religious associations, and tribal, lineage and ethnic affiliations played important roles in defining the mode and conditions of domination in the military and political apparatuses of the feudal state. Lineage and ethnicity in particular specified the conditions of access to political power, and hence the formal hierarchy of domination and subordination in the organiza-tional structure of the feudal state.

This preliminary definition entails two procedural rules for the conceptualization of Iranian feudalism. First, the economic structure is the point of departure in the analysis, focusing on the possession of and separation from the land and the set of production relations thereby generated. Second, the feudal production relations are specified in terms of the conditions of their existence provided in the political, legal, cultural and ideological forms of the feudal state. In an inverse order, these rules outline the levels of the conceptualization of Iranian feudalism, providing for the conceptual distinction between legal ownership and economic property, and the specific juridico-political and economic processes and practices underlying each.

The *iqta* was the dominant form of landed property in medieval Iran, exhibiting the characteristic features of feudal property relations up to the Constitutional period. The medieval *iqta* was constituted by the exchange of land revenue for military/administrative service between the Crown/state and the political-military notables. The connection between land revenue and military service was the foundation of the *muqta*'s rights to the land in his *iqta*. It was forged and sustained by the exigencies of the territorialization of state power in a predominantly agrarian social formation. The characteristic backwardness of the agrarian economic structure constantly militated against the centralizing functions of the state, widening the existing gulf between the spatial character of political power and its expanding territorial basis. The state thus resorted to military power as the most extensive and effective mechanism of political integration. The logistics of military power linked political power to the land, and ensured the dominance of the military in the hierarchy of domination and subordination, which was also the formal organization of the exchange of land revenue for military service; for the juridico-political rights of ownership associated with the grant of the *iqta* were characteristically bestowed on the position held by the *muqta* in the formal organization of the state. Hence the corresponding separation of the rights of ownership from the object of ownership which was the hallmark of landed property in feudal Iran.

The *muqta*'s position in the organizational structure of the state, on the other hand, was mostly a function of his tribal origins and ethnic background, which also defined the form and the extent of his military, administrative and fiscal obligations to the crown. These obligations formally appertained to the *iqta*, and defined the variation in its form. The typology of the *iqta* was therefore determined by the particular articulation of political and cultural relations in the formal organization of power in the feudal state.

The exchange of land revenue for military service which underpinned the logistics of military power also defined the structural limits of the politics of territorial centralism. The practice of land assignment resulted in the parcellization of the territory into semi-autonomous political/military units with their own domestic jurisdiction, an arrangement which effectively undermined the foundations of the functional autonomy of the state, politically and legally. Sovereignty was the price paid by the feudal state to retain its territorial integrity. The practice of land assignment left it with partial sovereignty, expressed in terms of the ability to impose a uniform coinage, land tax and foreign policy on its constituent units. In practice, however, the maintenance of this partial sovereignty depended strictly on the military support of these units, and on the overall balance of forces within the decentralized structure of the state. The basis of this curious development, which specified the dominance of the military in the institutional form of political power, was the *iqta*.

The articulation of the political and economic which specified the connection between land revenue and military service, however, only highlights the juridico-political process which constituted the *muqta* as a legal subject with specific rights over the land. The conditions and the mechanism of the appropriation of ownership rights are not given in this process, nor can they be deduced from it. This point, though crucial, is often obscured by the characteristic separation of the ownership rights from the land, leading to the conflation of the economic process of appropriation of ownership rights with the juridico-political conditions governing their existence within the state. Hence the common but erroneous view that the juridico-political conditions of the surrender of land to the *muqta* sufficed to ensure the appropriation of land revenue which provided for the upkeep of the military. The conceptual distinction between the process of formation and the conditions of appropriation of ownership rights renders this view untenable. It also provides a basis for the conceptual distinction between the state taxes and land rents, though both were mostly collected/extracted by the *muqta* in his double capacity as landlord and governor.

The ownership rights associated with the *iqta* were appropriated in the process of production of the economic surplus, the source of land revenue which sustained the connection between land and military service. It presupposed an exchange of rights to land use in return for a portion of the produce, regulated by tradition or convention, between the *muqta* and the peasants living and labouring on his *iqta*. The separation of the peasant from the land, and his subsequent subsumption to it, was the essential condition of production under feudalism. It follows that the exchange relations governing the appropriation of surplus resulted from the effective possession of the land by the *muqta*, and his control over the process of production.

Possession of and separation from the land is therefore the

foundation of feudal landed property. It is specified with reference to the following forms and conditions:

(i) forms and conditions of the distribution of the land to the unit of production, specified in the forms and conditions of tenancy

(ii) forms and conditions of the articulation of land and labour in the process of production, involving the subsumption of the latter by the former

(iii) forms and conditions of the distribution of the product from the unit of production to the social formation at large, specified in the rent form.

Feudal production was organized in different forms, each signifying a specific combination of labour process and relations of production. The variation in the organization of production was determined by variations in the mode and conditions of the landlord's distribution of land (and water) to the peasants; these conditions, formally expressed by the terms and conditions of tenancy, specified the peasant's rights to use the landlord's land, in return for a portion of the produce. The conditions of exchange were generally stipulated in the contract of tenancy, which specified the form and boundaries of the unit of production, and the technical division of labour within it.

Share-cropping and fixed rent were the two main forms of organization of production in Iran. Both were based on the same structure of production relations, characterized by the effective possession of the land by the landlord; but the conditions of the distribution of land to the unit of production, and hence the mode of articulation of labour process and relations of production in each case, were different. The effective separation of the direct producer from the land was the essential condition of feudal production in Iran in general.

The conditions of tenancy specified the mode and outcome of the involvement of the unit of production in commodity relations in two ways: first, by determining the size of the marketable surplus accruing to the economic agents; and second, by defining their overall relationship with the commodity market in general. Insecure tenancy, reinforced by the adverse geographic and demographic conditions, was the main reason for the prevalence of high rents in agriculture, which more often than not forced the peasant to take out loans at high interest for consumption and production. The combination of ground rent and usury pushed up the rate of exploitation, leaving the peasants with little or no marketable surplus. The bulk of the economic surplus was appropriated by the landlords, who usually sold what remained after their own annual domestic consumption to merchants in local and distant markets, or paid it to the soldiery (in kind) in lieu of salary.

The specific form of economic class relations associated with feudal landed property determined the mode and the condition of involvement of the unit of production in commodity relations. It was not the peasants but their overlords who were able to engage in commodity relations; and these relations did not affect either the calculation of the labour input to the unit of production or the relations of the appropriation of surplus in any significant way. Although merchant capital was, through control of local and distant commodity markets, an invariant of the structure of exploitation, its economic activity scarcely affected the organization of production and the economic calculation operating in it. Its more or less exclusive relationship with the land-owning class only reinforced the prevailing structure of feudal property relations.

Feudal production was organized on the basis of the peasant household or of the production team, usually an aggregate of households, whose productive capacity secured the connection between land revenue and military service. The historical force which eventually severed this connection, removing the military from the intersection of the political and the economic, arose out of the process of production; it was the expansion of commodity production in the late nineteenth and early twentieth centuries, which linked the value of the land to the market price of agricultural commodities. Although the prevailing economic class relations—high land rents and usury, and the consequent lack of marketable surplus—seriously curtailed the possibility of large-scale peasant involvement in commodity relations, the bulk of the land-owning class was rapidly drawn into production for the market. Land became the focal point of a complex process of struggle amongst the contending factions of this class and their external and internal allies, eventually leading to the abolition of the age-old practice of land assignment.

The institutionalization of private property in land which followed the advent of the Constitutional state was however by no means the end of Iranian feudalism. The creation of a market with specified legal boundaries for the sale and purchase of land did not alter the character of the dominant relations of production; the growing tendency towards large land-ownership on the one hand, and the underdevelopment of commodity relations on the other, sustained feudal economic class relations in agriculture. Feudal ground rent, and the underlying form of possession of and separation from the land, continued to form the structure of agrarian production. This was the form and the condition of exploitation in Iranian agriculture until the land reform of 1962.

REFERENCES*

Chapter 1

1. For studies of agrarian relations and production in Iran prompted by the land reform, see Keddie N., 'The Iranian Village Before and After Land Reform', *Journal of Contemporary History* vol.III no.3, 1963; Lambton A.K.S., *The Persian Land Reform*, Oxford 1963; Khamsi F., 'The Development of Capitalism in Rural Iran', M.A. thesis, Columbia University 1968; Khosravi K., *Pazhuheshi dar Jameh Shenasi-ye Rusta' i-ye Iran*, Tehran 1985; Momeni B., *Masaleh-e Ardhi va Jang-e Tabaqati dar Iran*, Tehran 1981; Soudagar M., *Nezam-e Arbab-Ra'iyati dar Iran*, Tehran 1979.
2. On this issue see Ashraf A., 'Historical Obstacles to the Development of a Bourgeoisie in Iran', in Cook M.A. (ed.), *Studies in the Economic History of the Middle East*, 1975; Akbari A.A., *Ellal-e Za'af-e Tarikhi-ye Bourgeoisie dar Iran*, Tehran 1979; Keddie, N., *Historical Obstacles to Agrarian Change in Iran*, Claremont 1960.
3. For studies focusing on aspects of the economic transformation of Iran in the Constitutional period, see Abrahamian E., 'The Causes of the Constitutional Revolution in Iran', *International Journal of Middle East Studies* vol. 10, 1979; Ashraf A. and Hekmat H., 'The Traditional Bourgeoisie and the Developmental Processes of Nineteenth-Century Iran', Princeton University mimeo, 1974; Entner M., *Russo-Persian Commercial Relations 1828–1914*, Gainsville 1965; McDaniel R., *The Shuster Mission and the Persian Constitutional Revolution*, Minneapolis 1974, esp. chapter 2; Nomani F., 'Tahavvol-e Tabaqat-e Nowkhasteh-e Iran', *Ketab-e Alefba* vol. 4, Tehran 1975, and 'Towse'eh-ye Sana'at dar Dowreh-e Qajar', ibid.; Tabari E., *Forupaoshi-ye Nezam-e Sonnati va Zayesh-e Sarma'i-dari dar Iran*, Stockholm 1975. For the development of capitalism in the post-Constitutional period see Soudagar M., *Roshd-e Sarma'i-dari dar Iran 1304–1340*, Tehran 1979; Nowshirvani V. and Knight A., 'The Beginning of Commercial Agriculture in Iran', Princeton University mimeo, 1974.
4. Pigulevskaya N.V. et al., *Tarikh-e Iran az Dowreh-e Bastan ta Payan-e Sadeh-e Hezhdahom*, trans. K. Keshavarz, Tehran 1968. This work

---

* Place of publication London unless otherwise stated

presupposes a universal schema of history, and the correspondence between the Marxist concepts of modes of production and Iranian history is taken for granted.

5. For a succinct study of the introduction of Marxism to Iran and especially the rise and fall of the Tudeh (Communist) Party of Iran during 1941–53, see Abrahamian E., *Iran between Two Revolutions*, Princeton 1982. See also Alavi B., *Panjah va Seh Nafar*, Tehran 1979; Khamei A., *Panjah Nafar va Seh Nafar*, Tehran n.d.; Mazdak, *Asnad-e Tarikhi-ye Jonbesh-e Kargari, Social Demokratic, va Komunisti-ye Iran*, 7 vols., Florence 1972–1978.

6. For studies of these debates before and after the Russian revolution see Walicki A., *The Controversy over the Development of Capitalism in Russia*, Oxford 1969; Bailey A. and Llobera J.R. (eds.), *The Asiatic Mode of Production: Science and Politics*, 1981, especially the editors' introductory remarks on Part II, 'The Fate of the Asiatic Mode of Production from Plekhanov to Stalin', pp. 37–109; Sawer M., 'The Politics of Historiography: Russian Socialism and the Question of the Asiatic Mode of Production', *Critique* nos. 10–11, 1978–79.

7. Stalin J., *Dialectical and Historical Materialism*, Peking 1959. Articles expounding this view are to be found in various issues of *Donya*, the theoretical journal of the Tudeh Party, during this period.

8. For examples of traditional historiography see Pirnia H., *Tarikh-e Iran-e Bastan*, 3 vols., Tehran 1960; Eqbal A., *Tarikh-e Iran: az Aghaz ta Engheraz-e Qajarieh*, Tehran 1320/1942; Nafisi S., *Tarikh-e Ejtema'i va Siyasi-ye Iran dar Dowreh-e Mo'aser*, 2 vols., Tehran 1956. For two relatively interesting histories of the Constitutional era see Kasravi A., *Tarikh-e Mashruteh-e Iran*, Tehran 1961, and Malekzadeh M., *Tarikh-e Enqelab-e Mashrutiyat-e Iran*, 5 vols., Tehran 1949.

9. See Malcolm J., *History of Persia*, 2 vols., 1829; Curzon G., *Persia and the Persian Question*, 2 vols. 1892; Jackson W., *Persia: Past and Present*, 1906; Herzfeld E., *Iran in the Ancient East*, 1914; Sykes P., *A History of Persia*, 1930.

10. See Wilber D.N., *Iran: Past and Present*, Princeton 1950; Christensen A., *L'Iran sous les Sassanides*, Copenhagen 1944 (Persian trans. *Iran dar Zaman-e Sassanian*, Tehran 1953); Lambton A.K.S., *Landlord and Peasant in Persia*, Oxford 1953; Upton J.M., *The History of Modern Persia: An Interpretation*, Cambridge Mass. 1968.

11. Abrahamian E., op.cit. 1982, pp.281–326.

12. Maleki K., *Hezb-e Tudeh cheh Miguyad va cheh Mikonad*, Tehran 1951, and *Political Memories*, ed. and introduced M.A.H. Katouzian, Hanover 1981. Maleki was the leading figure in the Third Force and the main critic of Tudeh's Stalinism and subservience to Moscow.

13. See issues of *Elm va Zendegi* and *Nabard-e Zendegi*, both published by the Third Force intelligentsia.

14. See Pouyan A.P., *Rad-e Nazarieh-e Baga va Zarurat-e Nabard-e Mosalla-haneh*, Tehran n.d.; Ahmadzadeh M., *Jang-e Mosallahaneh: Ham Strategi Ham Taktik*, Tehran n.d.; Jazani B., *Capitalism and Revolution in Iran*, 1980.

15. See for example Ashrafian K.Z. and Aroonova M.R., *Dowlat-e Nader Shah: Tarh-e Koli-ye Ravabet-e Ejtema'i dar Iran dar Daheha-ye Chaharom va Panjom-e Qarn-e Hezhdahom*, Persian translation and introduction by H. Momeni, Tehran 1974.

16. It should be noted that State repression under the Pahlavis (1925–1979) was the main and most effective measure contributing to the general poverty of Marxism and Marxist scholarship in Iran. Supplements added to the 1906 Constitution under Reza Shah outlawed Communism, and adherence to Marxism brought prison charges. During this period, Marxist literature as a rule circulated underground, with the exception of historiography, which enjoyed a relative freedom, but had to conceal Marxist terminology and Marxist sources in order to pass the State censorship.

17. It was a common view among the Marxist intelligentsia in Iran, especially before the 1979 revolution, that the Tudeh's crushing defeat in the early 1950s was largely self-inflicted; see for example Mazdak, *Karnameh-e Mosaddeq va Hezb-e Tudeh*, Florence 1979.

18. The work of Pigulevskaya et al. (1968) alone covers eighteen centuries of Iranian history, slavery and feudalism. Keshavarz, the translator, introduces it as follows: 'This book is the first experiment containing the views of the Soviet Iranologists, and has been written in accordance with their own particular style. The authors attempt to divide Iranian history during the Ancient and Middle Ages into periods ... The laws of development and the peculiarity of the relations of production in feudal society have been considered from a social [i.e. Marxist] point of view'; Translator's introduction, Pigulevskaya et al. op.cit. 1968. The term 'social', which replaces 'Marxist' in this quotation, is an indication of the sensitivity of the State censorship.

19. See Diakonov I.M., *Tarikh-e Maad*, Tehran 1967; Dandamayev M.A., *Iran dar Dowran-e Nakhostin Padeshahan-e Hakhamaneshi*, Tehran 1973; Diakonov M.M., *Ashkanian*, Tehran 1968.

20. See Lukonin V.G., *Tammadon-e Iran-e Sasani*, Tehran 1972.

21. Kulsnikov A.I., *Iran dar Astaneh-e Yuresh Tazian*, Tehran 1973; Pigulevskaya et al. op.cit. Vol.I, 1968, pp.151–237.

22. See Pigulevskaya et al., op.cit. Vol.I, 1968, pp.238–324.

23. For the Mongol period see Petrushevsky I.P., *Keshavarzi va Monasebat-e Ardhi dar Ahd-e Moghol*, 2 vols., Tehran 1966, and 'The Socio-Economic Conditions of Iran under the Il-Khans', in *The Cambridge History of Iran* vol.V 1968, Boyle J.A. (ed.), *The Saljuq and Mongol Periods*; Barthold V., *Turkestan Down to the Mongol Invasion*, 1928. Petrushevsky's works display the most elaborate conception of Iranian feudalism in Soviet historiography; this conception will be considered in some detail in chapter 3.

24. The short-lived Sarbedaran State established in north-east Iran is an example of these provincial governments, which sprang up in different localities in the final period of Mongol rule in Iran. See Petrushevsky, *Nahzat-e Sarbedaran-e Khorasan*, Tehran 1971.

25. See Pigulevskaya et al., op.cit. Vol.II, 1968, pp.491–529, pp.530–596.

26. On Nadir's rule see Reisner, op.cit. 1973.
27. Pigulevskaya et al., op.cit. Vol.II, 1968, pp.651–654.
28. Iransky S. et al., *Enqelab-e Mashrutiyat-e Iran va Risheha-ye Ejtema'i va Eqtesadi-ye An*, Tehran 1951; Ivanov M.S. *Enqelab-e Mashrutiyat-e Iran*, Tehran 1979.
29. From the Reza Shah period (1925–41), see Melikov A.S., *Esteqrar-e Diktatori-ye Reza Khan dar Iran*, Tehran 1980; and Ivanov's work on the post-Constitutional period (1900–1975), Ivanov M.S., *Tarikh-e Novin-e Iran*, Stockholm 1978.
30. See Ashraf op.cit. 1970; Khonji M.A., 'Tarikh-e Maad va Mansh'a-ye Nazarieh-e Diakonov', *Rahnema-ye Ketab*, 1967; Katouzian M.A.H., op.cit. 1981.
31. The concepts of 'Asiatic patrimonial despotism' and 'Aridisolatic society' are used by Ashraf and Katouzian respectively. Both authors stress the restructuring of Iranian Asiatism by an imported capitalist system; the latter leads to the prolongation of the former. Ashraf op.cit. 1970; Katouzian op.cit. 1981.
32. The uniqueness of Iranian history is implicit in Ashraf's argument, while Katouzian asserts the notion explicitly.
33. The interpretation of Iranian history in terms of a conflict between centralizing and decentralizing forces and tendencies, i.e. conflict between the State and the tribes, is not specific to Asiatic definitions; numbers of other historians also subscribe to this view, e.g. N. Keddie, who uses the notion of 'tribal feudalism', to define pre-Constitutional Iran. See Keddie N., 'The Impact of the West on Iranian Social History', Ph.D. thesis, University of California at Berkeley, 1955. The notion is reiterated in her later works.
34. The concept of 'Orientalism' has enjoyed a wide currency in social sciences in recent years, following the publication of Edward Said's controversial work on the subject; Said E., *Orientalism*, 1978, especially Introduction pp.1–28. Said's concept and his definition of the Orientalist problematic have since been widely criticized from different standpoints; for a resume of responses to Said's work see Mani L. and Frankenberg R., 'The Challenge of Orientalism', *Economy and Society* vol. XIV no. 2. So far as the question of history and historical writing is concerned, Said's critique of the Orientalist discourse systematically undermines any notion of 'historical specificity' that can be attributed to non-European societies. It effectively subsumes their histories under a universal history, whereby their diversities can be reduced only to their diverse cultural formations.
35. Marx refers to the Asiatic mode of production as a concept designating a specific period in the history of human societies only in his 1859 Preface to *A Contribution to the Critique of Political Economy*, 1971 p.21. He expounds the characteristic features of the concept in his other work, mainly in *Grundrisse*, only in passing, with the exception of his journalistic writings on the British rule in India. His remarks in *Grundrisse*, however, appear in the form of a series of contrasts with the pre-capitalist economic forms in the West, which follow the main logic of Marx's writings on pre-capitalism. They are intended primarily to throw light on the development of his main object of investigation, i.e. the capitalist mode of production.

36. Weber expounds the notion of 'patrimonial' rule in the context of his discussion of 'The Three Pure Types of Legitimate Authority'—legal, traditional and charismatic. 'Patrimonial authority', which belongs to the second type, is then discussed in *contrast* with the legal/rational type, which presupposes rational processes and practices specific to market relations and institutions; Weber M., *The Theory of Social and Economic Organization*, ed. with an introduction by T. Parsons, New York 1947, pp. 341–358.

37. Among Western adherents to the concept of the Asiatic mode of production, Krader recognizes this point. He defines the Asiatic mode and Asiatic society in contrast not with feudalism but with capitalism; see Krader L., *The Asiatic Mode of Production*, van Assen 1975, esp. pp.286–96.

38. For this mode of analysis and interpretation of Iranian society and history, see Banani A., *The Modernization of Iran, 1921–1941*, Stanford 1961; Avery P., *Modern Iran*, 1965; Keddie N., op.cit. 1955; Upton, op.cit. 1968; Bill J., *The Politics of Iran: Groups, Classes and Modernization*, Columbus 1972; Binder L., *Iran: Political Development in a Changing Society*, Berkeley 1962; Amirsadegi H. and Ferrier R. (eds.), *Twentieth Century Iran*, 1977.

Chapter 2

1. See the works cited in Chapter 1.
2. Broadly speaking, historians have registered four main categories of land-ownership in pre-capitalist Iran:

(i) *Aradhi-ye Khaleseh* (Crown lands), mainly originating in conquest or confiscation, were owned by the reigning monarch as his private holding. No assignment, administrative or military, was made of this category of land. The monarch retained exclusive rights over the Crown lands, although transfer or sale of ownership rights was not uncommon. Crown lands were usually leased out by bailiffs to the peasants; the bailiff, in his capacity as representative of the Crown, distributed land and seed to the peasants, controlling the process of production and the conditions of tenancy. Crown lands were exempted from state taxation.

(ii) *Aradhi-ye Divani* (State lands) also originated from conquest and confiscation of various other categories of land-ownership. State lands were the main source of land assignment, and were always subject to government taxation.

(iii) *Aradhi-ye Waqfi*, Muqufat, (ecclesiastial lands, charitable lands). *Waqf* is an Islamic institution by which private donations of land or its revenue are made to ecclesiastical institutions for charitable purposes. *Waqf* lands were administered by the *mutavalli*, an agent appointed by the institution concerned (sometimes the donor in person functioned as *mutavalli*) who often leased out the land, either directly to the peasants living on it, or to local merchants for a lump sum paid in advance. In either case the peasant paid a portion of produce as rent. This category of land-ownership was taxable; the *mutavalli* usually collected the taxes and paid them to the government agent in lump sums. The argument developed in Chapter 4 suggests that *waqf* lands were effectively private holdings, and should be considered as such.

(iv) *Aradhi-ye Arbabi, Amlak-e Arbabi* (private holdings). This category of land-ownership had diverse sources, but its main origin was the conversion of land assignments into private property, often developing at the expense of the *divani* lands. Private lands resembled fee-simple holdings in character, and the holders enjoyed rights of appropriation and disposal; they could transfer or sell their rights in it.

This fourfold categorization of land-ownership, with variations in the relative size and significance of each category, persisted until the late Qajar period, when the expansion of commodity production for the market and the subsequent struggle for land among the contending sections of the land-owning class led to a major redefinition of the *khaleseh* lands. The category of *khaleseh* during this period was substantially expanded, mostly by means of confiscation and forced expulsion, at the expense of other categories of land-ownership, especially the *waqf* and *arbabi* lands.

The *khaleseh* was thus divided into five sub-categories, as follows: (i) *Amlak-e divani* (real *khaleseh*), administered by the government directly, or indirectly through the *mubasher* who organized and controlled production; this category of *khaleseh* was subject to state taxation. (ii) *Amlak-e zabti*, or *mutassarifi*, which consisted of the *arbabi* and *waqf* lands, as well as *tuyuls* and *soyurghals* confiscated by the state, usually leased out to the peasants in return for a portion of the produce; these lands were taxable. (iii) *Amlak-e sabti* included lands whose ownership had previously been unspecified, brought into state possession and leased out to the peasant in return for a specified rent. (iv) *Amlak-e bazri* were originally private holdings or personal assignments to a specific individual, which had over the course of time fallen barren and abandoned; the state then took possession, providing seed and working capital to the peasant living on the land, in return for a specified rent. (v) *Amlak-e enteqali* referred to the sale of the fee-tail of land originally from the category of *amlak-e sabti*; the holder of this category of land possessed no rights of disposal over it, and it was subject to high government taxes.

This brief discussion of the categories of land-ownership in pre-Constitutional Iran shows that various categories were subject to different tax regimes and legal relations which clearly affected the conditions of production and appropriation of surplus, i.e. the size of the produce and the level of rent, hence also the extent of the involvement of the unit of production in commodity exchange relations. But the variation in the juridico-political conditions of the formation of ownership rights over the land had no bearing on the actual economic processes of the formation and appropriation of private property in land, as it did not affect either the character of the relations of production or the mode of appropriation of surplus. The separation of the peasants from the land and their subsumption in the process of production was the invariant of the process of formation and appropriation of feudal landed property in all categories of land-ownership. This point, which reaffirms the necessity of the conceptual distinction between legal ownership and economic property and their respective juridico-political and economic processes and practices, is also the reason why this study does not devote a separate chapter to the categories of land-ownership in feudal Iran. For detailed and systematic discussion of the categories of land-ownership in pre-Constitutional Iran, see Lambton A.K.S., *Landlord and Peasant in Persia: A Study of Land Tenure and Land Revenue Administration*, 1953; Nomani, op.cit. 1980; Petrushevsky, op.cit. 1965.

3. Ashraf, op.cit. 1975; Katouzian, op.cit. 1981.
4. Katouzian mostly identifies Marxist scholarship with the publications of the Tudeh party and the writings of the Tudeh intelligentsia—his ideological opponents as a committed Persian nationalist.
5. For different definitions of the concept of the Asiatic mode of production in Marx's discourse, see: Wittfogel K., *Oriental Despotism*, 1981, pp.369–388; Anderson P., *Lineages of the Absolutist State*, 1974, pp.462–484; Eberhard W., *Conquerors and Rulers: Social Forces in Medieval China*, 1970, pp.48–60 and 66–74; Lichtheim G., 'Marx and the Concept of the "Asiatic Mode of Production"', *St Antony's Papers* no. 14, 1963; Hindess B. and Hirst P.Q., *Pre-Capitalist Modes of Production*, 1975, pp.178–220; Bailey A.M. and Llobera J.R. (eds.), *The Asiatic Mode of Production: Science and Politics*, 1981, pp.23–37.
6. See the works cited in note 5, especially Wittfogel, op.cit. pp. 388–409; Anderson op.cit. pp.484–549; Bailey and Llobera, op.cit. pp.237–334. Also Danilova L.V., 'Controversial Problems of the Theory of Pre-Capitalist Societies', *Soviet Anthropology and Archaeology* IX, 1971, pp.269–328.
7. See Balibar in Althusser L. and Balibar E., *Reading Capital*, 1970, pp.209–225; Taylor J.G., *From Modernization to Modes of Production*, 1979, pp.172–186; Mandel E., *The Formation of the Economic Thought of Karl Marx*, 1971, pp.116–139.
8. See for example the work of Godelier M., 'The Concept of the "Asiatic Mode of Production" and Marxist Models of Social Evolution' in Seddon D. (ed.), *Relations of Production: Marxist Approaches to Economic Anthropology*, 1978, pp.209–259. For a critique of this view, see Mandel op. cit. 1971.
9. See Amin S., *Unequal Development*, 1976, pp.13–58. Wickham, following Amin, also uses the notion of the tributary mode of production; see Wickham C.J., 'The Uniqueness of the East', *Journal of Peasant Studies* vol. 12 nos. 2–3, 1985, pp.166–196, especially pp.170–171.
10. See Wittek P., *The Rise of the Ottoman Empire*, 1971.
11. Ibn Khaldun, *The Muqaddimah: An Introduction to History*. Translated from Arabic by Frank Rosenthal, edited and abridged by N.J. Dawood, 1967. For some contemporary discussions of Ibn Khaldun's conception of history, see Mahdi M., *Ibn Khaldun's Philosophy of History*, 1982; al-

Azmeh A., *Ibn Khaldun in Modern Scholarship*, 1981, and *Ibn Khaldun: An Essay in Reinterpretation*, 1982; Lacoste Y., *Ibn Khaldun: The Birth of History and the Past of the Third World*, 1984.

12. Gibb H.A.R. and Bowen H., *Islamic Society and the West: A Study of the Impact of Western Civilisation on Moslem Culture in the Near East*, 1953 and 1962 (2 vols.). Turner also refers to this point, indicating that 'Gibb and Bowen's text also provides the major source for Anderson's study of the "House of Islam" ... Anderson derives his distinction between "civil society" and the "state" from Gramsci, but his information on the general characteristics of Islamdom is heavily dependent on Gibb and Bowen's account. The oddity of this dependence is striking, since Anderson is explicitly aware of the dangers of the Orientalist tradition but continues to flirt with that perspective.' Turner B.S., *Capitalism and Class in the Middle East: Theories of Social Change and Economic Development*, 1974, p.73.

13. See for example Lambton, op.cit. 1953, Katouzian, op.cit. 1981; both argue for the retarding effects of Islamic law on the development of landed property in medieval Iran.

14. See relevant sections in Wittfogel, op. cit. 1981; Bailey and Llobera, op.cit. 1981; Hindess and Hirst, op. cit. 1975.

15. This argument is often raised in defence of the concept, substantiating the functional necessity of the Asiatic state by attributing an economic character to it. See Taylor's review of Hindess and Hirst, *Critique of Anthropology* vol. I nos. 4–5, 1975, pp.127–155, and vol. II no. 6, 1976, pp.56–69; and their response to his critique in *Mode of Production and Social Formation*, 1977, p.42.

16. See for example Cutler A. et al., *Marx's Capital and Capitalism Today*, vol. I, 1977, pp.207–222.

17. Cutler A., 'Letter to Etienne Balibar' and 'Response', *Theoretical Practice*, nos. 7/8, 1973, pp.51–5, 73–85.

18. See Hindess and Hirst, op.cit. 1975, pp.183–200, 223–232, op.cit. 1977, pp.34–46, 63–73; and Cutler A. et al., op.cit. 1977, pp.103–167, 243–262.

19. Communal production, by definition, requires communal property, without which it cannot exist. In a discussion of Marx's commentary on India, Thorner points out that in early modern times communal property did not exist in the Indian village, and production was organized on an individual household basis; Thorner D., 'Marx on India and the Asiatic Mode of Production', *Contribution to Indian Sociology* IX, 1966. Many of Marx's remarks on communal production in the Indian village emphasize its self-sufficient, isolated and egalitarian character, an issue much disputed in modern historical and sociological research; see Anderson, op.cit. 1974, pp.458–488; Hindess and Hirst, op.cit. 1975, pp.243–244. Asad questions the relevance of the concept of equality to forms of production in nomadic social forms, with wider theoretical implications for pre-capitalist forms in general; Asad A., 'Equality in Nomadic Social

Systems: Notes towards the Dissolution of an Anthropological Category', *Critique of Anthropology* vol. 3 no. 11, 1978.

20. The prevailing forms of land tenure and the conditions of tenancy in pre-capitalist Iran were essentially incompatible with the economic and juridico-political requisites of a communal form of production. Historical evidence testifies to the absence of communal property capable of forming the basis for a communal form of production in agriculture; see Lambton, op.cit. 1953, 1968, 1987, 1988; Nomani, op.cit. 1980. Stack, visiting Iran in the late nineteenth century, writes: 'I sought in vain for any satisfactory traces of the village community as exemplified in India. It is certain that the population of a Persian village, if it be of any size, cannot be merely casual; indeed, the village has perhaps greater permanence in Persia than elsewhere, because in the general aridity of the country, village sites are marked out by nature, and a water-supply which supports a village now, has probably served the same purpose for a thousand years. It follows that the arbabs must be related to each other . . .' Stack E., *Six Months in Persia*, 1882, p.261. Stack's account of the effect of aridity on the geographical organization of Iranian villages, too, runs counter to Katouzian's exposition.

21. The post-1962 period witnessed the rise of populist thought on the Iranian intellectual scene. Characteristically heterogeneous in form and substance, the populist trend came to dominate the literary and social scientific fields in the following two decades. The agrarian populists, rural sociologists, economists and agronomists, who worked and wrote in the political and ideological climate of the post-reform period, could be broadly divided into two groups: first, the 'traditionalists', such as Houshang Keshavarz and Javed Safi Nejad, whose works were not directly influenced by Western and Russian populist thought, and secondly the 'modern' populists, such as Houshang Saedlou, Ismail Ajami and Fatemeh Etemad Mughadam, who were strongly influenced by the theoretical writings of Western and Russian populists, especially Alexander Chayanov. See for instance Safi Nejad J., *Nezamha-ye Towlid-e Zera'i-ye Jami: Boneh, Qabl va Ba'ad az Eslahat-e Ardhi*, Tehran 1975; Saedlu H., *Masa'el-e Keshavarzi-ye Iran*, Tehran 1979; Ajami I., 'Social Classes, Family Demographic Characteristics and Mobility in Three Iranian Villages', *Sociologica Ruralis* 9 no. 1, 1969.

22. See Hossein Mahdavy's introductory remarks on Ashraf's article in the same volume (Cook, op.cit. 1975), p.258.

23. For discussions of the concept of domination in Weber's discourse see Bendix R., *Max Weber: An Intellectual Portrait*, 1962; Mommesen W., *The Age of Bureaucracy*, 1974; Hirst P.Q., *Social Evolution and Sociological Categories*, 1976. For Weber's thesis on the development of capitalism see Giddens A., *Capitalism and Modern Social Theory*, 1971, and 'Marx, Weber and the Development of Capitalism', *Sociology* vol.4, 1970, pp.289–310; Birnbaum N., 'Conflicting Interpretations of the Rise of Capitalism: Marx and Weber', *British Journal of Sociology* vol. 4, 1953, pp.125–41; Turner B.S., *For Weber*, and op.cit. 1984, esp. pp.30–43.

Chapter 3

1. Marx K., *A Contribution to the Critique of Political Economy*, 1971, 'Introduction to a Critique of Political Economy', p.190. '*Production in general*', Marx writes, 'is an abstraction, but a sensible abstraction in so far as it actually emphasizes and defines the common aspects and thus avoids repetition'. In *Capital* Marx defines the concept of 'production in general' in the following terms: 'Whatever the social form of production, labourers and means of production always remain factors of it. But in a state of separation from each other either of these factors can be such only potentially. For production to go on at all they must unite. The specific manner in which the union is accomplished distinguishes the different economic epochs of the structure of society from one another.' *Capital* Vol. II, 1967, pp.36–37.

2. This, however, is the case in the discourse of *Capital*, where the dominance of the relations over the forces of production is ensured by the form of the possession of and separation from the means and conditions of production which underlie the processes of the production and appropriation of surplus value. Marx's conceptualization of the transition from the 'formal' to the 'real' subsumption of labour to capital and his analysis of the transformation of 'absolute' to 'relative' surplus value in Volume I, and his conceptualization of the 'metamorphoses of capital and their circuits' in Volume II, are cases in point. Marx's analyses here are informed by a mode of causality arising from the primacy of the relations of production in the discourse. This order of causality, however, is not maintained in all his writings. In the well-known 1859 *Introduction*, for example, and in *The Poverty of Philosophy*, the order is reversed, and the forces of production are assigned the dominant position. The two different orders of causality in Marx's discourse have given rise to diverse conceptions of history and politics in Marxist theory, classical and contemporary. Plekhanov's 'The Development of the Monist View of History' (*Selected Philosophical Works* vol. I, Moscow 1974), and Lenin's *The Development of Capitalism in Russia* (*Collected Works* vol. III, 1970), are classical examples, emphasizing the primacy of the forces and the relations of production in the development of history and politics respectively. In contemporary Marxist theory Althusser pioneered an influential theoretical trend to reconstruct the Marxist theory of the modes of production in terms of the primacy of the relations of production; see *Reading Capital*, 1970. Gerry Cohen, on the other hand, has produced a powerful statement of the primacy of the forces of production in historical materialism in his *Karl Marx's Theory of History: A Defence*, 1978. For a concise comparative account of the contributions of Althusser and Cohen to the Marxist theory of history see Lock G., 'Louis Althusser and G. A. Cohen: A Confrontation', *Economy and Society* vol. 17, 1988, pp.499–517.

3. The inclusion of the conditions of existence and the effects of the relations of production in the definition of the concept of the mode of

production has led to a confusion between the two concepts of mode of production and social formation; see for example Anderson's definition of the concept of the feudal mode of production in *Passages from Antiquity to Feudalism*, 1974a, esp. pp.147–173, and in its sequel *Lineages of the Absolutist State*, 1974b.

4. See Marx's analysis of 'so-called primitive accumulation of capital', *Capital* vol. I, 1970, part VIII, pp.713–774.

5. *Capital* vol.III, 1971, chapter XLVII, pp.782–813, and *Grundrisse*, chapter on 'Capital', Notebooks IV, V, 1974; the relevant sections in *Pre-Capitalist Economic Formations*, 1964.

6. This point will be further elaborated below in examining Anderson's concept of the feudal mode of production, pp.84–96.

7. For historiographies of Western feudalism informed by the political definition of the concept of the feudal mode of production, see Duby G., *The Early Growth of the European Economy: Warriors and Peasants from the Seventh to the Twelfth Centuries*, 1974; Hilton R., *Bond Men Made Free*, 1977. For studies of the transition from feudalism to capitalism, see Dobb M., *Studies in the Development of Capitalism*, and the controversy prompted by Dobb, Hilton R. (ed.), *The Transition from Feudalism to Capitalism*, 1976. See also Brenner R., 'Agrarian Class Structure and Economic Development in Pre-Industrial Europe', *Past and Present* no. 70, 1976, and the debate it generated on the historical specificities of capitalist development in Europe, in Aston T.H. and Philpin C.H.E. (eds.), *The Brenner Debate*, Cambridge 1985. For studies on the character of socio-economic development in Europe in the latest stages of feudalism see Aston T. (ed.), *Crisis in Europe 1560–1600*, 1965, and the important work of Lublinskaya A.D., *French Absolutism: The Crucial Phase*, Cambridge 1968, especially her summary of the debate on the nature of the seventeenth-century crisis.

8. This point is forcefully made by Hirst in his influential review of Anderson's work; see Hirst P.Q., 'The Uniqueness of the West', *Economy and Society*.

9. Anderson's work prompted a wide response from both historians and sociologists, Marxist and non-Marxist. See MacRae D.G., 'Chains of History', *New Society* 31, 1975; Runciman W.G., 'Comparative Sociology or Narrative History: A Note on the Methodology of Perry Anderson', *Archives Européennes de Sociologie* 21, 1980; Heller A., 'Review of *Passages* and *Lineages*', *Telos* no. 33, 1977; Miliband R., 'Political Forms and Historical Materialism', *The Socialist Register*, 1975; Thomas K., 'Jumbo-History', *New York Review of Books*, April 1975; Fulbrook M. and Skocpol T., 'Destined Pathways: The Historical Sociology of Perry Anderson', in Skocpol T. (ed.), *Vision and Method in Historical Sociology*, Cambridge 1984.

10. See Fulbrook and Skocpol, op.cit. 1984.

11. Petrushevsky, op.cit. 1966, vol. II, pp.156–168.

12. Hindess and Hirst, op.cit. 1975.

13. All quotations from the works of Petrushevsky and Nomani in this study are translated from Persian by the author.

14. In fact Petrushevsky refers to Marx's often-quoted remarks on the character of the relations of exploitation in Asiatic societies, but without mentioning the concept of the Asiatic mode of production (Petrushevsky, op.cit. vol. II, pp.5–7). This omission, along with Petrushevsky's vacillation between rent and tax-rent, should be attributed to the suppression of the concept in official Soviet historiography. For discussions of the fate of the concept of the Asiatic mode of production in the Soviet Union, see Bailey and Llobera, op. cit. 1981, pp.49–106, and Wittfogel, op.cit., pp.389–411; for an account of the later Soviet response to the concept, and especially to Wittfogel's definition of Asiatic society, see Gellner E., 'Soviets against Wittfogel: or the Anthropological Preconditions of Mature Marxism', in Hall J.A. (ed.), *States in History*, Oxford 1986, pp.78–108.

15. Petrushevsky relies on Juwayni's account of the *yasa* in *Tarikh-e Jahan Gusha* vol. I, p.24; see Petrushevsky, op.cit. Vol. II, pp.171–2. For a detailed account of the political, legal and military organization of the Mongol state in Iran see Spuler B., *Die Mongolen in Iran: Politik, Verwaltung und Kultur der Ilchanzeit 1220–1350*, translated into Persian by M. Miraftab, Tehran 1972. For a more general discussion of the Mongol state see Morgan D., *The Mongols*, Oxford 1986. Morgan's work contains a useful guide to the Chinese, Persian, European and contemporary sources, pp.5–32. The military and legal organization of the Mongol polity, especially the *yasa*, is discussed in some detail below, pp.84–112.

16. See Spuler, op.cit. and Morgan, op.cit. especially pp.158–170.

17. Nomani's account of the development of feudalism in Iran is loosely chronological, sustaining an order of continuity. But his genealogy of the *iqta* does not follow a chronological order, due mainly to the scarcity of the primary source on which he relies. This makes it difficult to present a systematic view of the development of the *iqta* in his work.

Chapter 4

1. The concept of 'production in general' (Marx, 'Introduction to a Critique of Political Economy', 1971, p.190) is a theoretical construct. It refers primarily to the relationship of man to nature common to all societies, in which 'labour time' is a 'unique real cost' regulating the 'production' process. The concept leaves out property relations other than those arising from the labour of transformation. The labour of the human subject is the source of economic property and the foundation of the process of production. The concept has given rise to much criticism in Marxist theory. See for example Rancière J., 'The Concept of Critique and the Critique of Political Economy', *Theoretical Practice* no. 1, 1971, pp.35–52, no. 2, 1971, pp.30–48, no. 6, 1972, pp.31–49; and Lippi M., *Value and Naturalism*, 1979, especially pp.20–37.

2. For a discussion of the anthropological concept of economic property and ownership in Marx's early writings see Rancière, op.cit. no. 1, 1971; Tribe K., 'Ground Rent and the Formation of Classical Political Economy', Ph.D. thesis, Cambridge University 1975, and 'Economic

Property and the Theorization of Ground Rent', *Economy and Society* vol. 6, 1977, pp.69–88.

3. Tribe, op.cit. 1977.

4. See Althusser L., *For Marx*, 1969, especially the essay 'On the Young Marx', pp.49–86; and Rancière, op.cit. 1971.

5. Althusser develops this concept in *For Marx*, and it subsequently informs the discourse of *Reading Capital*. For a discussion of the concept in Althusser's discourse see Cutler A., 'The Concept of the Epistemological Break', *Theoretical Practice* nos. 3 & 4, 1971, pp.63–81.

6. Marx's conceptualization of the forms and conditions of the sub-sumption of labour to capital in *Capital* Volume I are instructive in this respect. Marx identifies two forms of subsumption: formal and real, each corresponding to a specific stage in the development of the capitalist mode of production. Formal subsumption relates to the period of manufacture and is characterized by a non-correspondence between the social division of labour in society and the technical division of labour in the organization of production; the non-correspondence and the prevailing organization of labour hinder the real control of the capitalist over the process of production. The transition from manufacture to modern industry which ensures the real subsumption of labour to capital, hence bringing the process of production under the complete control of the capitalist, is analyzed in terms of the increasing dominance of capitalist relations of production in society, which radically restructures the organization of labour and production. However, in Volume I, capitalist relations appear only in terms of their effects, i.e. the changing technical division of labour, and its effect on productivity; *Capital* vol. I, 1970, pp.322–368. For additional remarks on the formal and the real subsumption of labour to capital in the capitalist mode of production see the Appendix to the Penguin edition of *Capital* Volume I, 1976, pp.1019–1038.

7. The labour theory of value forms the core of Marx's analysis of the capitalist mode of production in *Capital*. The theory has been subject to criticism by non-Marxist economists and social scientists since the early decades of this century. Critics have variously emphasized the logical inconsistency and the fictitious character of the labour theory of value, noting its non-correspondence to the facts of experience in real economic life. It is also, critics have argued, irrelevant to the analysis of the process of capitalist distribution, in which prices rather than the value of commodities constitute the measure of exchange; e.g. Bohm-Bawerk E. von, *Karl Marx and the Close of his System*, published with Rudolf Hilferding's response, *Bohm-Bawerk's Criticism of Marx*, edited with an introduction by Paul Sweezy, 1974. Marxist theoreticians argued in response that the critics have radically misconceived the precise nature and status of the theory in Marx's discourse. Marx's theory is not economic in character —is not intended to explain capitalist exchange relations—but rather a tenet of historical materialism, and as such concerned with the social relations underlying the processes of capitalist production and distribution; e.g. Hilferding, op.cit. 1974. The shift of emphasis from the

economic to the social has since remained the fundamental argument in the Marxist defence of the labour theory of value, e.g. Colletti's response to Bernstein's critique of the theory, 'Bernstein's Marxism' in Colletti L., *From Rousseau to Lenin: Studies in Ideology and Society*, 1974, pp.45–108. The revival of interest in Marxist theory in the late 1960s and 1970s, and the subsequent attempts by Marxist theoreticians to analyze the complex social and economic structure of contemporary capitalism, laid the ground for the re-evaluation of the labour theory of value; e.g. Steedman et al., *The Value Controversy*, 1981. Orthodox Marxist critics came to acknowledge the validity of the bourgeois critique of the theory, while rejecting the empiricist epistemology in which it was grounded; the conventional Marxist defence of the theory, emphasizing its social rather than economic character, is (it was now argued) but a *de facto* recognition of the validity of this critique. The question of the pertinence of the labour theory of value to capitalist exchange relations cannot be resolved in the context of contemporary re-theorizations of the 'transformation problem' in *Capital*, and the main points of the bourgeois critique of the theory, viewed in isolation from their specific ideological context, have serious implications for the consistency of Marxist economic theory as a whole. An economic theory in which the labour of transformation is the sole means of validation of economic exchange and property cannot come to terms with the host of problems arising from the radical changes in the structure of capitalist relations of production. Contemporary statements of orthodoxy, philosophical and economic, however rigorous and sophisticated, fail to meet the challenge, and their ideological commitments obscure the urgent need for an effective political strategy. For the critics of the Marxist orthodoxy, the question was thus no longer one of defence or rectification, but of a radical restructuring of the discourse of *Capital;* can it be sustained without the labour theory of value? See Cutler A. et al., op.cit. 1977, esp. Part I 'Value', pp.9–10; Lippi M., op.cit. 1976, esp. pp.109–133. For a neo-Ricardian argument see Steedman I., *Marx After Srafa*, 1977. A rigorous defence of the labour theory of value and theorization of the 'transformation problem' is found in Fine B. and Harris L., *Re-reading Capital*, 1979. Rubin's work remains the most rigorous and subtle exposition of the labour theory of value to date; Rubin I. I., *Essays on Marx's Theory of Value*, Detroit 1972.

8. See Cutler et al., op.cit. 1977; Tribe, op.cit. 1975, 1976.

9. The conception of economic property and ownership associated with the labour theory of value cannot explain the formation and appropriation of property in 'natural objects', i.e. objects which are not products of human labour; in the economic field, they remain as objects which have no value, but are exchanged at a definite price. In relation to land, Marx writes: *'Rent is the price paid to the owner of natural forces or mere productions of nature* for the right of using those forces, or appropriating (by labour) those productions. This is in fact the form in which all rent appeared originally. But then the question still remains to be solved of how things which have no *value* can have a *price*, and how this is compatible with the general theory of *value'* (*Theories of Surplus Value*, 1969, Part II, p.247).

The bulk of Marx's writings on capitalist rent in *Capital* Volume III is devoted to the resolution of this apparent paradox, but to no avail. The inconsistencies of Marx's theorization of capitalist ground rent have been the source of a major controversy amongst Marxist theoreticians. See Walker R., 'Contentious Issues in Marxian Value and Rent Theory: A Second and Longer Look', *Antipode*, 1975; Scott A. J., 'Land and Land Rent: An Interpretative Review of the French Literature', in Board C. et al. (eds.), *Progress in Geography* 9, 1976, pp.101–47; Tribe, op.cit. 1977; Cutler A., 'The Concept of Ground Rent and Capitalism in Agriculture', *Critique of Anthropology* nos. 4 & 5, 1975, pp.72–89; Fine B., 'On Marx's Theory of Agricultural Rent', *Economy and Society* vol. 8 no. 3, 1979, pp.241–278.

10. See Tribe, op.cit. 1977. Fine disputes this point, arguing that 'Marx's theory of agricultural rent is not an adjunct of his theory of capital at the level of distribution but is separate from it', op.cit. 1979, p.241. Fine's argument, a rigorous statement of the orthodox position, fails to transcend the theoretical inconsistencies of the classical theory. See also the responses to Fine's essay: Catephores G., 'The Historical Transformation Problem: A Reply', and Ball M., 'On Marx's Theory of Agricultural Rent: A Reply to Ben Fine', both in *Economy and Society* vol. 9 no. 3, 1980; and Fine's rejoinder to Catephores, 'On the Historical Transformation Problem', ibid.

11. See Althusser, op.cit. 1969, esp. the essay 'Marxism and Humanism', pp.219–247, and op.cit. 1970, esp. 'The Basic Concepts of Historical Materialism', pp.199–254. For critical evaluation of the works of Althusser and his contribution to Marxist theory see: Glucksmann A., 'A Ventriloquist Structuralism', *New Left Review* no. 72, 1972; Benton T., *The Rise and Decline of Structural Marxism*, 1983; Callinicos A., *Is There a Future for Marxism?*, 1982; Elliot G., *Althusser: The Detour of Theory*, 1987; Hirst P.Q., *On Law and Ideology*, 1979; Craib I., *Modern Social Theory*, 1984.

12. Asad T. and Wolpe H., 'Concepts of Modes of Production', *Economy and Society* vol. 5 no. 4, 1976. See also reviews of Hindess and Hirst's *Pre-Capitalist Modes of Production* by Taylor J.G., *Critique of Anthropology*, vols. 4–5, 6, 1975–6; Dobb M., *History*, 1976; Cook S., *Journal of Peasant Studies* vol. 4 no. 4, pp.360–389.

13. Elsewhere Tribe rightly points out that the origin of this argument is found in Marx's critique of Ricardo's theory of rent. Marx criticizes Ricardo for falsely generalizing his analysis of capitalist rent for all ages and countries; Tribe, op.cit. 1977, p.75.

14. On this see Kula W., *An Economic Theory of the Feudal System*, 1976.

15. See Hindess and Hirst, op.cit. 1975, pp.234–5.

16. Marx's writings on landed property and ground rent contain remarks alluding to such a definition. In *The Poverty of Philosophy*, for example, he clearly distinguishes economic property from legal ownership, identifying the former with social relations of production: 'In each historical epoch, property has developed differently and under a set of entirely different social relations. Thus to define bourgeois property is nothing else than to

give an exposition of all the social relations of bourgeois production ... to give a definition of property as an independent relation, a category apart, an abstract and eternal idea, can be nothing but an illusion of metaphysics or jurisprudence ... M. Proudhon affirms that there is something mystical and mysterious about the origin of property. Now to see mystery in the relation between production itself and the distribution of the instruments of production—is not this, to use M. Proudhon's language, a renunciation of all claims to economic science?' (pp.148–9). In this essay Marx states clearly that the relations of production are constitutive of property in general, and cannot be reduced to juridico-political intervention in the process of production (ibid. p.167). The conception of property as relations of production, not given but constructed in the process of production, is further affirmed in a letter to Annenkov explaining his critique of Proudhon's *Philosophie de la misère* (Marx and Engels, *Selected Correspondence*, 1975, pp.29–39 esp. p.38). In *Capital*, Marx refers in unambiguous terms to the economic character of ground rent, stating that 'the mere legal ownership of land does not create any ground rent for the owner' (Volume I 1970, p.739). Further remarks to this effect can be found in various of Marx's works, but they are effectively marginalized by the category of value which dominates the order of his discourse on the subject.

Chapter 5

1. For studies of the origins and the history of the *iqta* in the medieval period see Cahen C. 'L'Evolution de l'*iqta* du II au XIII siècle', *Annales—Economies—Sociétés—Civilisations*, VIII, 1953, pp.25–52; Lambton A.K.S., 'Reflections on the *iqta*', in Makdisi G. (ed.), *Arabic and Islamic Studies in Honor of Hamilton A. R. Gibb*, Leiden 1965, pp.358–376, and 'The Evolution of the *Iqta* in Medieval Iran', *Iran* V, 1967, pp.41–50.

2. Spencer clearly attributes the origins of the state to warfare and conquest, claiming that pre-industrial societies were dominated by military states, and military power was the driving force of social change and development in 'militant societies'; Spencer H., *Principles of Sociology* 1969. See also Hintze 0. (ed. Gilbert F. *The Historical Essays of Otto Hintze*, New York 1975, esp. pp.128–215, 422–52; Andreski S., *Military Organization and Society*, Berkeley 1971; Eisenstadt S.N., *The Political Systems of Empires*, New York 1969. Three major recent works in historical sociology variously influenced by different military conceptions of the state are: Skocpol T., *States and Social Revolutions*, Cambridge 1980; Giddens A., *The Nation-State and Violence*, Cambridge 1987; Mann M., *Sources of Social Power*, Vol. I, Cambridge 1987. Mann's contribution will be discussed in detail below.

3. The term is borrowed from Mann M., *States, War and Capitalism*, Oxford 1988.

4. Anderson here provides an entirely subjectivist view of serfdom; the absence of juridico-political relations of domination and subordination is attributed to the subjective action of the 'Arabs': 'Indifference or

contempt for agriculture precluded even a stabilized serfdom; labour was never regarded as so precious by the exploiting class that peasant adscription became a main desideratum' (op.cit. 1974b, p.501). This argument by implication means that the consolidation of serfdom in the West was primarily due to the subjective will and rational action of the land-owning class, with no foundation in the process of the formation and appropriation of feudal landed property.

5. Mann points out the erroneous character of the military conception of the state, and argues in particular against the assumption that the organizational structure of the state is coterminous with the military organization (Mann, op.cit. 1988, pp.59–68).

6. Anderson's conception of the Islamic state and society is best expressed in his discussion of the historical specificity of the Ottoman state (op.cit. 1974b, pp.361–397). Following Lybyer, Anderson argues that the Ottoman state was composed of ruling (military-bureaucratic) and religious institutions, which together formed the structure of patrimonial rule in Ottoman society (ibid. p.366). The primacy of the ruling institutions in the structure of Ottoman Sultanism (another term borrowed from Weber), he further argues, was an expression of its very nature as a warrior and predatory institution. In his essay on the 'House of Islam' Anderson equates the Ottoman social formation with the territorial basis of the Ottoman state, the boundaries of which are determined by a ceaseless quest for military mobilization and territorial expansion. The Marxist concept of social formation, with its hierarchy of determinations, thus dissolves into a political entity, the 'economic bedrock' of which is the 'complete absence of private property in land' (ibid. p.365). There is in Anderson's analysis of the Ottoman social formation virtually no demarcation line between the social and the political; the social is either subsumed within the political or collapses into it; and his persistent inability or unwillingness to define the form and character of the prevailing production relations and organization in Ottoman agriculture leads him back to the theoretical premises of the concept of the Asiatic mode of production. His own analysis of the Ottoman state thus belies his call to give this concept 'the decent burial it deserves' (ibid. pp.548–9).

7. See the works cited above, note 3.

8. On this point Mann differs from Spencer (from whom he borrows the notion of the militant state), arguing that Spencer declined to attribute functionality to military force, and thus overlooked its role in the economic development of the militant states (op.cit. 1988, p.64).

9. See Mann, op.cit. 1988, pp.37–8; Anderson's review of *The Sources of Social Power*, *Times Higher Education Supplement*, 1988, and his comments in 'A Culture in Counterflow', *New Left Review* 180, 1990, pp.41–78. Also Christopher Wickham's review of Mann's work, 'Historical Materialism, Historical Sociology', *New Left Review* 171, 1988.

10. Mann's comments on *Pre-Capitalist Modes of Production* suggest that he is in agreement with the authors' critique and subsequent rejection of the classical Marxist concept of pre-capitalist relations of production

characterized by the non-separation of the direct producers from the means and conditions of production (op.cit. 1988, p.36).

11. Mann's method is thoroughly empiricist; the correspondence of the concept with the real is the proof of its validity. See footnote op.cit. 1988, p.36.

12. See for example J. G. Taylor's review of *Pre-Capitalist Modes of Production* in *Critique of Anthropology*, 1975–1976, already considered in Chapter 3.

13. See for example Lambton, op.cit. 1965.

14. Clearly Lambton's writings on the *iqta* largely predate Anderson's remarks in *Lineages of the Absolutist State*. Anderson cites Lambton's early work *Landlord and Peasant in Persia* in the context of his conception of ownership in medieval Islam (Anderson 1974b, p.515). The similarity of their approaches to *iqta* may be attributed to the influence of Cahen.

15. Lambton's article 'The Evolution of the *Iqta* in Medieval Iran' (op.cit. 1967) was initially presented as a lecture to a meeting of the British Institute of Persian Studies, held in Tehran in November 1965; the lecture draws on her article 'Reflections on the *Iqta*' published earlier the same year in a collection edited by George Makdisi (op.cit. 1965). The choice of subject and the timing of the lecture leave little doubt as to its main purpose. The lecture is an explicit attack on and refutation of the concept of Iranian feudalism deployed by the radical Iranian intelligentsia, especially the Marxist left, in their analyses of the social, economic and political conditions and consequences of the Land Reform of 1962 (for a detailed discussion of this issue see Chapter 1). Lambton was quick to detect the political and ideological undercurrents of the revival of interest in studies of Iranian pre-capitalism. Her lecture opens thus: 'The title of my lecture may, perhaps, have puzzled some of you. The term *iqta* ceased to be commonly used in Persian from the time of the Ilkhans. My purpose this evening is to examine the *iqta*, the parent or forerunner of the *tuyul*, in order to show to what extent, if at all, medieval Persian society can be called feudal in the narrow sense, and Persian institutions, in a legal sense, feudal. I am not concerned with the all too frequent current misuse of the word feudalism, which has become a term of abuse, just as it did during the French revolution when it was adopted as a general description to cover many abuses of the *ancien régime*' (op.cit. 1967, p.41).

16. This general scenario, as we have seen (Chapter 3 above), has its ancestry in Ibn Khaldun's work; Nomani gives a revamped version of the same scenario (op.cit. 1972, pp.33–40).

17. The concept of spatial centralism is borrowed from Mann, op.cit. 1988.

18. This section draws on the following histories and studies of the Saljuq state: Nizam ul-Mulk, *Siyasat Nameh*, English trans. H. Darke, 1960; *Atabat al-Kataba*, ed. Eqbal A. with introduction by Qazwini M., Tehran 1950; Hamdullah Mustawfi Qazwini, *The Tarikh-i Guzida*, trans. and ed. Browne E.G., 2 vols., 1910 and 1913; Muhammad b. Ali b. Sulaymani al-Ravandi, *Rahat al-Sudur va Ayat al-Surur*, ed. Muhammad Eqbal, 1921; Eqbal A., *Vezarat dar Ahd-e Salatin-e Bozorg-e Saljuq*, Tehran 1959–60; Klausner C.L., *The Saljuq Vezirate: A Study of Civil*

Administration 1055–1194, Cambridge Mass., 1973; Lambton A.K.S., (i) 'The Internal Structure of the Saljuq Empire', in Boyle J. A. (ed.), *The Cambridge History of Iran*, vol. V, Cambridge 1968, pp.203–82 (ii) *Continuity and Change in Medieval Persia*, 1988 (iii) 'Administration of Sanjar's Empire as Illustrated in the *Atabat al-Kataba*', *Bulletin of the School of Oriental and African Studies* vol. XX, 1957, pp.367–388 (iv) 'Saljuq-Ghuzz Settlement in Persia' in Richards D.S. (ed.), *Islamic Civilization 950–1150*, Oxford 1973, pp.105–26; 'Diwan', in *Encyclopaedia of Islam*, new ed. vol. 1, pp.731–2; Houtsma M.I., 'Some Reflections on the History of the Saljuks', *Acta Orientalia* vol. III, 1924, pp.136–152; Bowen, H., 'Notes on Some Early Seljuqid Viziers', *Bulletin of the School of Oriental and African Studies* vol. XX, 1957, pp.105–10; Goitein S.D., 'The Origin of the Vizierate and its True Character', *Islamic Culture* vol. XVI nos. 3, 4, 1942, pp.255–63, 380–92.

Chapter 6

1. For example, definitions of pre-capitalist Iran as an Asiatic society which argue for the absence of private property in land implicitly or explicitly entail a notion of absolute sovereign/state ownership; e.g. Katouzian, op.cit. 1981; Ashraf, op.cit. 1975. Medieval political discourse is the authority and the point of reference commonly invoked by such studies.
2. The influence of the Sassanian theory of kingship and rule on conceptions of government in medieval political discourse is widely acknowledged by contemporary scholars; see Bosworth C.E., 'The Heritage of Rulership in Early Islamic Iran and the Search for Dynastic Connections with the Past', *Iran* XI, 1973, pp.51–62; Busse H., 'The Revival of the Persian Kingship under the Buyids', in Richards D.S. (ed.), *Islamic Civilization 950–1150*, 1973; Amir Arjomand S., *The Shadow of God and the Hidden Imam*, Chicago 1984, esp. pp. 85–101; Binder L. 'Al-Ghazali's Theory of Islamic Government', *The Muslim World*, 1955, pp. 229–41; Lambton A.K.S., 'Quis Custodiet Custodes: Some Reflections on the Persian Theory of Government', *Studia Islamica*, vols. V, VI, 1956, pp.125–48, 125–46, and 'Justice in the Medieval Persian Theory of Kingship', ibid. vol. XVII, 1962, pp.91–119, and 'Theory of Kingship in Nasihat ul-Muluk of Ghazali', *Islamic Quarterly* I, 1954, pp.47–55.
3. See for example Anderson, op.cit. 1974b, p.515.
4. Petrushevsky argues that Nizam ul-Mulk's drive for centralization and concentration of state power in the royal court, and his opposition to the decentralizing feudal forces, was the main reason for the assertion of the theory of absolute ownership in *Siyasat Nameh*; he contends that Nizam ul-Mulk was fighting a losing battle against the rising feudal forces in the Saljuq polity (Petrushevky, op.cit. Vol.I, 1966, p.50).
5. Lambton argues that *Siyasat Nameh* is not a 'Mirror for Princes', but an administrative manual written by a professional politician engaged in a political power struggle; she refers to the formal organization of the text and its difference from the format of the 'Mirrors', which were generally

written by men of letters. She pays little attention, however, to the conceptual structure of *Siyasat Nameh* and its striking similarity to those of the 'Mirrors'; nor does she note the resemblance in the political and ideological conditions of the formation of the discourse of *Siyasat Nameh* and the discourse of the 'Mirrors', e.g. *Nasihat ul-Muluk*; Lambton A. K.S., 'Islamic Mirrors for Princes', in *La Persia nel Medioevo*, Academia Nazionale dei Lincei, Rome 1971, pp.419–442 (esp. p.420).

6. For this issue see the following: Busse H., 'Iran under the Buyids', *Cambridge History of Iran* IV, 1975, pp.250–304; Amir Arjomand S., op.cit. 1984; Siddiqi A.H., 'Caliphate and Kingship in Medieval Persia', *Islamic Culture* vol. IX 1935, pp.560–79, vol. X 1936, pp.97–126, 260–79, 390–408, vol. XI 1937, pp.37–59; Madelung W., 'The Assumption of the Title Shahanshah by the Buyids and "The Reign of Daylam (Dawlat al-Daylam)" ', *Journal of Near East Studies* XXVIII, 1969, pp.84–108, 168–183; Lambton A.K.S., *State and Government in Medieval Islam*, Oxford 1981, esp. pp.103–153, and op.cit. 1954, 1956, 1962, 1971; Rosenthal E. I. J., *Political Thought in Medieval Islam*, Cambridge 1958, esp. pp.21–84.

7. For example, al-Mawardi's (d. 450/1058) discourse entails a 'formal' concept of justice, denoting a state of moral and religious perfection, as opposed to the 'substantive' notion shared by the authors of the three major 'Mirrors'. See Gibb H.A.R., 'Al-Mawardi's Theory of Khilafah', *Islamic Culture* XI 3, 1937, pp.291–302; Lambton, op.cit. 1981, pp. 83–102; Rosenthal, op.cit. 1958, pp.27–37.

8. Lambton, op.cit. 1968 pp.206–7, 1970 pp.241–2, 1981 pp.43–69; Mottahedeh R., 'The Shu'ubiyah Controversy and the Social History of Early Islamic Iran', *International Journal of Middle East Studies* VII, 1976, pp.161–182; Gibb H.A.R., 'The Social Significance of the Shu'ubiyah', in Shaw S.J. and Polk W.R. (eds.), *Studies on the Civilisation of Islam*, 1962, pp.62–73.

9. Noting this point, Amir Arjomand argues that Ibn al-Muqaffa's failure prevented 'the incorporation of Islamic law into the State law', and that 'religious law became largely theoretical while the State developed a secular jurisdiction of its own' (op. cit. 1984, p.50). He then draws on Schacht's commentary on this issue to substantiate Weber's argument that 'the sacred law of Islam is throughout specifically a jurist law' rather than a 'judges' law' (ibid.). Arjomand generalizes this argument to the development of the legal institutions and processes in the Islamic polity in subsequent epochs.

10. The assimilation was not unproblematic; it created a lasting tension in the body of Islamic political and juridical discourse between the constituent elements of the Sassanian tradition on the one hand, and the juridical and ethical precepts of *sharia* and *sunna* on the other. See the sources cited above, notes 6 and 8.

11. For example, Ghazali, too, expresses concern about the development of such trends within the polity. See the relevant sections in *Nasihat ul-Muluk*, ed. Homai J., Tehran 1936/37; English translation Bagley F.R. C., *Ghazali's Book of Counsel for Kings*, Oxford 1964. See also Lewis B., 'Al-Ghazali's Theory of Kingship', *Bulletin of the School of Oriental and*

African Studies XVII, 1954; Dawood, op.cit. 1965; Lambton, op.cit. 1954, 1971, 1981; Binder, op.cit. 1955; Hillenbrand C., 'Islamic Orthodoxy or Realpolitik? Al-Ghazali's Views on Government', *Iran* XXVI, 1988, pp.81–94.

12. The theory of the absolute ownership of the king is also expressed in *Qabus-Nameh*. In this text, too, the theory is associated with the Persian concept of kingship, and features in the context of a discussion of ideal rule. Kai Kaous Ibn Iskandar, *Qabus-Nameh*, ed. and trans. Levy R., *A Mirror for Princes*, 1951. See also Dawood, op.cit. 1965.

13. *Ahd-e Ardashir* is an *andarz nameh* (advice book). It purports to be the words of Ardashir (founder of the Sassanian dynasty, ruled 224–42 A.D.) to his successors, bequeathing to them good counsel and political wisdom. The text is included in Dehkhoda's *Amsal va Hekam* Vol. III, Tehran 1931; also see Mashkur M.J. (ed.), *Karnameh-e Ardashir Babakan*, Tehran 1951; *Ahd-e Ardashir*, Persian translation Ali Iman Shushtari, Tehran 1348/1970; Minovi M. and Rizvani, M.I. (eds.), *Nameh-e Tansar*, Tehran 1932/3, reprinted Tehran 1975; English translation by M. Boyce, *The Letter of Tansar*, Rome 1968. Minovi and Boyce both note the close resemblances between the two texts; Boyce comments that 'the resemblances in places are so close that it seems that there must have been some interdependence of texts' (op.cit. 1968, p.14).

14. For the ethos of universal kingship and the Zoroastrian cosmology see Zaehner R.C., *The Dawn and Twilight of Zoroastrianism*, New York 1961; Christensen A., *L'Iran sous les Sassanides*, Copenhagen 1944, Persian translation by Rasid Yasami, *Iran dar Zaman-e Sassanian*, Tehran 1972, esp. Chapter 8; Frye R.N., 'The Charisma of Kingship in Ancient Iran', *Iranica Antiqua* IV, 1964, pp.36–54; Widengren G., 'The Sacral Kingship of Iran', in *Sacral Kingship*, Leiden 1959, pp.242–258.

15. See for example the section entitled, 'Enquiry into Religious Matters', esp. p.60; 'Kingship and Religion are like two (twin) brothers . . .'

16. The marginalization of the *sharia* and the historic *imama* in defining the nature of authority and the conditions of legitimate rule is characteristic of the discourse of the 'Mirrors' in general. In relation to *Nasihat ul-Muluk* and *Qabus Nameh* see Lambton, op.cit. 1962, 1971, 1981; Dawood, op.cit. 1965; Rosenthal E.I.J., op.cit. 1958.

17. Nizam ul-Mulk and Ghazali both consider justice as the condition of kingship and the quality of kings. Nizam ul-Mulk, invoking the *sunna*, argues, 'Kingship remains with the unbeliever but not with injustice'. Justice is defined as the manner of discharging one's duty and satisfying the creator, the Truth. 'It is for the Kings to observe His pleasure (His name be glorified) and the pleasure of the Truth is in the charity which is done to his creatures and in the justice which is spread among them' *(Siyasat Nameh*, trans. H. Darke, 'The Book of Government or Rules for Kings', 1960, p. 12). Elsewhere in the same section (Chapter II), he reiterates, 'A Kingdom may last while there is irreligion but it will not endure when there is oppression'. On the concept of justice in the discourse of the 'Mirrors' see the sources cited in note 16 above.

18. The functional division of society into fixed stratified orders was by no

means specific to the discourse of *Siyasat Nameh*. Rather, as Lambton indicates, 'this functional division of society was largely accepted by the medieval Islamic theory of the state, and the duty of the ruler was seen largely to be the preservation of a due equipoise which was to be achieved by keeping each individual in his proper place' (op.cit. 1962, p.97).

19. Hafiz Abru, *Jughrafia*, p.178a.

Chapter 7

1. Khosravi K., 'Muzara'eh', *Rahnema-ye Ketab* nos. 7–9, Tehran 1353/ 1975, and *Nezamha-ye Bahreh Bardari az Zamin dar Iran*, Tehran 1352/ 1974; Soudagar M.A., *Nezam-e Arbab va Rayyati dar Iran*, Tehran 1337/ 1959; Bahrami T., *Tarikh-e Keshavarzi dar Iran*, 1330/1952; Momeni B., *Masaleh-e Ardhi va Jang-e Tabaqati*, Tehran 1359/1981; Nomani, op.cit. 1980; Petrushevsky I.P., op.cit. 1966 Vol. II; Lambton A.K.S., op.cit. 1953; Keddie N., *The Historical Obstacles to Agrarian Change in Iran*, Claremont 1960, and 'The Iranian Village Before and After Land Reform', *Journal of Contemporary History* vol. III no. 3, 1963.

2. The official figures referred only to *arbabi* (private) land, thus excluding share-cropping on large tracts of *khaleseh* and *waqf* lands, so the actual area of agricultural land under share-cropping was larger; see Behnam and Rasekh, op.cit. p.41.

3. The official figures for the total amount of land under share-cropping in Azarbayjan, Khorasan and Kurdistan were respectively 72.86%, 76% and 38.3%; *Tehran Economist* 1962, nos. 485, 487, 497.

4. For analysis of share-cropping relations in Iranian agriculture in the pre-Safavid era see Lambton, op.cit. 1953; Petrushevsky, op.cit. 1966, vol. II; Nomani, op.cit. 1980; Khosravi, op.cit. 1974, 1975.

5. See the sources cited in note 4, especially the works of Khosravi.

6. The prevailing rent relations seem to have continued uninterrupted down to the eve of the 1962 land reform. Black, for example, writing in the 1940s, confirms this point; Black A.G., 'Iranian Agriculture—Present and Prospective', *Journal of Farm Economics* vol. 30, 1948.

7. For authoritative Shii and Sunni sources on *muzara'eh* see Khosravi, op.cit 1974, 1975. Zia ul-Haque provides a detailed account of share-cropping relations in early Islam; ul-Haque Z., *Landlord and Peasant in Early Islam: A Study of the Legal Doctrine of Muzara'a or Sharecropping*, Islamabad 1977.

8. Despite disagreement on details, the Islamic jurists hold fairly similar views on the general condition of share-cropping. They are unanimous that share-cropping should satisfy the following conditions:

    (i) the period of the contract must be specified;
    (ii) the land specified in the contract must be cultivable, i.e. it should have water;
    (iii) the proceeds of the specified land must be divided between the two parties proportionately, for the period of time likewise specified in the contract. The portions of produce accruing to

each party may be equal or not, but neither of the two may collect all the produce.

(Mohaqeq-e Avval, *Shara-ye al-Islam*, Tehran 1346–9/1968–71, Vol. I pp.273–274, in Khosravi, op.cit. 1974, pp.20–75).

9. In Islamic law, share-cropping is a conditional contract, *aqd-e lazem;* it cannot be nullified without the consent of both parties, the peasant and the land-holder, who may or may not be the legal owner of the land—legal ownership of the land is not requisite for share-cropping contracts. The period of the contract agreed by the two parties is, according to the *sharia*, unalterable. The land-holder is charged with provision of seed, while the provision of labour and draught animals is generally the responsibility of the share-cropping peasant. Aside from these general points, Khosravi maintains, there is no unity of opinion among the Islamic jurists as to the rules and conditions of the provision of the means of production by the landlord and the peasant. His exposition of share-cropping relations in *sharia* is based primarily on Shii sources, namely: Helli, Mohaqeq-e Avval, *Shara-ye al-Islam* (Persian trans.), 3 vols., Tehran 1346–9/1968–71, esp. vol. I, and *Mukhtasar Nafe'* (Persian trans.), Tehran 1343/1965; Shahid-e Thani, *Sharhi al-Lama* (Persian trans.), 2 vols., Tehran 1380 (Hijra). Of the Sunni sources, Khosravi refers to the works of the Shafe'i scholars: Shaikh al Islam Kurdistani S.M., *Rahnama-ye Madh'hab-e Shafe'i*, Tehran 1337/1959; Kanimishkani, Abu al-Vafa b. Muhammad b. Abdul-Karim, *Usul-e Fiqh-e Shafe'i*, Tehran 1332/1954. Khosravi's exposition indicates that the rules and conditions of share-cropping relations in the *sharia* on the whole favoured the landholder rather than the peasants.

10. The Civil Code of 1936 was ratified by a *majles* which was predominantly composed of large landowners, who were also strongly represented in the government. Chapter IX of the Code, which specifically deals with share-cropping, took further steps to protect the economic interests of the land-owning class; the principles of the Shii *sharia* were deployed to enhance this aim. See for example Lambton 1953, pp.206–209.

11. See the sources cited above, notes 1, 4.

12. This view is held by the majority of contemporary scholars writing on agrarian relations; e.g. Nomani, op.cit. 1980; Khosravi, op.cit. 1974, 1975; Soudagar, op.cit. 1979. A few, however, disagree, attributing the origins of share-cropping relations to the Islamic period; e.g. Ebadi M.A., *Eslahat-e Ardhi dar Iran*, Tehran 1340/1962.

13. Marx criticizes the concept of efficiency employed by the classical political economists by focusing on the conditions of the productivity of labour and the modes of extraction of surplus in various modes of production; *Capital* Vol.III 1971, Part VI, esp. pp.640–648.

14. McCulloch is also critical of the practice of crop-sharing; his reasoning is much the same: 'The practice of letting lands by proportional rents is very general on the continent, and wherever it has been adopted, it has put a stop to all improvement and has reduced the cultivators to the most abject poverty', *Principles of Political Economy*, Edinburgh 1843, p.471.

15. Sismondi as a critic of capitalism adopted a different position on share-cropping relations; he favoured the practice for its flexibility, which he believed was advantageous to the peasants; *Political Economy*, New York 1966, pp.41–42.

16. For a detailed exposition of the neo-classical position on share-cropping see Cheung S.N.S., *The Theory of Share-Tenancy*, Chicago 1969, esp. pp. 42–55.

17. Pearce points out that 'this [partial equilibrium] level of analysis was accepted as long as such relationships remained a fact, and a regretted one, of the capitalist nations which fostered the precursors of such analytical techniques'; 'Towards a Marxist Analysis of Share-Cropping', mimeo., The Peasant seminar series, Centre for International and Area Studies, University of London 1979, p.2; reprinted as 'Share-Cropping: Towards a Marxist View' in *Journal of Peasant Studies* vol. X, 1982–3.

18. See ibid.

19. This mode of analysis, however, is not specific to the neo-classical economists alone; it is also deployed by contemporary economists to examine the effects of land tenure on the productivity of the labour force. See Cheung, op.cit. pp.47–48.

20. This point should not be generalized. There are factors other than the size of the marketable surplus which influence the share-cropper's relationship with the commodity market. The type of crop, for instance, is an important factor; the production of subsistence and cash crops presuppose two different forms of relation with the commodity market. In the case of the cash crops the producer's relationship with the market is not a function of the marketable surplus alone.

21. The prevailing tradition provided for two distinct forms of tenancy, temporary and permanent. In the case of the former, the land was usually leased out for a period not exceeding a full production cycle, i.e. usually eighteen months; in the latter case the peasant held the right to land use for life, and in certain cases the tenancy rights could be transmitted to his heirs. The permanent tenancy was by no means the norm; it was granted in exceptional circumstances, and even then to very few share-croppers. The practice of *nasaq-bandi*, periodic redistribution of land, militated against the conditions for permanent tenancy arising from continuous occupation of the land. See Soudagar, op.cit., p.157.

22. *Sahrā* seems to have been a widespread practice, surviving the vicissitudes of time. Contemporary writers researching the state of Iranian agriculture in the post-reform era have variously registered the existence of production teams known as *sahra* in different provinces. For example Morio Ono, writing about the state of large-scale capitalist farming in the province of Ghorgan during the late 1960s, refers to the prevalence of *sahrā* in the area; his description of the forms, organization and functioning of the *sahrā* closely resembles that provided by nineteenth-century travellers such as Fraser and Stack. Ono M., 'On the Socio-Economic Structure of Iranian Villages', *Developing Economics* vol. V no. 3, 1967.

23. Although Fateh's commentary is primarily concerned with the state of

Iranian agriculture in the early decades of the twentieth century, the available historical evidence indicates clearly that the character of the prevailing economic relations, and in particular the forms and conditions of tenancy, had undergone little if any change since the Safavid era. See for example Lambton, op.cit. 1953; Issawi, op.cit. 1971.

24. In this context, the concept of 'working capital' is more appropriate than the means of production; it refers not only to the means of production required to renew the production cycle, but also to the minimum consumption needs of the share-cropper, traditionally provided by the landlord—a factor which signifies the strength of pre-capitalist relations in the Iranian countryside before 1962.

25. On this point see Marx, *Capital* Vol. III, 1971, p.795.

26. See ibid. p. 797; Kula, op.cit. 1976, pp.29ff. It should be noted that the presence of monetary expenditure in the economic calculation of the unit of production under money rent did not make it either proto-capitalist or transitory. Classical Marxism has emphasized this important point; e.g. *Capital* Vol. III, 1971. See also Kosminsky's studies of agrarian relations in medieval England, op.cit. 1955, 1956.

27. Chayanov excludes the *ikos*, the household of antiquity, from this typology; the *ikos*, he insists, did not constitute a 'pure' economic type. See *The Theory of Peasant Economy*, Illinois 1966, pp.5–22.

28. Littlejohn notes that Chayanov's subjectivism is restricted to the on-farm process, and even then the labour-consumer balance is not merely an effect of the conscious calculation of the economic subjects. The subjective evaluation of the economic objects is not determined by the specific psychology of the peasant, but is a result of the specificity of the objective conditions of production, i.e. specific conditions which cannot be attributed simply to the absence on the farm of the traditional categories peculiar to the capitalist unit of production. Littlejohn G., in Hindess B. (ed.), *Sociological Theories of Economy*, 1977.

29. See *Capital* Vol.III 1971, pp.760–762.

30. For the concentration of landed property and the prevalence of large land-ownership in pre-capitalist Iran see Lambton, op.cit. 1953; Keddie, op.cit 1956, 1960, 1963; Issawi, op.cit. 1971; Houman, op.cit. 1334/ 1956.

31. The economic conditions and social status of the *khosh neshinan* in the Iranian countryside are discussed in various studies of the 1962 land reform and its socio-economic consequences. See for example Keddie, op.cit. 1963; Momeni B., op.cit. 1359/1981; Soudagar, op.cit. 1979.

32. The major studies of agrarian relations in the pre-reform era suggest that money rent was a marginal mode of appropriation of economic surplus in the Iranian countryside. See for example the sources cited in notes 30, 31 above.

33. See the relevant sections in the studies of agrarian relations in pre-capitalist Iran cited notes 30, 31 above.

34. In this respect, Kurdistan was an exception; demesne production was sporadically practised in parts of the territory, where the Kurdish landlords retained a portion of their arable land (rather than leasing it out

to the peasants) and worked it using the *corvée* labour of their subordinate peasants. The peasants performing *corvée* labour received only their daily food; no other payment, in cash or in kind, was made to them. The *corvée* was locally known as the *gal*. It was in addition to the labour service carried out by the peasants in general, and consisted mainly of non-agricultural work; see Lambton, op.cit. 1953, p.332.

SELECTED BIBLIOGRAPHY

1. Persian Sources*

Adamiyat F., *Amir Kabir va Iran*, 1346/1968

Akbari A. A., *Ellal-e Za'af-e Tarikhi-ye Bourgeoisie dar Iran*, 1357/1979

Amin B., *Dar Bareyeh Feodalism-e Iran Qabl az Mashruteh*, 1357/1979

Ashraf A., 'Dar Bareyeh Nezam-e Asia'i', *Jahan-e Now* vol. 24 no. 3, 1348/1970

—— 'Nezam-e Asia'i ya Nezam-e Feodali', *Jahan-e Now* vol. 22 nos. 5–7, 1346/1968

—— 'Nezam-e Ejtema'i-ye Iran dar Dowreh-e Islami', *Jahan-e Now* vol. 23 nos. 1–3, 1347/1969

Ashraf A., 'Vizhegiha-ye Shahr Neshini dar Iran', *Nameh-e Ulum Ejtema'i* vol. I no. 4, 1353/ 1975

Bahrami T., *Tarikh-e Kheshavarzi-ye Iran*, 1330/1952

Bayhaqi, Khaja Abu'l Fadhl Muhammad b. Hussain, *Tarikh-e Bayhaqi*, ed. A. K. Fayyaz, Mashhad 1350/1972

Bastani Parizi, M. I. *Siyasat va Eqtesad-e Asr-e Safavi*, 1348/1968

Behnam J., Rasekh S., 'Jameh Shenasi-ye Rusta'i-ye Iran', *Sokhan* no. 1, 1342/1964

Dehkhoda A. A., *Amsal va Hekam*, vol. 3. 1931

Ebadi M. A., *Eslahat-e Ardhi dar Iran*, 1340/1962

Ensafpur G. R., *Sakht-e Dowlat dar Iran az Islam ta Yuresh-e Moghol*, 1356/1978

Eqbal A., *Tarikh-e Mofasal-e Iran az Estila-ye Moghol ta Engeraz-e Qajariyeh*, 1320/1942

—— *Vezarat dar Ahd-e Salatin-e Bozorg-e Saljuq*, 1337/1959

Eskandar Beg Turkaman, Monshi, *Tarikh-e Alam-ara-ye Abbasi*, 2 vols, 1350/1972

Hafiz Abru, *Jughrafia-ye Hafiz Abru Qesmat-e Robi Harāt*, ed. Ma'yel Haravi, 1349/1971

Hedayati H., 'Mokhtasari dar Bareh-e Vaqa-ye Negariha va Nosakh-e Khatti-ye Farsi Marbut beh Tawarikh-e Qarn-e Davazdahom-e Hejri', *Majalleh-e Daneshkadeh-e Adabiyat-e Tehran*, vol. II part 3, 1332/1954

Hindu Shah b. Sanjar, *Tajarib al-Salaf*, ed. A. Eqbal, 1313/1935

---

* Place of publication Tehran unless otherwise stated

Hodud al-Alam, ed. M. Sotudeh, 1340/1962
Houman A., *Eqtesad-e Keshavarzi*, 3 vols., 1334/1956
Ibn al-Balkhi, *Fars Nameh*, ed. A. N. Behruzi, Shiraz 1343/1965
Jamalzadeh M. A., *Ganj-e Shayegan*, Berlin 1335/1957
Khonji M. A., 'Tarikh-e Maad va Mansh'a-e Nazarieh-e Diakonov', *Rahnama-ye Ketab* vol. 3, 1347/1969
Kasravi A., *Tarikh-e Pansad Saleh-e Khuzestan*, 1330/1952
Khosravi K., 'Abyari va Jameh-e Rusta'i dar Iran', *Ulum-e Ejtemai*, I, 1348/1970
—— *Pazhuheshi dar Jameh Shenasi-ye Rusta' i-ye Iran*, 1351/1973
—— *Nezamha-ye Bahreh Bardari az Zamin dar Iran*, 1353/1975
—— 'Muzare'a', *Rahnama-ye Ketab* nos. 7–9, 1353/1975
Mashkur M. J. (ed.), *Karnameh-e Ardashir Babakan*, 1329/1951
Mashkur, M. J. *Tarikh-e Ejtema'i-ye Iran dar Ahd-e Bastan*, 1347/1969
Minovi M. and Rizvani, M. I. (eds.), *Nameh-e Tansar*, 1311/1933, reprinted 1354/1976
Mirhaydar H., *Az Tuyul ta Enqelab-e Ardhi*, 1355/1977
Momeni B., *Masaleh-e Ardhi va Jang-e Tabaqati*, 1359/1981
Mortazavi M., *Tahqiq dar Bareh-e Dowreha-ye Ilkhanan-e Iran*, 1341/1963
Mostowi A., *Sharh-e Zendegani-ye Man Tarikh-e Ejtema'i va Edari-ye Dowreh-e Qajariyeh*, Tehran 1324–5/1944–5, 3 vols.
Muntakhab al Din Badi' al-Kateb al-Juvayni, *Atabat al-Kataba*, ed. A. Eqbal, 1329/1950
Nafisi S., *Tarikh-e Ejtema'i va Siyasi-ye Iran dar Dowreh-e Mo'aser*, 2 vols., 1334/1956
Nayshabouri Zahir al-Din, *Saljuq Nameh*, 1332/1954
Nomani F., 'Tahavvol-e Tabaqat-e Nowkhasteh-e Iran', *Ketab-e Alefba* vol. 4, 1353/1975
—— 'Towse'eh-e Sana'at dar Dowreh-e Qajar', ibid.
—— *Takamol-e Feodalism dar Iran*, 1358/1980
—— 'Elm-e Ejtema'i va Shiveh-e Towlid-e Asia'i', *Baran* no. 10, 1357/1979
Rajabzadeh H., *Ayn-e Keshvar Dari dar Ahd-e Vezarat-e Rashid al-Din Fadhl ullah Hamadani*, 1352/1975
al-Ravandi, Muhammad b. Ali b. Sulayman, *Rahat al-Sudur va Ayat al-Sorur*, ed. M. Eqbal, 1333/1955
Ravandi M., *Tarikh-e Ejtema'i-ye Iran*, 3 vols., 1355/1957
Saedlu M., *Masa'el-e Keshavarzi-ye Iran*, 1357/1979
Safi Nejad, J., *Nezamha-ye Zera'i-ye Jami: Boneh, Qabl va Ba'ad az Eslahat-e Ardhi*, 1353/1975
Shushtari, A. I. (ed.), *Ahd-e Ardashir*, 1348/1970
Soudagar M., *Nezam-e Arbab-Ra'iyati dar Iran*, 1357/1979
—— *Roshd-e Sarma'idari dar Iran, 1304–1340*, 1357/1979
Zarinkub A. H., *Dow Qarn-e Sokut*, 1336/1958

2. Persian sources in English translation*

Fasa'i H., *History of Persia under Qajar Rule*, trans. H. Busse, New York 1972

---

* Place of publication London unless otherwise stated

Ghazali, *Nasihat ul-Muluk*, trans. F. R. C. Bagley, *Ghazali's Book of Counsel for Kings*, Oxford 1964
Hamdullah Mustawfi Qazwini, *Tarikh-i Guzida*, vol. I trans. E. G. Browne, 1910
—— *Nuzhat al-Gulub*, 2 vols., trans. G. LeStrange, London 1915–19
Juwayni, Ata Malik, *Tarikh-e Jahan Gusha*, trans. J. A. Boyle, *The History of the World Conqueror*, Manchester 1958
Kai-Kaous Ib Iskandar, *Qabus-Nameh*, trans. R. Levy, *A Mirror for Princes*, 1951
Minorsky V., *Tadhkirat ul-Mulk: A Manual of Safavid Administration*, 1943
Nizam ul-Mulk, *Siyasat Nameh*, trans. H. Darke, *The Book of Government and Rules for Kings*, 1960
Tansar, *Nameh-e Tansar*, trans. M. Boyce, *The Letter of Tansar*, Rome 1968

3. Other languages translated into Persian*
Ashrafian K. Z. and Aroonova M. R., *Dowlat-e Nader Shah*, 1352/1974
Barthold V. V., *Uluq Bay va Zaman-e Vay*, trans. H. A. P. Tabrizi, Tabriz 1336/1958
Christensen A., *Iran dar Zaman-e Sassanian*, trans. Rashid Yasami, 1351/1973
—— *Vaze'e-e Mellat va Dowlat va Darbar dar Dowreh-e Shahanshahi-ye Sassanian*, trans. M. Minovi, 1314/1936
Dandamayer M. A., *Iran dar Dowran-e Nakhostin Padeshahan-e Hakhamaneshi*, 1973
Diakonov I. M., *Tarikh-e Maad*, trans. K. Keshavarz, 1345/1967
Diakonov M. M., *Ashkanian*, trans. K.Keshavarz, 1344/1966
—— *Tarikh-e Iran-e Bastan*, trans. R. Arbab, 1346/1968
Iransky S. et al., *Enqelab-e Mashrutiyyat-e Iran: Rishe'hayeh Eqtesadi va Ejtema'i*, trans M. Houshyar, 1330/1951
Lukonin V.G., *Tammadon-e Iran-e Sasani*, trans. A. Reza, 1350/1972
Petrushevsky I. P., *Keshavarzi va Monasebat-e Ardhi dar Ahd-e Moghol*, 2 vols., trans. K. Keshavarz, 1966
—— *Nahzat-e Sarbedaran-e Khorasan*, trans. K. Keshavarz, 1972
Pigulevskaya N. V. et al., *Tarikh-e Iran az Dowreh-e Bastan ta Payan-e Sadeh-e Hizhdahom*, 2 vols., trans. K. Keshavarz, 1346/1968
Spuler B. *Die Mongolen in Iran: Politik, Verwaltung und Kultur der Ilchanzeit, 1220–1350*, Persian trans. M. Miraftab, 1972
Tabari, Abu Ja'afar Muhammad b. Jorayev, *Tarikh-e Tabari*, trans. A. Payendeh, vols. X, XIV, 1353/1975, 1354/1976

4. English language sources†
Abbott K. E., 'Notes Taken on a Journey Eastwards from Shiraz . . .', *Journal of the Royal Geographical Society* vol. XXVII, 1857
Abrahamian E. 'The Crowd in Iranian Politics', *Past and Present* 41, 1968

---

* Place of publication Tehran unless otherwise stated
† Place of publication London unless otherwise stated

—— 'Oriental Despotism: the Case of Qajar Iran', *International Journal of Middle East Studies* vol. 5, 1974

—— 'European Feudalism and Middle Eastern Despotism', *Science and Society* vol. 39, 1975

—— *Iran Between Two Revolutions*, Princeton 1982

Abrams P., *Historical Sociology*, Somerset 1982

Adamiyat F., 'Problems in Iranian Historiography', trans. T. M. Ricks, *Iranian Studies* IV Part 4, 1971

Adorno T. W., *Against Epistemology*, 1982

Ajami, I., 'Social Classes, Family Demographic Characteristics and Mobility in Three Iranian Villages', *Sociologica Ruralis* 9, no. 1, 1969

Algar H., *Religion and the State in Iran 1785–1906*, Berkeley 1969

Althusser L., *Lenin and Philosophy*, 1971

—— and Balibar E., *Reading Capital*, 1970

Amin S., *Unequal Development: An Essay on the Social Formations of Peripheral Capitalism*, Brighton 1976

Amir Arjomand S., *The Shadow of God and the Hidden Imam*, Chicago 1984

Anderson P., *Passages from Antiquity to Feudalism*, 1974(a)

—— *Lineages of the Absolutist State*, 1974(b)

—— 'A Culture in Counterflow', *New Left Review* 180, 1990

Andreski S., *Military Organization and Society*, Berkeley 1971

Antoniadis-Bibicou H., 'Byzantium and the Asiatic Mode of Production', *Economy and Society* vol. 6, 1977

Antoun R. and Harik I. (eds.), *Rural Politics and Social Change in the Middle East*, Bloomington 1972

Asad A. 'Equality in Nomadic Social Systems? Notes towards the Dissolution of an Anthropological Category', *Critique of Anthropology* vol. 3 no. ii, 1978

Asad T., 'Ideology, Class and the Origins of the Islamic State', *Economy and Society* vol. 9, 1980

—— and Wolpe H., 'Concepts of Modes of Production', *Economy and Society* vol. 5 no. 4, 1976

Ashraf A., 'Historical Obstacles to the Development of a Bourgeoisie in Iran', in M. A. Cook (ed.), *Studies in the Economic History of the Middle East*, 1975

—— and Hekmat H., 'The Traditional Bourgeoisie and the Developmental Processes of Nineteenth-Century Iran', Princeton University mimeo, 1974

Ashtor E., *A Social and Economic History of the Near and Middle East in the Middle Ages*, 1976

Aston T. (ed.) *Crisis in Europe 1560–1660: Essays from Past and Present*, 1970

—— and Philpin C. H. E. (eds.), *The Brenner Debate*, 1985

Attridge D. et al. (eds.), *Post-Structuralism and the Question of History*, 1988

Aymard M., 'The *Annales* and French Historiography, 1929–1972', *Journal of European Economic History* I, 1972

al-Azmeh A., *Ibn Khaldun in Modern Scholarship*, 1981

—— *Ibn Khaldun: an Essay in Reinterpretation*, 1982

Bagchi A., 'Crop-sharing Tenancy and Neo-Classical Economics', *Economic and Political Weekly* no. 17, 1976

Baharier J., 'A Note on the Population of Iran 1900–1966', *Population Studies* vol. XXII no. 2, July 1968

—— *Economic Development in Iran*, Oxford 1971
Bailey A. M. and Llobera J. R., 'The Asiatic Mode of Production: An Annotated Bibliography', *Critique of Anthropology* no. 2, 1974
—— (eds.) *The Asiatic Mode of Production: Science and Politics*, 1981
Bailey H. W., *Zoroastrian Problems in the Ninth-Century Books*, Oxford 1971
Bakhash S., *Iran; Monarchy, Bureaucracy and Reform under the Qajars*, 1978
Ball M. J., 'Differential Rent and the Role of Landed Property', *International Journal of Urban and Regional Research* vol. I no. 3, 1977
—— and Massay D., Taylor G., '*Marx's Capital and Capitalism Today:* A Review Article', *Capital and Class* no. 7, 1979
Banaji J., 'A Summary of Kautsky's "The Agrarian Question"', *Economy and Society* no. 5, 1976
—— 'Modes of Production in a Materialist Conception of History', *Capital and Class* no. 2, 1977
—— 'The Peasantry in the Feudal Mode of Production; Towards an Economic Model', *Journal of Peasant Studies* vol. III no. 3, 1976
Banks J. A., 'From Universal History to Historical Sociology', *British Journal of Sociology* vol. 40 no. 4, 1989
Baron S. H., 'Marx's *Grundrisse* and the Asiatic Mode of Production, *Survey* 21, 1975
Barthold W., *Turkestan Down to the Mongol Invasion*, trans. and revised with the assistance of H. A. R. Gibb, 1928
Belyaev E. A., *Arabs, Islam and the Arab Caliphate*, New York 1969
Bendix R., *Kings or People: Power and the Mandate to Rule*, Berkeley 1978
—— *Force, Fate and Freedom: On Historical Sociology*, Berkeley 1984
Ben-Shemesh A., *Taxation in Islam* vol. I, Leiden 1958
Bent J., 'Village Life in Persia', *The New Review* V, 1891
Benton T., *The Rise and Fall of Structural Marxism*, 1983
Berger P., 'Charisma and Religious Innovation: The Social Location of Israelite Prophecy', *American Sociological Review* vol. 28, 1963
Berktay H., 'The Feudalism Debate: The Turkish End', *Journal of Peasant Studies* vol. 14 no. 3, 1987
Bernstein H., 'Modernization Theory and the Sociological Study of Development', *Journal of Development Studies* vol. 7 no. 2, 1972
Bettelheim C., *Economic Calculation and Forms of Property*, 1976
Bhaduri A., 'A Study of Agricultural Backwardness under Semi-Feudalism', *Economic Journal* 1973
—— 'On the Formation of Usurious Interest Rates in Backward Agriculture', *Cambridge Journal of Economics* 1977
Binder L., 'Al-Ghazali's Theory of Islamic Government', *The Muslim World* 1955
Birnbaum N., 'Conflicting Interpretations of the Rise of Capitalism: Marx and Weber', *British Journal of Sociology* vol. 4 1953
Black A. G., 'Iranian Agriculture – Present and Prospective', *Journal of Farm Economics* vol. 30, 1948
Bloch M., *The Historian's Craft*, Manchester 1954
—— *Feudal Society*, 2 vols., 1961

Blum J., 'The Rise of Serfdom in Eastern Europe', *American Historical Review* no. 62, 1957
—— *Landlord and Peasant in Russia from the 9th to the 19th Century*, New York 1968
Bohm-Bawerk, E. von, *Karl Marx and the Close of his System*, ed. and introduced by P. M. Sweezy, 1975 (see also Hilferding)
Bosworth C. E., 'Military Organization Under the Buyids of Persia and Iraq', *Oriens* XVIII–XIX, 1967
—— (ed.) *Iran and Islam: In Memory of the late Vladimir Minorsky*, Edinburgh 1971
—— *The Ghaznavids* (2nd. ed.), Beirut 1973
—— 'The Heritage of Rulership in Early Islamic Iran and the Search for Dynastic Connections with the Past', *Iran* XI, 1973
Bowen H. C., 'Notes on Some Early Seljuqid Viziers', *Bulletin of the School of Oriental and African Studies* vol. XX, 1957
—— 'Nizam al-Mulk', *Encyclopaedia of Islam*, 1st ed.
Braudel F., *On History*, 1980
Brenner R., 'Agrarian Class Structure and Economic Development in Pre-Industrial Europe', *Past and Present* no. 70, 1976
—— 'The Origins of Capitalist Development: A Critique of Neo-Smithian Marxism', *New Left Review* no. 105, 1977
Buchanan D., 'The Historical Approach to the Rent and Price Theory', *Economica* 1929
Bulliet R. W., *The Patricians of Nishnapur*, Cambridge 1972
—— 'Local Politics in Eastern Iran under Ghaznavids and Seljuks', *Iranian Studies* vol. II, 1978
Burke P., *Sociology and History*, 1980
—— (ed.) *Economy and Society in Early Modern Europe: Essays from Annales*, 1972
—— (ed.) *A New Kind of History: From the Writings of Febvre*, 1973
Busse H., 'The Revival of Persian Kingship under the Buyids', in D. S. Richards (ed.), *Islamic Civilisation, 950–1150*, Oxford 1973
—— 'Iran Under the Buyids', *Cambridge History of Iran* vol. IV, 1975
Butler M. A., 'Irrigation in Persia by Kanats', *Civil Engineering* vol. 3, 1933
Buxton W., *Talcott Parsons and the Capitalist Nation State*, Toronto 1985
Byres T. J., 'Historical Perspectives on Share–cropping', *Journal of Peasant Studies* vol. X nos. 2–3, 1983
Cahen C., 'L'Evolution de l'iqta du ix au xiii siecle', *Annales ESC* vol. VIII, 1953
—— 'The Body Politic' in G. E. von Grunebaum (ed.), *Unity and Variety in Muslim Civilization*, Chicago 1955
—— 'The Turkish Invasion: The Selchukids', in K. M. Setton (ed.), *History of the Crusades* vol. I, Philadelphia 1955
—— 'The Historiography of the Seljuqid Period', in B. Lewis and P. M. Holt (eds.), *Historians of the Middle East*, 1962
—— 'Atabak', *Encyclopaedia of Islam*, new ed., vol. I pp.731–2
Callinicos A., *Is There a Future for Marxism?*, 1982
—— *Making History: Agency, Structure and Change in Social Theory*, Cambridge 1987

Cambridge History of Iran
—— Vol. I, *The Land of Iran*, ed. W. B. Fisher, 1968
—— Vol. II, *The Median and Achaemenian Period*, ed. I. Greshevitch, 1985
—— Vol. III, *The Seleucid, Parthian and Sassanian Periods*, ed. E. Yarshater, 1983
—— Vol. IV, *From the Arab Invasion to the Saljuqs*, ed. R. N. Frye, 1975
—— Vol. V, *The Saljuq and Mongol Periods*, ed. J. A. Boyle, 1968
—— Vol. VI, *The Timurid and Safavid Periods*, eds. P. Jackson and L. Lockhart, 1980
—— Vol. VII, *From Nadir Shah to the Islamic Republic*, eds. P. Avery, G. R. G. Hambly and C. Melville, 1990
Cambridge History of Islam, eds. P. M. Holt, A. K. S. Lambton and Bernard Lewis, 2 vols. 1970
Carr E. H. *What is History?* 1967
Chardin, Sir John, *Travels in Persia 1673–1677*, New York 1988
Chayanov A. V., *The Theory of Peasant Economy*, Illinois 1966
Cheung S., 'Private Property Rights and Share–cropping', *Journal of Political Economy*, 1968
—— *The Theory of Share-Tenancy*, Chicago 1969
—— 'The Structure of a Contract and the Theory of Non-Exclusive Resources', *Journal of Law and Economics* vol. XIII, 1970
Clarke J., 'Some Problems in the Conceptualization of Non-Capitalistic Relations of Production',*Critique of Anthropology* vol. II no. 8, 1977
Clawson P., 'The Internationalization of Capital and Capital Accumulation in Iran and Iraq', *The Insurgent Sociologist* vol. VII no. 2, 1977
Cook J. M., *The Persian Empire*, 1983
Cook M. (ed.), *Studies in the Economic History of the Middle East: From the Rise of Islam to the Present Day*, 1975
Cook S., '"Beyond the Foremen": Towards a Revised Marxist Theory of Pre-Capitalist Formations and the Transition to Capitalism', *Journal of Peasant Studies* vol. 4, 1976–7
Coulborn R., *Feudalism in History*, Princeton 1956
Craib Ian, *Modern Social Theory*, Brighton 1984
Critchley J., *Feudalism*, 1978
Crone P., *Slaves on Horses*, Cambridge 1980
Curzon G. N., *Persia and the Persian Question*, 1892
Cutler A., 'The Concept of Ground Rent and Capitalism in Agriculture', *Critique of Anthropology* nos. 4–5, 1975
—— and Taylor J., 'Theoretical Remarks on the Theory of the Transition from Feudalism to Capitalism', *Theoretical Practice* no. 6, 1972
—— et al., *Marx's Capital and Capitalism Today*, 2 vols., 1977, 1978
Dalton G. (ed.), *Tribal and Peasant Economies*, New York 1967
Danilova L. V., 'Controversial Problems of the Theory of Pre-Capitalist Societies', *Soviet Anthropology and Archaeology* LX, 1971
Dawood A. H., 'A Comparative Study of Arabic and Persian Mirrors from the Second to the Sixth Century A. D.', unpublished Ph.D. thesis, London University 1965
Diakanoff I. M., 'The Commune in the Ancient East as treated in the works of Soviet Researchers', *Soviet Anthropology and Archaeology* II no. 1, 1963

——— 'Main Features of the Economy in the Monarchies of Ancient Western Asia', *Third International Conference of Economic History*, Munich 1965, Paris 1969

Dobb M., *Studies in the Development of Capitalism*, 1975

——— 'Review of *Pre-Capitalist Modes of Production*', *History* Jan. 1976

Downing T. E. et al. (eds.), 'Irrigation's Impact on Society', *Anthropological Papers of the University of Arizona* no. 25, Tucson 1974

Duby G., *Rural Economy and Country Life in the Medieval West*, 1968

——— *The Early Growth of the European Economy: Warriors and Peasants from the Seventh to the Twelfth Centuries*, 1974

——— *The Three Orders: Feudal Society Imagined*, 1978

Dumont L., 'The Village Community from Munro to Maine', *Contributions to Indian Sociology* IX, 1966

Dunn S. P., *The Fall and Rise of the Asiatic Mode of Production*, 1982

Eberhard W., *Conquerors and Rulers: Social Forces in Medieval China*, Leiden 1970

Edel M., 'Marx's Theory of Rent', paper presented to the Conference of Socialist Economists, Housing Group, 1976

Eisenstadt S. N., 'Religious Organizations and Political Process in Centralized Empires', *Journal of Asian Studies* vol. XXI no. 3, 1962

——— *The Political Systems of Empire*, 1963

Engels F., *The Role of Force in History*, 1968

——— *The Origins of Family, Private Property and the State*, New York 1977

English P. W., 'The Origin and Spread of Qanats in the Old World', *Proceedings of the American Philosophical Society* CXII, 1968

Entner M. L., *Russo–Persian Commercial Relations 1828–1914*, Florida 1965

Fateh M. K., *The Economic Position of Persia*, 1926

Fine B., 'On Marx's Theory of Agricultural Rent', *Economy and Society* vol. 8 no. 3, 1979

——— and Harris L., *Re-reading Capital*, 1979

Fisher, Commodore B., 'Irrigation Systems of Persia', *Geographical Review* vol. XVIII, 1928

Floor W. M., 'The Guilds in Iran ...', *Zeitschrift der Deutschen Morgen Landischen Gesselschaft* no. 125, 1975

Forbes-Leith F. A. C., *Checkmate: Fighting Tradition in Asia*, 1928

Fraser J. B., *Historical and Descriptive Account of Persia*, New York 1833

——— *Narrative of the Residence of the Persian Princes in London in 1835 and 1836*, 1838

——— *Travels and Adventures in the Persian Provinces on the Southern Banks of the Caspian Sea*, 1926

Frye R. N., *The Heritage of Persia*, Cleveland 1963

——— 'The Charisma of Kingship in Ancient Iran', *Iranica Antiqua* IV, 1964

Ganshof F. L., *Feudalism*, 1971

Garthwaite G. R., *Khans and Shahs*, Cambridge 1983

Gellner E., 'Soviets against Wittfogel: or, the Anthropological Preconditions of Mature Marxism', in J. A. Hall (ed.), *States in History*, Oxford 1986

Gibb H. A. R., 'Al-Mawardi's Theory of Kingship', *Islamic Culture* vol. XI no. 3, 1937

—— 'Al-Mawardi's Theory of the Caliphate', in S. J. Shaw and W. R. Polk (eds.), *Studies on the Civilization of Islam*, 1962

—— and Bowen H., *Islamic Society and the West: A Study of the Impact of Western Civilization on Moslem Culture in the Near East*, Oxford 1957

Giddens A., 'Marx, Weber and the Development of Capitalism', *Sociology* vol. 4, 1970

—— *Capitalism and Modern Social Theory: An Analysis of the Writings of Marx, Durkheim and Max Weber*, Cambridge 1971

—— *The Nation-State and Violence*, Cambridge 1987

Gilbar G., 'Demographic Developments in Late Qajar Persia, 1870–1906', *Bulletin of the School of Oriental and African Studies* vol. XI no. 2, 1976

—— 'The Big Merchants and the Persian Constitutional Revolution of 1906', ibid. vol. XI no. 3, 1977

Ginsberg N. (ed.), *The Pattern of Asia*, New Jersey 1958

Godelier M., *Rationality and Irrationality in Economics*, 1970

Goitein S. D., 'The origin of the Vizierate and its True Character', *Islamic Culture* vol. XVI nos. 3–4, 1942

—— 'A Turning-Point in the History of the Muslim State', *Islamic Culture* XXIII, 1949

—— *Studies in Islamic History and Institutions*, Leiden 1966

Goldstone J., 'East and West in the Seventeenth Century: Political Crises in Stuart England, Ottoman Turkey and Ming China', *Comparative Studies in Society and History* vol. XXX no. 1, 1988

Goodfellow P. M., *Principles of Economic Sociology*, 1939

Grunebaum G. E. von, *Medieval Islam*, Chicago 1953

Gurevich A., 'Medieval Culture and Mentality according to the New French Historiography', *European Journal of Sociology* vol. XXIV no. 1, 1983

—— 'Representations of Property during the Middle Ages', *Economy and Society* vol. 6, 1977

Hadary G., 'The Agrarian Reform Problem in Iran', *The Middle East Journal* vol. V no. 2, 1951

Haldon J., 'The Feudalism Debate Once More: The Case of Byzantium', *Journal of Peasant Studies* vol. 17 no. 1, 1989

Hall J. A., *Powers and Liberties*, 1985

—— (ed.), *States in History*, Oxford 1986

Hambly G., 'An Introduction to the Economic Organization of Early Qajar Iran', *Iran* II, 1964

Hanway J., *The Revolutions of Persia*, 1753

—— *An Historical Account of the British Trade over the Caspian Sea*, 1753

Haque, Zia ul, *Landlord and Peasant in Early Islam: A Study of the Legal Doctrine of Muzara'a or Sharecropping*, Islamabad 1977

Harbsmeier M., 'Critique of Political Economy, Historical Materialism and Pre-Capitalist Social Forms', *Critique of Anthropology* vol. III no. 12, 1978

Hechter M., 'Review of Anderson, *Lineages of the Absolutist State*', *American Journal of Sociology* vol.82 no. 2, 1977

Hegel G. W. F., *The Philosophy of History*, New York 1956

Heller A., 'Review of Anderson, *Passages from Antiquity to Feudalism* and *Lineages of the Absolutist State*', *Telos* no. 33, 1977

Hershlag Z. Y., *Introduction to the Modern Economic History of the Middle East*, Leiden 1964
—— *The Economic Structure of the Middle East*, Leiden 1975
Hilferding Rudolf, *Bohm-Bawerk's Criticism of Marx*, ed. and intro. P. M. Sweezy, 1975 (see also Bohm-Bawerk)
Hillenbrand C., 'Islamic Orthodoxy or Realpolitik? Al-Ghazali's Views on Government', *Iran* XXVI, 1988
Hilton R. 'A Critique of M. Dobbs' *Studies in the Development of Capitalism*', *The Modern Quarterly* vol. II no. 3, 1947
—— 'Capitalism, What's in a Name?', *Past and Present* no. 1, 1952
—— 'Rent and Capital Formation in Feudal Society', *Second International Conference of Economic History 1962*, Paris 1965
—— *The Decline of Serfdom in Medieval England*, 1969
—— *The Transition from Feudalism to Capitalism*, 1976
—— 'Feudalism and the Origins of Capitalism', *History Workshop Journal* 1, 1976
Hindess B. and Hirst P. Q., *Pre-Capitalist Modes of Production*, 1975
—— *Mode of Production and Social Formation*, 1977
Hintze O., *The Historical Essays of Otto Hintze*, ed. F. Gilbert, New York 1975
Hirst P. Q., review of Sahlins, *Journal of Peasant Studies* vol. II no. 2, 1974
—— *On Law and Ideology*, 1979
—— 'The Necessity of Theory', *Economy and Society* vol. VII, 1979
—— *Marxism and Historical Writing*, 1985
Hobsbawm E., 'From Social History to the History of Society', *Daedalus* vol. 100, 1971
Hodgson G., 'Marxian Epistemology and the Transformation Problem', *Economy and Society* vol. III no. 4, 1974
Hoogland E. J., 'The Khushnishin Population of Iran', *Iranian Studies* 6, 1973
Hourani A. H. and Stern S. M. (eds.), *The Islamic City: A Colloquium*, Oxford 1970
Houtsma M. T., 'Some Reflections on the History of the Saljuks', *Acta Orientalia* Vol. III, 1924
—— 'The Death of the Nizam ul-Mulk and its Consequences', *Journal of Indian History* ser. III vol. II, 1924
Inalak H., *The Ottoman Empire*, 1973
—— 'Centralisation and Decentralisation in Ottoman Administration', in T. Naff and R. Owen (eds.), *Studies in Eighteenth-Century Islamic History*, Cambridge 1977
Issawi C., *The Economic History of the Middle East 1800–1914*, Chicago 1966
—— *The Economic History of Iran 1800–1914*, Chicago 1971
Jacobs N., *The Sociology of Development: Iran as an Asian Case Study*, New York 1966
Jamalzadeh M. A., 'Some Aspects of Labour Conditions in Persian Agriculture', *Asiatic Review* CVI, 1935
—— 'An Outline of the Social and Economic Structure of Iran', *International Labour Review* vol. LXIII nos. 1 and 2, 1951
Jones R., *An Essay on the Distribution of Wealth and the Sources of Taxation*, 1831

—— *An Introductory Lecture on Political Economy*, 1833

Katouzian H., *The Political Economy of Modern Iran: Despotism and Pseudo-Modernism 1926–1979*, 1981

Kaye B., *The British Marxist Historians: An Introductory Analysis*, Cambridge 1984

Kazemzadeh F., 'Iranian Historiography', in B. Lewis and M. Holt (eds.), *Historians of the Middle East*, 1962

Keddie N., 'The Impact of the West on Iranian Social History', Ph.D. dissertation, University of California, Berkeley, 1955

—— *The Historical Obstacles to Agrarian Change in Iran*, Claremont 1960

—— 'The Iranian Village Before and After Land Reform', *Journal of Contemporary History* vol. 3 no. 3, 1963

—— (ed.) *Scholars, Saints and Sufis: Muslim Religious Institutions since 1500*, Berkeley 1972

—— *Roots of Revolution*, New Haven 1981

Kennedy H., 'Central Government and Provincial Elites in the Early Abbasid Caliphate', *Bulletin of the School of Oriental and African Studies* vol. 44, 1981

Kennedy P., *The Rise and Fall of the Great Powers: Economic Change and Military Conflict from 1500 to 2000*, 1988

Klausner C. L., *The Seljuk Vezirate: A Study of Civil Administration 1055–1194*, Cambridge Mass., 1973

Knapp P., 'Can Social Theory Escape from History? Views of History in Social Science', *History and Theory* vol. 23 no. 1

Koebner R., 'Despot and Despotism: Vicissitudes of a Political Term', *Journal of the Warburg and Courtauld Institutes* vol. XIV, 1951

Kolegar F., 'The Concept of "Rationalisation" and Cultural Pessimism in Max Weber's Sociology', *The Sociological Quarterly* vol. 5, 1964

Kolko G., 'A Critique of Max Weber's Philosophy of History', *Ethics* vol. 70, 1959

Kosminsky E. A., 'Services and Money-Rents in the Thirteenth Century', *Economic History Review* no. 5, 1935

—— 'The Evolution of Feudal Rent in England: the XI to the XV Centuries', *Past and Present* no. 7, 1955

—— *Studies in the Agrarian History of England in the Thirteenth Century*, Oxford 1956

Krader L., *The Asiatic Mode of Production*, Van Assen, Netherlands 1975

Kriedte P., Medick H. and Schlumbohm J., *Industrialisation before Industrialisation*, Cambridge 1981

Kula W., *An Economic Theory of the Feudal System*, 1976

—— *Measures and Men*, Princeton, N.J. 1986

LaCapra D., *History and Criticism*, Cornell 1985

Lacoste Y., *Ibn Khaldun: The Birth of History and the Past of the Third World*, 1984

Lambton A. K. S., *Landlord and Peasant in Persia: A Study of Land Tenure and Land Revenue Administration*, Oxford 1953

—— 'The Theory of Kingship in *Nasihat ul-Muluk* of Ghazali', *Islamic Quarterly* I, 1954

—— 'Quis Custodiet Custodes: Some Reflections on the Persian Theory of Government', *Studia Islamica* V & VI, Paris 1956

—— 'The Impact of the West on Persia', *Journal of the British Institute of International Affairs* XXXIII, 1957

—— 'The Administration of Sanjar's Empire as illustrated in the *Atabat al-Kataba*', *Bulletin of the School of Oriental and African Studies* vol. XX, 1957

—— 'Persian Society under the Qajars', *Journal of the Royal Central Asian Society* vol. XLVIII no. 4, 1961

—— 'Justice in the Medieval Persian Theory of Kingship', *Studia Islamica* XVII, Paris 1962

—— *The Persian Land Reform*, Oxford 1963

—— 'Reflections on the *iqtā*', in G. Makdisi (ed.), *Arabic and Islamic Studies in Honour of Hamilton A. R. Gibb*, Leiden 1965

—— 'The Evolution of *iqtā* in Medieval Iran', *Journal of the British Institute of Persian Studies* V, Tehran 1967

—— 'The Internal Structure of the Saljuq Empire', *The Cambridge History of Iran* vol. V, J. A. Boyle (ed.), 'The Saljuq and Mongol Periods', Cambridge 1968

—— 'Islamic Mirrors for Princes', in *La Persia nel Medioevo*, Rome 1971

—— 'Saljuq-Ghuzz Settlement in Persia', in D. S. Richards (ed.), *Islamic Civilisation 950–1150*, Oxford 1973

—— 'Tribal Resurgence and the Decline of the Bureaucracy in the Eighteenth Century', in T. Naff and R. Owen (eds.), *Studies in Eighteenth-Century Islamic History*, Cambridge 1977

—— *State and Government in Medieval Islam. An Introduction to the Study of Islamic Political Theory: The Jurists*, Oxford 1981

—— *Qajar Persia: Eleven Studies*, 1987

—— *Continuity and Change in Medieval Persia*, 1988

—— 'Diwan', *Encyclopaedia of Islam* vol. IV, New Ed.

Lapidus Ira M., 'The Evolution of Muslim Urban Society', *Comparative Studies in Society and History* vol. XV no. 10, 1973

—— 'Arab Settlements and Economic Development in Iraq and Iran in the Age of the Umayyad and Early Abbasid Caliphs', in A. L. Udovitch (ed.), *The Islamic Middle East, 700–1900*, Princeton N.J., 1981

—— *Muslim Cities in the Later Middle Ages*, Cambridge 1984

Lattimore O., 'Feudalism in History', *Past and Present* 12, 1957

Leach E., 'Hydraulic Society in Ceylon', *Past and Present* 15, 1959

Lecourt D., *Marxism and Epistemology*, 1975

LeRoy Ladurie E., *The Territory of the Historian*, Brighton 1979

Levy R., *The Social Structure of Islam*, Cambridge 1957

Lewis B., 'Al-Ghazali's Theory of Kingship', *Bulletin of the School of Oriental and African Studies* XVII, 1954

—— and Holt P. M. (eds.), *Historians of the Middle East*, Oxford 1962

Lichtheim G., 'Marx and the "Asiatic Mode of Production"', *St Antony's Papers* no. 14, Oxford, 1963

Lippi M., *Value and Naturalism in Marx*, 1976

Lloyd C., *Explanation in Social History*, Oxford 1988

Lock G., 'Louis Althusser and G. A. Cohen: A Confrontation', *Economy and Society* vol. XVII, 1988

Lockhart L., *Nadir Shah: A Critical Study*, 1938

Loewith K., 'Weber's Interpretations of the Bourgeois-Capitalist World in Terms of the Guiding Principles of Rationalization', in D. Wrong (ed.), *Max Weber*, New Jersey, 1970

Lokkegard F., *Islamic Taxation in the Classical Period*, Copenhagen 1950

Lublinskaya A. D., *French Absolutism: The Crucial Period, 1620–1629*, Cambridge 1968

Lyber A. H., *The Government of the Ottoman Empire*, Cambridge Mass., 1963

Madelung W., 'The Assumption of the Title Shahanshah by the Buyids and "The Reign of Daylam" (Dawlat al-Daylam)', *Journal of Near East Studies* XXVIII, 1969

Mahdi M., *Ibn Khaldun's Philosophy of History*, 1982

Malcolm J., *History of Persia*, 2 vols., 1829

—— *Sketches of Persia*, 1829

Mandel E., *The Formation of the Economic Thought of Karl Marx*, 1971

Mandelbaum M., *The Problem of Historical Knowledge*, New York 1967

Mann M., *The Sources of Social Power* vol. I, Cambridge 1986

—— *States, War and Capitalism: Studies in Political Sociology*, Oxford 1988

Marglin S., 'What do Bosses Do?', *Review of Radical Political Economy*, Summer 1974

Marshall A., *The Principles of Economics*, 1961

Martin J. E., *Feudalism to Capitalism*, 1986

Marx K., *Capital*, vols. I (1970), II (1967), III (1971), London/Moscow (Progress Publishers)

—— *Capital* vol. I, 1976 (Penguin ed.)

—— *Economic and Philosophical Manuscripts of 1844*, 1970

—— *A Contribution to the Critique of Political Economy*, 1971

—— *Grundrisse*, 1973 (Penguin ed.)

—— *The Poverty of Philosophy*, Peking 1957

—— *Theories of Surplus Value*, 3 parts, Moscow 1968, 1969, 1972

—— and Engels F., *On Colonialism*, Moscow 1974

—— and Engels F., *Selected Correspondence*, Moscow 1975

McCullock J. R., *Principles of Political Economy*, 1907

McLellan G., *Marxism and the Methodologies of History*, 1981

—— 'History and Theory: Contemporary Debates and Directions', *Literature and History* vol. 10 no. 2, 1984

MacRae D. G., 'Chains of History', *New Society* 31, 1975

Melotti U., *Marx and the Third World Order*, 1977

Meredith C., 'The Administrative Structure of Early Qajar Iran', *Iranian Studies*, Spring 1972

Miliband R., 'Political Forms and Historical Materialism', *The Socialist Register* 1975

Mill J. S., *Principles of Political Economy*, 1909

Minorsky V., 'The Aq Qoyunlu and Land Reforms', *Bulletin of the School of Oriental and African Studies* vol. XVII no. 3, 1955

—— and Minovi M., 'Nasir al-Din Tusi on Finance', ibid. vol. IX, 1937–9

Modarressi Tabataba'i H., *Kharaj in Islamic Law*, 1983

Momigliano A., *The Classical Foundations of Modern Historiography*, Berkeley 1990

Mommsen W., 'Max Weber's Political Sociology and his Philosophy of World History', *International Social Science Journal* vol. 17, 1965
—— *The Age of Bureaucracy*, 1974
Morgan D. O., (ed.), *Medieval Historical Writings in Christian and Islamic Worlds*, 1982
—— 'Persian Historians and the Mongols', in ibid.
—— *The Mongols*, Oxford 1986
Morgen J. de, 'Feudalism in Persia: Its Origin, Development and Present Condition', *Smithsonian Institute Annual Report 1913*, Washington 1914
Morier, *A Journey through Persia, Armenia and Asia Minor to Constantinople, in the Years 1808 and 1809*, 1812
—— *A Second Journey through Persia, Armenia and Asia Minor to Constantinople, between the Years 1810 and 1816*, 1818
Morony M. G., 'Landholding in Seventh Century Iraq: Late Sassanian and Early Islamic Patterns', in A. L. Udovitch (ed.), *The Islamic Middle East 700–1900*, Princeton N.J., 1981
Mottahedeh R., 'The Abbasid Caliphate in Iran', *Cambridge History of Iran* vol. IV, R. N. Frye (ed.), 'From the Arab Invasion to the Saljuqs', Cambridge 1975
—— 'The Shu'ubiyah Controversy and the Social History of Early Islamic Iran', *International Journal of Middle Eastern Studies* VII, 1976
Mukhia H., 'Was There Feudalism in Indian History?', *Journal of Peasant Studies* vol. VIII no. 3, 1981
Neale R. S., *Writing Marxist History*, Oxford 1988
Newman K., *Law and Economic Organisation: A Comparative Study of Pre-Industrial Societies*, Cambridge 1983
Nield K., 'Theoretical Poverty or the Poverty of Theory: British Marxist Historiography and the Althusserians', *Economy and Society* vol. VIII, 1979
Nomani F., 'The Origin and Development of Feudalism in Iran, 300–1600 A.D.' (Part I), *taqiqat'e eqtesadi* vol. IX nos. 27–28, 1972
—— 'Notes on the Origins and Development of Extra-Economic Obligations of Peasants in Iran, 300–1600 A.D.', *Iranian Studies* vol. IX nos.2–3, 1976
Nowshirvani V. F. and Knight A., 'The Beginnings of Commercial Agriculture in Iran', Princeton University mimeo, 1974
Okazaki, Shoko, *The Development of Large-Scale Farming in Iran*, Tokyo 1968
Ono, Morio, 'On the Socio-Economic Structure of Iranian Villages', *Developing Economics* vol. V no. 3, 1967
Oppenheim A. L., 'Comment on Diakonoff's "Main features . . .", *Third International Conference of Economic History, Munich 1965*, Paris 1969
Otsuka H., 'Max Weber's View of Asian Society', *Developing Economics* vol. IV 1966
Owen R., 'The Middle East in the Eighteenth Century', *Review of Middle Eastern Studies* vol. I, 1975
—— *The Middle East in the World Economy 1800–1914*, 1981
Pach Z. P., The Development of Feudal Rent in Hungary in the Fifteenth Century', *Economic History Review* 19, 1966
Parsons T., 'Economics and Sociology: Marshall in Relation to the Thought of his Time', *Quarterly Journal of Economics* vol. XLVI, 1932

—— *Societies: Evolutionary and Comparative Perspectives*, New Jersey 1966
—— et al. (eds.), *Theories of Society*, New York 1961
Patnaik Ulsa et al., *Studies in the Development of Capitalism in India*, Lahore 1978
Pearce R., 'Share-cropping: Towards a Marxist View', *Journal of Peasant Studies* vol. 10, 1982–3
Peel J. D. Y., *Herbert Spencer*, 1971
Perry J. R., *Karim Khan Zand: A History of Iran 1747–1779*, Chicago 1979
Petrushevsky I. P., *History of Iranian Studies, Fifty Years of Oriental Studies: A Brief Review*, (USSR Academy of Sciences) Moscow 1968
Pirenne H., *Medieval Cities*, Princeton, N.J., 1952
Plekhanov G., *Selected Philosophical Works*, Moscow 1974
Polanyi K., *The Great Transformation: The Political and Economic Origins of Our Time*, New York 1944
Poliak A.N., *Feudalism in Egypt, Syria, Palestine and Lebanon (1250–1900)*, 1939
—— 'Classification of Land in the Islamic Law', *American Journal of Semitic Languages and Literatures*, 1940
—— 'The Influence of Chinghiz-Khan's Yasa upon the General Organization of the Mamluk State', *Bulletin of the School of Oriental and African Studies* vol. X, 1942
Polk R. W. and Chambers R. L. (eds.), *The Beginnings of Modernization in the Middle East*, Chicago 1968
Postan M. M., 'Medieval Agrarian Society in its Prime: England', in M. M. Postan (ed.), *The Cambridge Economic History of Europe* 2nd ed. vol. I, Cambridge 1966
—— *Essays on Medieval Agriculture and General Problems of the Medieval Economy*, Cornell 1973
—— 'The Feudal Economy: A Review of W. Kula's *An Economic Theory of the Feudal System*', *New Left Review* no. 103, 1977
Rabino H. L., 'Banking in Persia', *Institute of Bankers' Journal*, Jan. 1892
—— 'An Economist's Notes on Persia', *Journal of the Royal Statistical Society*, 1901
Ramtin R., 'Asiatic Village Communities and the Question of Exchange', *Zaman* no. 1, 1979
Razi G. H., 'Religion and Politics in Iran: A Study of Social Dynamics', Ph.D. dissertation, University of California at Berkeley, 1957
La Regalita Sacra. The Sacral Kingship: Contributions to the Central Theme of the VIIIth International Conference of the History of Religions, Rome 1955, Leiden 1959
Reid J. D., 'Share–cropping in History and Theory', *Agricultural History* vol. 49 no. 2, 1975
—— 'The Theory of Share Tenancy Revisited – Again', *Journal of Political Economy* vol. 85 no. 2, 1977
Rey P. P., 'The Lineage Mode of Production', *Critique of Anthropology* vol. 3, 1975
Richards D. S. (ed.), *Islamic Civilization 950–1150*, Oxford 1973
Rodinson M., *Islam and Capitalism*, 1966

Rosenthal E. I. J., *Political Thought in Modern Islam*, Cambridge 1958
Rosenthal F., *A History of Muslim Historiography*, Leiden 1968
Roth G., 'History and Sociology in the Works of Max Weber', *British Journal of Sociology* vol. 27 no. 3, 1976
Rubin I. I., *Essays on Marx's Theory of Value*, Detroit 1972
—— *A History of Economic Thought*, 1979
Runciman W. G., 'Comparative Sociology or Narrative History? A Note on the Methodology of Perry Anderson', *Archives Européennes de Sociologie* 21, 1980
Salzman P. C., 'National Integration of the Tribes in Modern Iran', *Middle East Journal*, Summer 1971
Samuel R. (ed.), *People's History and Socialist Theory*, 1981
Sanaullah M. F., *The Decline of the Saljuqid Empire*, Calcutta 1938
Sato T., 'The *Iqta* System of Iraq under the Buwayhids', *Orient* (Tokyo) XVIII, 1982
Savory R. M., 'The Principal Offices of the Safavid State during the Reign of Ismail I', *Bulletin of the School of Oriental and African Studies* XXIII, 1960
—— 'The Provisional Administration of the Early Safavid Empire', ibid. XXVII, 1964
—— 'The Office of Khalifat al-Khulafa under the Safavids', *Journal of the American Oriental Society* 85, 1965
—— 'The Safavid State and Polity', *Iranian Studies* VII, 1974
—— *Iran Under the Safavids*, Cambridge 1980
Sawer M., 'The Politics of Historiography: Russian Socialism and the Question of the Asiatic Mode of Production', *Critique* nos. 10–11, 1978–9
Schacht J., *Origins of Muslim Jurisprudence*, Oxford 1950
—— *An Introduction to Islamic Law*, Oxford 1964
Scott A. J., 'Land and Land Rent: An Interpretative Review of the French Literature', in C. Board et al. (eds.), *Progress in Geography* 9, 1976
Seddon D., (ed.) *Relations of Production: Marxist Approaches to Economic Anthropology*, 1978
Shaban M. A., *Islamic History: A New Interpretation*, 2 vols., Cambridge 1971, 1976
Shanin T., 'The Nature and Logic of the Peasant Economy', *Journal of Peasant Studies* vol. I nos. 1–2, 1973–4
Sharma R. S., 'Methods and Problems of the Study of Feudalism in Early Medieval India', *Indian Historical Review* vol. I no. 1, 1974
Sheil, Sir Justin, 'Notes on a Journey from Tabriz . . .', *Journal of the Royal Geographical Society* vol. VIII, 1838
Siddiqi A. H., 'Caliphate and Kingship in Medieval Persia', *Islamic Culture* vol. IX no. 4, vol. X nos. 1–3, vol. XI no. 1, 1935, 1936, 1937
Sjoberg G., 'The Pre-Industrial City', *American Journal of Sociology* IX, 1955
Skocpol T., *States and Social Revolutions*, Cambridge 1985
—— (ed.), *Vision and Method in Historical Sociology*, Cambridge 1984
—— and Fullbrook M., 'Destined Pathways: The Historical Sociology of Perry Anderson', in ibid.
Smelser N. J., *The Sociology of Economic Life*, New Jersey 1963
—— (ed.), *Readings in Economic Sociology*, New Jersey 1965

Smith A., *The Wealth of Nations*, New York 1937
Smith D., 'History, Geography and Sociology', *Culture and Society* 5, 1988
—— *The Rise of Historical Sociology*, Cambridge 1991
Smith J. M. Jr., *The History of the Sarbidar Dynasty 1336–1381 A.D, and its Sources*, The Hague/Paris 1970
Sourdel D., *Medieval Islam*, 1986
Spencer H., *The Study of Sociology*, 1880
Spooner B., 'Irrigation and Society: The Iranian Plateau', in T.E. Downing et al (eds.), *Irrigation's Impact on Society*, Tucson 1974
Stack E., *Six Months in Persia*, 2 vols., 1882
Stamp D., *A History of Land Use in Arid Regions*, Paris 1961
Stauffer T. R., 'The Economics of Nomadism in Iran', *Middle East Journal* vol. 19 no. 3, 1965
Stauth G. (ed.), *Iran: Pre-Capitalism, Capitalism and Revolution*, Saarbrucken 1980
Stedman Jones, G., 'History: The Poverty of Empiricism', in R. Blackburn (ed.), *Ideology in Social Science*, 1972
—— 'From Historical Sociology to Theoretical History?' *British Journal of Sociology* vol. 27 no. 3, 1976
—— 'History and Theory', *History Workshop Journal* 6, 1978
Stinchcombe A., *Theoretical Methods in Social History*, New York 1978
Sweezy P. M., *The Theory of Capitalist Development*, New York 1970
Tagieva S. A., 'The State of the Persian Peasants at the end of the 19th and the beginning of the 20th Centuries' (Azari text), *Baku* VIII 1, 1969
Taylor J. G., *From Modernisation to Modes of Production*, 1979
Thomas K., 'Jumbo-History', *The New York Review of Books*, April 17 1975
Thompson E. P., 'On History, Sociology and Historical Relevance', *British Journal of Sociology* vol. 27 no. 3, 1976
—— *The Poverty of Theory*, 1979
Thorner D., 'Marx on India and the Asiatic Mode of Production', *Contribution to Indian Sociology* IX, 1966
Tigar M. E., *Law and the Rise of Capitalism*, New York 1977
Tilly C., *As Sociology Meets History*, New York 1981
—— *Coercion, Capital and European States, A.D. 990–1990*, Oxford 1990
—— (ed.), *The Formation of National States in Europe*, Princeton 1975
Tribe K., 'Ground Rent and the Formation of Classical Political Economy: A Theoretical History', Ph.D. thesis, Cambridge University 1976
—— 'Economic Property and the Theorization of Ground Rent', *Economy and Society* vol. VI no. 1, 1977
—— *Land, Labour and Economic Discourse*, 1978
—— *Genealogies of Capitalism*, 1981
—— (ed.), *Reading Weber*, 1989
Turner B. S., *Weber and Islam*, 1974
—— *Marx and the End of Orientalism*, 1978
—— *Capitalism and Class in the Middle East: Theories of Social Change and Economic Development*, 1984
—— 'Feudalism in Iran', in G. Stauth (ed.), *Iran: Pre-Capitalism, Capitalism and Revolution*, Saarbrucken 1980

Udovitch A. L., *Partnership and Profit in Medieval Islam*, Princeton, N.J. 1970
—— (ed.), *The Islamic Middle East 700–1900*, Princeton, N.J. 1981
USSR Academy of Sciences, *History of Iranian Studies: Fifty Years of Soviet Oriental Studies (Brief Reviews)*, Moscow 1968
Vafadari K., 'Some Ideas on the Unity of Town and Countryside in Asiatic Society', *Zaman* no. 1, 1979
Vahidi M., 'Water and Irrigation in Iran', *Plan Organization*, Tehran 1968
Varga Y., *Politico-Economic Problems of Capitalism*, Moscow 1968
Vilar P., 'Problems of the Formation of Capitalism', *Past and Present* no. 10, 1956
—— *A History of Gold and Money, 1450–1920*, 1976
Walker R., 'Contentious Issues in Marxian Value and Rent Theory: A Second and Longer Look', *Antipode* 1975
Wallerstein I., *The Modern World System*, New York 1974
—— *Historical Capitalism*, London 1983
Weber M., *The Theory of Social and Economic Organization*, New York 1947
—— *Economy and Society*, 3 vols., New York 1968
—— *General Economic History*, New Brunswick 1981
—— *The Agrarian Sociology of Ancient Civilizations*, 1988
White H., *The Historical Imagination in Nineteenth-Century Europe*, Baltimore 1973
Whyte R. O., 'Evolution of Land Use in South-Western Asia', in D. Stamp (ed.), *A History of Land Use in Arid Regions*, Paris 1961
Wickham C. J., 'The Other Transition: From the Ancient World to Feudalism', *Past and Present* no. 103, 1984
—— 'The Uniqueness of the East', *Journal of Peasant Studies* vol. XII nos. 2–3, 1985
—— 'Historical Materialism, Historical Sociology', *New Left Review* 171, 1988
Widengren G., 'The Sacral Kingship of Iran', in idem. *Sacral Kingship*, 1959
Williams K., 'Problematic History', *Economy and Society* vol. 1, 1972
Wittfogel K. A., *Oriental Despotism: A Comparative Study of Total Power*, New York 1981
Wolpe H., *The Articulation of Modes of Production*, 1980
Wolf E. R., *Europe and the Peoples Without History*, Berkeley 1982
Wood J. E., *The Aqquyunlu: Class, Confederation, Empire*, Minneapolis and Chicago 1976
Worsley P., 'The Origins of the Family Revisited', *The Marxist* vol. IV no. 1, 1965
Zaehner R. C., *The Dawn and Twilight of Zoroastrianism*, New York 1961
Zeldin T., 'Social History and Total History', *Journal of Social History* vol. X no. 2, 1976
Zubaida S., 'Economic and Political Activism in Islam', *Economy and Society* vol. I, 1972

INDEX

Names

Abu Yusuf 167
Agha Muhammad Khan 10
Ahmadzadeh, M. 8
Ajami, I. 243 n21
Alp Arsalan 166
Althusser, L. 27, 101, 244 n2, 247 n5,
   249 n11
Amir Arjomand, S. 254 n9
Anderson, P. 24–7, 59, 60–8, 73–4,
   126–32, 133, 135–6, 138, 142,
   242 n12, 250 n4, 251 n6
Anushirvan the Just 177, 184
Ardashir 172–3, 175, 177–8, 255 n13
Ardawan 178
Asad, A. 242 n19
Asad, T. 108
Ashraf, A. 4, 16, 22, 34, 46–51,
   238 n31

Balibar, E. 27–30, 101
Banaji, J. 218, 222–3
Behnam, J. 193
Black, A. G. 197, 214
Bowen, H. C. 25, 26
Boyce, M. 177, 178, 255 n13
Buzurjmihre-e Bakhtgan 184

Cahen, C. 142
Chardin, Sir John 198
Chayanov, A. V. 218, 219–22, 243 n21,
   259 n27 and n28
Chengiz Khan 77, 78
Cheung, S. N. S. 203
Christensen, A. 177

Cutler, A. 117, 207

Dawood, A. H. 167, 168
Debray, R. 8
Demin, A. I. 216
Dehkhoda, A. A. 172
Djamalzadeh, M. A. *see* Jamalzedeh

Engels, F. 9, 37

Fateh, M. K. 210, 212
Fine, B. 248 n10
Frank, A. G. 8
Fraser, J. B. 197

Ghazali, Imam Muhammad 166,
   254 n11, 255 n17
Ghazan Khan 78
Gibb, H. A. R. 25, 26
Goitein, S. D. 168
Gramsci, A. 242 n12
Guevara, Ernesto Che 8
Gusnusp 175, 178

Hafiz Abru 189–90
Hershlag, Z. Y. 211
Hindess, B. 30–2, 102–7, 108–9, 112,
   114, 117–8, 133, 139–42
Hirst, P. 30–2, 102–7, 108–9, 112,
   114, 117–8, 133, 139–42

Ibn Khaldun 25, 241 n11, 252 n16
Issawi, C. 198, 211, 216

279